INVESTIGATION NARRATIVE

On Mon., 7/22/91, at approximately 11:30PM, officers responded to a call for help from a citizen who directed them to an apartment at 924 N. 25th St., Apt. #213. Upon arrival of the officers on Sq. 31, they observed various photographs in the apartment, depicting dismembered bodies. When they opened the refrigerator, the officers observed the dismembered head of a human being inside. The suspect was subsequently placed under arrest and admitted this offense.

DAHMER'S CONFESSION

The Milwaukee Cannibal's Arrest Statements

By John Borowski

Waterfront Productions

DAHMER'S CONFESSION:
THE MILWAUKEE CANNIBAL'S ARREST STATEMENTS

Copyright ©2017 by John Borowski
johnborowski.com

Cover Art by Annie Clift - annieclift.com

Published By:
Waterfront Productions
P.O. Box 607085
Chicago, IL 60660
U.S.A.

ISBN
978-0-9976140-2-2

OTHER BOOKS BY AUTHOR JOHN BOROWSKI

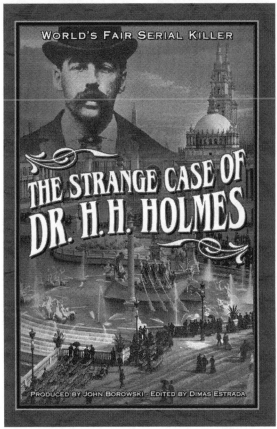

OTHER FILMS BY FILMMAKER JOHN BOROWSKI

serialkillerculture.com

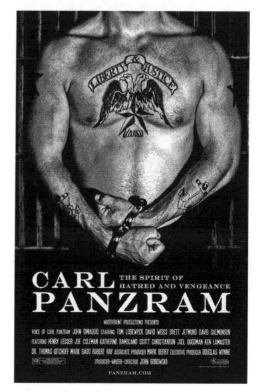

panzram.com

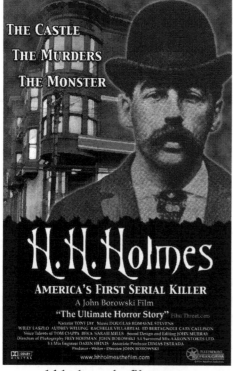

hhholmesthefilm.com

albertfishfilm.com

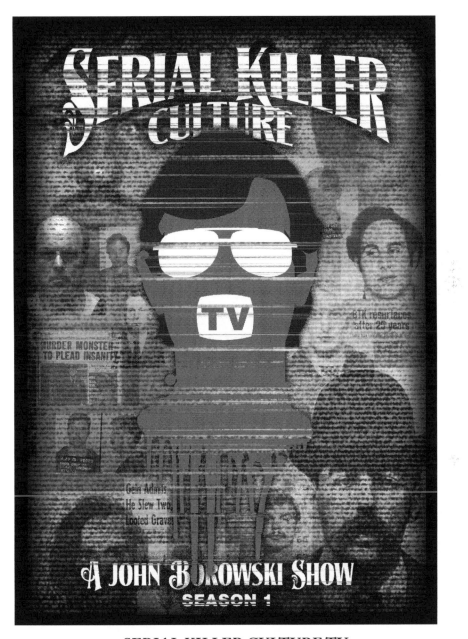

SERIAL KILLER CULTURE TV
A TV Show by filmmaker John Borowski.

Serial Killer Culture TV is an episodic true crime TV series featuing intimate interviews with those involved in the culture of serial killers and true crime. Included are collectors, artists, survivors, authors, forensic psychologists, museums, universities, and more.

AVAILABLE VIA STREAMING ON AMAZON PRIME AND DVD.

CONTENTS

FOREWORD

by John Borowski

Dahmer was the first serial killer that really hit home with me because he was not only local to me being a Chicago native, but also because he was the first serial killer in which I viewed live news broadcasts as the horrors of apartment 213 unfolded on national television. Watching Universal monster movies, I had realized that many of the early monster stories and movies were based on real people: Dracula was based on Vlad the Impaler, Dr. Frankenstein was based on grave robbing cases grave robbing, etc. Although some say serial killers are monsters, the only thing I regret in making my films on serial killers is that I called H.H. Holmes a monster. Once serial killers are apprehended they do not grow horns and three eyes, nor does their skin turn green. They are still human beings and it is society's responsibility to attempt to try to figure out why and how they became what they became. I see serial killers as souls in torment as they too suffer in their own way by committing multiple murders and having to live with the continual compulsion, very much like the Wolf Man, they attack and then have a cooling off period.

When I was in high school, I practiced special makeup effects and I wanted to be a special makeup artist. My best friend would also create effects with me. His father was a detective when Dahmer was arrested. One day, my friend called me and told me that I had to come over. When I arrived at his house, he showed me what he discovered in his father's office. What he thought was a mask catalog was actually the Dahmer file, complete with Dahmer's confession as well as photocopies of the photographs that Dahmer took of the dismembered bodies. I will never get the images of those photos out of my head. Dahmer would take the heads of his victims, their eyes and mouths open in horror, and place them in his kitchen sink next to their dismembered hands, and sometimes their penis, and take photos of the body parts. The photos and confession made such an impression on me that years later, in film school, I made a short film called *State of Mind*, which is viewable on my youtube channel. I broke two rules of the filmmaking class: We were not allowed to attempt sync dialogue and we could not mix 16mm black and white and color film stock. It was my intention to film the current action of the detective interrogating Dahmer in black and white and show the horror of the actions he committed in highly saturated color flashbacks, rather than the typical black and white flashbacks. I also wanted Dahmer and the detective to speak to each other so I had the detective smoking and when he spoke, he moved his fingers and when Dahmer spoke, I showed extreme close-ups of his eyes, this way I could fake the sync sound. When my instructor finally saw the film, he just nodded his head as if there was something wrong with me. He stated that he had to rewind the footage several times when there were shots of heads in a freezer in the film. These were heads I made when I was making special makeup effects. In the end, the instructor gave me an "A" grade and the film was screened at the best of the year films for Columbia College Chicago 1992.

Dahmer was my introduction to contemporary serial killers. I became fascinated by serial killers and their ties to horror. I call it reality horror. Years later, when I was researching a Chicago history paper, I came across the story of Dr. H.H. Holmes and his Murder Castle in Chicago. I was again fascinated by another serial killer's extreme abnormal psychology. The building he designed contained elaborate maze-like structures, secret staircases, hidden rooms, trap doors, a greased chute, huge vaults and a basement containing a glass bending apparatus, which was actually a crematorium. The entire building was designed for murder and body disposal. Holmes was an evil genius. It wasn't until I read Harold Schechter's book, *Depraved*, where I learned so much more about Holmes' entire life of swindling and serial murder for profit. Since no one had ever made a film on Holmes, I decided that my first film out of college would focus on Holmes' entire life. My first film, *H.H. Holmes: America's First Serial Killer*, is still the most popular of all my works.

I have thought a lot about Dahmer over the years. I would eventually like to make a feature film on his life. It would have to be graphic. His story still fascinates me. When I read Stephen Giannangelo's psychological profile of Dahmer in his book, *Real-Life Monsters*, it struck me as the most thorough and thought provoking writings on Dahmer which I have ever read. His profile makes complete sense to me and has allowed me a better understanding of the psychological reasons behind why Dahmer may have done the horrific acts upon his victims.

Dennis Nilsen was very similar to Jeffrey Dahmer except Nilsen murdered 12 young men in the U.K. between 1978 and 1983. What I found interesting about both of their lives is that they were not only extremely lonely, but when they were apprehended, they were very calm and straight forward in describing in detail the victims which they murdered and what they did with their bodies. It makes sense that Dahmer wanted to create a shrine to his victims because I do believe that he, like Nilsen, adored his victims and truly didn't want them to leave him.

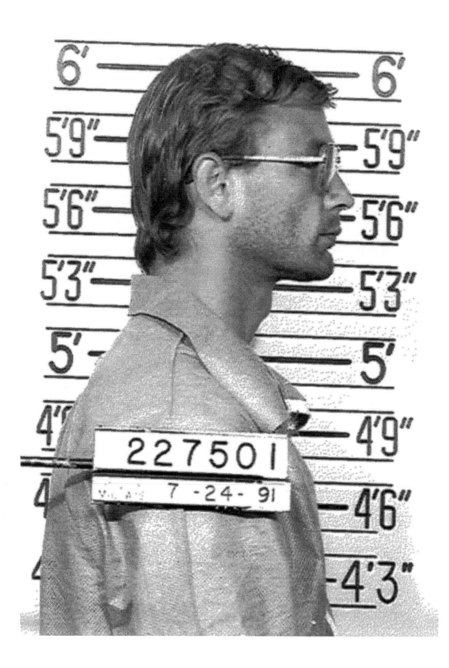

Jeffrey Dahmer
A Broken Mind or Broken Soul?

In January 1992, as a graduate student looking to integrate the psychology of the serial killer with clinical and abnormal psychology, I took a course called Serial Murder. The course was taught by international serial murder expert Dr. Steven Egger, and I probably never enjoyed another class as much.

A few months earlier, it was reported that a man in Milwaukee had been arrested and was accused of being a serial killer, and he was found to have had skulls and bones and body parts in his apartment. It was said he was a cannibal. He had body parts in his refrigerator "to eat later." The news, over and over, played the video of the blue vat of acid used to decay the remains of his victims, being removed from his home on a cart.

Not long afterwards, a contact I had from the Milwaukee PD provided me a copy of the killer's confession and crime scene photos. The details were stunning. The pictures, mesmerizing. These documents are available today, but on this day were unheard of, as was the crime. The media saturation of the criminal trial was in full swing during my time in class, and the confession was an amazing connection to the killer himself.

This was my introduction to Jeffrey Dahmer. I have always found his case, his mindset, his personality, to be fascinating. I still do.

It would be arrogant and unreasonable to purport to offer a psychological profile on a subject I've never spoken to. This essay is merely one person's observation and reactions to the mind and motivations of one of the most memorable serial murderers of our lifetimes.

CHILDHOOD

Jeffrey Dahmer was born in 1960 in Milwaukee, Wisconsin. His childhood fascination with dissection, animal bones and carcasses are well-known. He would collect road kill and bring them home to dismember, examine and store away. It's hard to ignore this in context with his later behavior as an adult. His early fixation with the inner workings of the animals carried right up to his placing his ear to a victim's stomach to hear the sounds inside.

Jeff always seemed to exhibit a lethargic attitude about most everything, noted by classmates and others alike. He appeared extremely, painfully introverted, although there were times he acted out in ways that made people remember him. It seemed he really didn't know who he was.

His underachievement, even in activities he demonstrated some success in, was an ongoing theme: through childhood, young adulthood, the military, a vocational school he never attended. His very lack of motivation and drive belied his belief he would fail again. Certainly with a potential lover. It's not shocking he would retreat deep into a fantasy world of rehearsing an event that would bring him the ownership of another person in the way he most desired.

It should be noted when he returned from prison for child molestation in 1990, it was claimed he'd been the victim of a sexual assault, which was unsubstantiated. However, his stepmother Shari stated that, "he'd lost his soul in there" and that he no longer had light in his eyes.

INFLUENCE OF HIS PARENTS

Along with Dahmer's interest in body parts and his distress over his sexuality and lack of success with partners, it seems the biggest influence in his mindset came from his parents.

His mother, Joyce, was a high-anxiety, stressed woman who never met a conflict she didn't like. She demanded attention and courted drama. She suffered from various psychological and physical maladies, including an unexplained form of "rigidity" to her body, months before Jeffrey's birth. She had at least one suicide attempt. It was always difficult to differentiate her illnesses from what appeared to be orchestrated performances.

The most obvious prenatal concern was her addiction to medications to address her many physical and emotional maladies. Joyce Dahmer was reportedly taking as many as 26 pills a day at the time she delivered Jeff. It's difficult to determine the effect this prenatal exposure had.

Jeffrey's father, Lionel, had his own influence on Jeff's development. Lionel has taken on a personal responsibility for Jeff's outcome in interviews and in his own book. Lionel, as a young person had his own destructive interests and violent fantasies and once bombed a child off a bike with explosives. Would these natural instincts towards violence be something he could have passed on and might have addressed with his son? It seems the only thing Lionel taught his son as a child was the bleaching of animals' bones, something that would serve him later in the preservation of human skulls and skeletal remains.

The most critical influence, however, seems to be the combined trauma both parents delivered with their contentious, selfish and angry divorce and more importantly, their abandonment of Dahmer and his little brother in the house at age 18. This final brutal, abject rejection was not inconsistent with the mutual neglectful lack of attention they paid their son, something he always carried with him. While it's true this act might not have affected all young men like it did Dahmer, the loneliness and isolation was a factor in his personality that shaped his actions to come. Different sorts of trauma affect people in diverse ways, and this act was as significant as it was devastating to Jeffrey.

HIS CRIMES

Jeffrey Dahmer murdered at least 17 men and boys by 1991. His crimes are legendary. His first murder was in response to a potential sexual partner who wanted to leave. Most of the later murders involved an attempt at obtaining and controlling a subservient partner who would never leave. He drilled holes and poured chemicals in a victim's skull in an experiment in trying to create a sex zombie. Committing necrophilia with a victim's' corpse was a perfect solution to the complete control Dahmer required in a partner. And finally, the act of cannibalism, was the ultimate act of control and ownership of another human being, one who would never leave him. The dismemberment that came with this act, while later described as distasteful by Dahmer, was an essential intimate prelude.

PSYCHOLOGICAL OBSERVATIONS

Dahmer's history is briefly summarized in order to provide a short background to his road to madness. Dahmer was reportedly diagnosed with a number of clinical conditions, including borderline personality disorder, antisocial traits, schizotypal personality disorder and psychosis. It's also reasonable to infer a degree of narcissism, obsessive-compulsive behavior and a reasonable degree of psychopathy. There's also an apparent childish emotional lack of development that's hard to overlook.

Dahmer seemed to suffer from depression throughout his adult life. He suffered in his loneliness at a terrible level. He exacerbated his problems with alcohol abuse, unsuccessfully self-medicating and also facilitated his crimes with the intentional use of alcohol to reduce his inhibitions. He eventually confessed to a Psychiatrist that he felt he could commit the crimes without the alcohol.

Dahmer's pathology stemmed from a severe intertwining of his extreme sexual desire of a very specific physical homosexual type, in a completely subservient role, along with a deep interest in bodily function, structure and the dismemberment of the human body. Dahmer's motivation in dismemberment cannot be dismissed as a mere attempt at hiding victims' bodies. This connection with his childhood fascination with animal body parts and sexual stimulation is clear.

At trial, Dahmer's defense team attempted to connect his murders with an irresistible impulse connected with his desire for necrophilia. They also tried to infer his horrific acts could only be committed by someone controlled by a mental disease. The prosecution's star expert witness could not discount the existence of a mental disease, but blamed his behavior on an absence of character, and insistently offered his capability for self-control was evidenced by his ability to lie when caught and to proactively avoid detection.

INSANITY

Dahmer's case, like many serial killers before him, came down to an unsuccessful insanity defense. To be fair, it's probably the only way one can describe the multiple killings, torture, dismemberment and cannibalism he committed. The behavior seems to describe itself. Of course it's crazy. Isn't it?

However, as with the other cases, it wasn't an excuse a jury was willing to accept. And on the surface, it almost seemed esoteric to attempt to find this multiple killer insane. He'd admitted his crimes. He begged for forgiveness in open court from the victims' families and from God. He stood there barely interested when one victim's family member appeared to attempt to assault him in open court. It did seem hollow, though, as Dahmer read his prepared statement in the same dull expressionless monotone that he'd mumble to his father when explaining his latest failure. Remorse? Who knows.

The end game here was to keep him out of prison's General Population where he'd be a high interest target. It was a worthy goal. It was here where Dahmer met his final punishment, beaten to death by a fellow inmate for motivations truly known only by his executioner.

AN ANSWER?

Dahmer's mental defects were many. His deep depression and abject loneliness seemed to mentally immobilize him. He seemed resigned to failure, rejection and disdain from others. His body language, affect and manner of speaking gave the impression he was taking medication; something that probably might have helped him through therapy.

This was replaced by alcohol in his daily routine. Dahmer, like Bundy, Gacy and other serial killers, reached a point in his life where he understood that there was a compartmentalized segment of his psyche that included the need to habitually murder other human beings in order to own them the way he needed to. This may have tortured him, but he had no intent to stop at the time Tracy Edwards ran to Milwaukee Police with handcuffs dangling from his wrist that night.

It's hard to rank and assess the various factors in Dahmer's life that brought him to that moment, the night of his arrest. I have to believe the breaking point was the abandonment of his parents, which left him rocking and chanting and moaning to himself, trying to speak to the dead, much like he was described years later by a would- be victim just before he attempted to take another life.

I tend to agree with the Prosecution's expert, Park Dietz, when he likened Dahmer's case to one of a pedophile. He might have liked to stop, but he didn't. His enjoyment of killing innocent men and having sex with their lifeless bodies was too great. His personal need and desire to own their bodies and defile them was more important than those people's rights to live. Jeffrey Dahmer's decision seems like a sane one, however insane it sounds to the rest of us.

by Stephen J Giannangelo

Author:
- Real-Life Monsters: A Psychological Examination of the Serial Murderer
-The Psychopathology of Serial Murder: A Theory of Violence

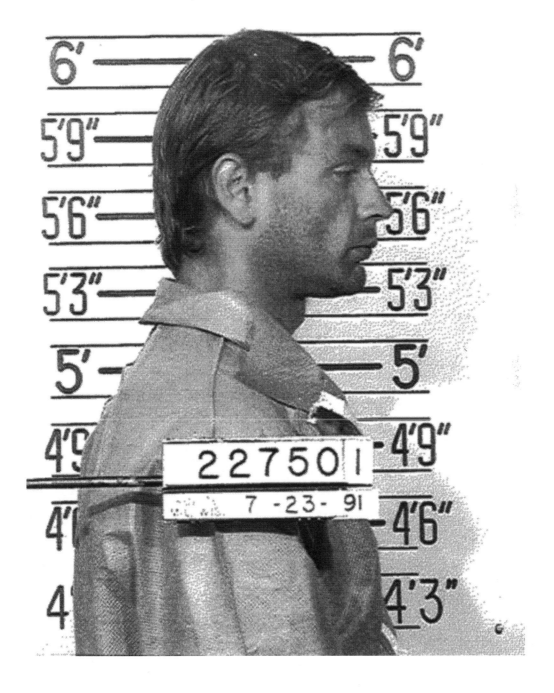

227501
7-23-91

11

DAHMER'S COMPLETE CONFESSION

SPECIAL	O	JUVENILE DIVISION
ROUTING:	O	VICE CONTROL DIVISION

INCIDENT #: 91-57463/M-2491

INCIDENT A: HOMICIDE	SS#	O C C	DAY	DATE Nov,-1987	TIME	T O	DAY	DATE	TIME

INCIDENT B: ADR AUG 13 1991 SS#

INCIDENT C: SS#

LOCATION OF INCIDENT (Address)
2308 W. Wisconsin Ave.-(Ambassador Hotel) CITY CO OF

DATE/TIME OF REPORT: Sun. 08-11-91 1135 DISTRICT 3 SQD AREA REP CON#

Location of Incident ---CHECK 1 ITEM ONLY----
- O 01-AIR/BUS/TRAIN TERM
- O 02-BANK/SAVINGS & LOAN
- O 03-BAR/NIGHT CLUB
- O 04-CHURCH/SYNAGOGUE/ETC
- O 05-COMMERCIAL/OFC BLDG
- O 06-CONSTRUCTION SITE
- O 07-CONVENIENCE STORE
- O 08-DEPART/DISCOUNT STORE
- O 09-DRUG STR/DR OFC/HOSP
- O 10-FIELD/WOODS
- O 11-GOV'T/PUBLIC BLDG
- O 12-GROCERY/SUPERMARKET
- O 15-JAIL/PRISON
- O 16-LAKE/WATERWAY
- O 17-LIQUOR STORE
- O 99-OTHER RESIDENCE
- O 96-OTHER TEMP LODGING
- O 93-OTHER VEHICLE
- O 90-PARK
- O 18-PARKING LOT/GARAGE
- O 19-RENTAL STORAGE BLDG
- O 21-RESTAURANT
- O 22-SCHOOL/COLLEGE/UNIV
- O 23-SERVICE/GAS STATION
- O 24-SPECIALTY STORE (Fur jewelry, etc)
- O 13-STREET/ALLEY/ROAD
- O 98-SUSP RESIDENCE
- O 95-SUSP TEMP LODGING
- O 92-SUSPECT'S VEHICLE
- O 97-VICT RESIDENCE
- O 94-VICT TEMP LODGING
- O 91-VICT VEHICLE
- O 25-UNKNOWN/OTHER

REPORTED FOR (VICT) Last	First	M.	RACE	SEX	DATE OF BIRTH	ETHNIC ORIG	HOME TELEPHONE #
TUOMI, STEVEN	W.		W	M	12-19-62	O HISP / Ø NON-HISP	

ADDRESS	RACE CODES	TYPE OF VICTIM	
1315 N. Cass St., Apt. 107	A-ASIAN B-BLK I-INDIAN W-WHI	Ø I-INDIVIDUAL O B-BUSINESS O F-BANK/SAV & LOAN	O G-GOVERNMENT O R-RELIGIOUS ORG. O S-SOCIETY

EMPLOYED BY	Name	Address	BUSINESS PHONE	VICTIM RESIDENT OF COUNTY?	Y N O O	VICTIM'S CONSENT? ORDERED TO VIEW PHOTOS?	Y N O O / O O

REPORTED BY	Last	First	M.	Same	RACE	SEX	DATE OF BIRTH	ETHNIC ORIG O HISP O NON-HISP	HOME TELEPHONE #

HOME ADDRESS	CONVEYED TO	None	CONVEYED BY	None

TYPE OF INJURY	O N-NONE O M-MINOR O B-BROKEN BONE	O I-INTERNAL O S-SEVERE CUT/LAC O T-TEETH LOST	Ø O-OTHER MAJOR INJURY O U-UNCONSCIOUS	EXTENT OF INJURIES	O N-NONE O M-MINOR O S-SERIOUS	O C-CRITICAL Ø F-FATAL O O-OTHER-expln	TYPE OF TREATMENT	O R-REFUSED O T-TREATED/REL O H-HOSPITALIZED

NARRATIVE

Incl. Elements of Crime- Known suspect caused the death of the above victim and dismembered him, disposing of the remains. NO SUPP

PROPERTY

Property Codes ---LIST CODE FOR EACH ITEM OF PROPERTY IN "CODE #" COLUMN. IF PROPERTY WAS DAMAGED BEGIN CODE W/ "D" (eg. D-00)

- 01-AIRCRAFT
- 02-ALCOHOL
- 04-BICYCLES
- 06-CLOTHES/FURS
- 07-COMPUTER WARES
- 08-CONSUMABLES
- 09-CREDIT CARDS
- 10-DRUGS/NARCOTICS
- 11-DRUG/NARC EQUIP
- 12-FARM EQUIPMENT
- 13-FIREARMS
- 14-GAMBLING EQUIP
- 15-HEAVY EQUIPMENT
- 16-HOUSEHOLD GOODS
- 17-JEWELRY/PREC METAL
- 18-LIVESTOCK
- 19-MERCHANDISE
- 20-MONEY
- 21-NEGOTIABLE INSTRMENT
- 22-NONNEGOT INSTRMENT
- 23-OF ICE EQUIPMENT
- 25-PURSE/BAG/WALLET
- 26-RADIO/TV/VCR
- 27-RECORD/AUDIO VISUAL
- 29-STRUCT-SINGLE DWL
- 30-STRUCT-OTHER DWL
- 31-STRUCT-OTHER COMM
- 32-STRUCT-INDUST MFG
- 33-STRUCT-PUBLIC
- 34-STRUCT-STORAGE
- 35-STRUCT-OTHER
- 36-TOOLS
- 38-VEH PART/ACC
- 39-WATERCRAFT
- 77-OTHER
- 99

QUAN	TYPE OF PROPERTY	DESCRIPTION	SERIAL #	CODE #	VALUE

2472 1 25
M_____ / SEC_____ / PAGE_____

PROPERTY INSURED BY	None	ADDITIONAL PROPERTY ON ATTACHED PO-15	TOTAL STOLEN $
RELATED INCIDENT #"s M-2472 thru M-2482	EVIDENCE INVENTORY #"s		TOTAL DAMAGED $
			TOTAL STOLEN/DAMAGED $

ADMIN

WARRANT INFO	DATE ENTERED	SYSTEM #	DATE CANCELED	WARRANT ISSUED-NUMBER
TELETYPE INFO	MESSAGE NUMBER	DATE/TIME	DATE CANCELED	CANCELED BY
DETECTIVE DET. K. MCHENRY	I.D. TECH	LATENT CASE #	C.I.B. SUPERVISOR Lt. K.M.
REPORTING OFFICER DET. K. MCHENRY	PAYROLL# 25815	LOC # 91	ASSISTING OFFICER	DIST. SUPERVISOR

SUSPECT NO. 1	LAST	FIRST	MID	RACE	SEX	DATE OF BIRTH		AGE	ETHNIC ORIG
	DAHMER,	JEFFREY	LIONEL	W	M	05-21-60		31	O HISP ⊘ NON-HISP
ADDRESS			CITY	STATE		HEIGHT	WEIGHT	BUILD	HAIR · EYES
	924 N. 25th St., Apt. 213								
ALIAS			ID#				SOCIAL SECURITY #		
	(SEE CLEARANCE REPORT-PO14).								

SCARS, MARKS, MOLES, DEFORMATIES, AMPUTATIONS, TATTOOS, FACIAL HAIR (Describe-i.e. scar L/HAND, mole R/CHEEK, tattoo on CHEST)

ATTIRE

SUSPECT NO. 2	LAST	FIRST	MID	RACE	SEX	DATE OF BIRTH		AGE	ETHNIC ORIG
									O HISP O NON-HISP
ADDRESS			CITY	STATE		HEIGHT	WEIGHT	BUILD	HAIR EYES
ALIAS			ID#				SOCIAL SECURITY #		

SCARS, MARKS, MOLES, DEFORMATIES, AMPUTATIONS, TATTOOS, FACIAL HAIR (Describe-i.e. scar L/HAND, mole R/CHEEK, tattoo on CHEST)

ATTIRE

VEHICLE YEAR	VEHICLE MAKE	VEHICLE MODEL	TYPE	COLOR	LICENSE #	STATE	EXP	TYPE	V.I.N. #

ADDITIONAL SUSPECTS INFO.

TOTAL SUSPECTS

SUSPECT WEAPONS: CHECK 1-3 ITEMS

1 2	1 2	1 2	1 2	1 2	1 2
O O ALTERED STOCK	O O CHROME/NICKEL	O O HANDGUN	O O OTHER	O O REVOLVER	O O SHOTGUN
O O AUTOMATIC	O O DOUBLE BARREL	O O IMPLIED WEAPON	O O OTHER FIREARM	O O RIFLE	O O SIMULATED WEAPON
O O BOLT ACTION	O O DRUG/NARCOTIC	O O KNIFE/CUTTING INSTR	O O PERSONAL WEAPON	O O SAWED OFF	O O SINGLE BARREL
O O BLUE STEEL	O O EXPLOSIVES	O O LIQUID GAS	O O POISON	O O SEMI AUTO	O O THROWN OBJECT
O O BLUNT OBJECT	O O FIRE/INCINDIARY	O O MOTOR VEHICLE	O O PUMP ACTION	O O SHORT/SNUB BBL	O O UNKNOWN

WPN SUSP NO. 1	MAKE	MODEL	CALIBER	SERIAL #	BUTT #	INVENTORY #	REPORTED Y N STOLEN O O

ADDED WPN INFO SUSP #1

WPN SUSP NO. 2	MAKE	MODEL	CALIBER	SERIAL #	BUTT #	INVENTORY #	REPORTED Y N STOLEN O O

ADDED WPN INFO SUSP #2

VICT RELATIONSHIP TO SUSPCT
CHECK 1 ITEM PER SUSPECT
1 2	1 2
O O AQ-ACQUAINTANCES	O O IL-IN-LAW
O O BE-BABYSITTEE-BABY/CHILD	O O NE-NEIGHBOR
O O BR-BABYSITTER	O O OB-OTHER BUSINESS RELATIONSHP
O O BG-BOYFRIEND/GIRLFRIEND	O O DV-OTHER DV VICTIM
O O CH-CHILD	O O OF-OTHER FAMILY
O O CF-CHILD OF BOY/GIRLFRHD	O O OK-OTHERWISE KNOWN
O O CO-COHABITANT	O O PA-PARENT
O O CS-COMMON LAW SPOUSE	O O CP-PROFESSIONAL CARE PROVIDER
O O EE-EMPLOYEE	O O CR-PROFESSIONAL CARE RECEIVER
O O ER-EMPLOYER	O O RO-ROOMATE
O O EX-EX SPOUSE	O O SB-SIBLING(BROTHER/SISTER)
O O FR-FRIEND	O O SE-SPOUSE
O O GC-GRANDCHILD	O O SC-STEP-CHILD
O O GP-GRANDPARENT	O O SP-STEP-PARENT
O O HR-HOMOSEX RELATIONSHIP	O O SS-STEP-SIBLING
	O O ST-STRANGER
	O O RU-UNKNOWN

SERIAL ASSAULTS
CHECK 1-3 ITEMS
- O A-ANAL PENETRATION BY PENIS
- O B-FONDLED BREASTS/GENITALS
- O C-FORCED VICTIM TO DISROBE
- O D-FORCED VICTIM PERFORM ORAL ACTS
- O E-FORCD VICT TO SPECIFIC POSITION
- O F-ENILE/VAGINAL PENETRATION
- O G-PENETRATED W/OTHER THAN PENIS
- O H-PERFORMED ORAL PERVERSION
- O J-OTHER

CRIMINAL ACTIVITY CODE
CHECK 1-3 ITEMS
- O K-BUY DRUGS/STOLEN PROPERTY
- O L-CULTIVATE/MANUFACTURE/PUBLISH
- O M-DISTRIBUTE/SELL
- O N-EXPLOIT CHILDREN

ASSAULT/HOMICIDE
CHECK 1-3 ITEMS
- O 1-ARGUMENT
- O 2-ASSAULT ON PO
- O 3-DRUG RELATED
- O 4-GANG RELATED
- O 5-LOVER'S QUARREL
- O 6-MERCY KILLING
- O 7-DURING FELONY ACR
- ⊘ 8-OTHER CIRCUMSTANCE
- O 9-UNKNOWN CIRCUMSTANCE

- O P-OPERATE/PROMOTE
- O Q-POSSESS DRUGS/PROP/ETC
- O R-TRANSPORT/IMPORT
- O S-USE/CONSUME DRUGS
- ⊘ T-OTHER

SUSPECT'S ACTIONS
CHECK 1-3 ITEMS
	O 11-GLOVES WORN	O 21-VICT ARGUED	O 31-VICT FORCED INTO OWN VEH
O 01-ASSIST VICT W/VEH TROUBLE	⊘ 12-MET VICT AT BAR/PARTY	O 22-VICT BOUND/GAGGED	O 32-AFTER/WHILE VICT PARKS VEH
O 02-ATTACKED FROM CONCEALMNT	O 13-PHONE DISABLED	O 23-VICT BURNED	O 33-VICT INJ W/HAND,FEET,TEETH
O 03-DAMAGE COMMITTED	O 14-PRINTS WIPED CLEAN	⊘ 24-VICT CHOKED	O 34-VICT KIDNAPPED/HOSTAGE TAKEN
O 04-DEMAND NOTE USED	O 15-RANSACKED PREMISES	⊘ 25-VICT CUT/STABBED	O 35-VICT LURED TO VEHICLE
O 05-DEMANDED VALUABLES	O 16-USED FACIL-Phone,Food	O 26-VICT DROWNED	O 36-VICT SHOT
O 06-DRUGS DEMANDED	O 17-VEH TROUBLE FAKED	O 27-VICT FOLLOWED ON FOOT	O 37-VICT VEH STOPPED ON STREET
O 07-ENTERED AFTER KNOCK/RING	O 18-VEH USED IN OFFENSE	O 28-VICT FOLLOWED/APPRCHED W/VEH	O 38-VICT VEHICLE TAKEN
O 08-FIRE SET	O 19-VEH USED TO MOVE PROP	O 29-VICT FORCED INTO SUSP VEH	O 39-WEAPON FIRED
			O 40-OTHER

TARGET
CHECK 1 ITEM
- O 50-CASH REGISTER
- O 51-GARAGE
- O 52-PERSON
- O 54-RESIDENCE
- O 55-SAFE BOX
- O 56-STORAGE AREA
- O 57-VENDING MACHINE
- O 58-OTHER

SUSPECT USED
CHECK 1-3 ITMES
- O A-ALCOHOL
- ⊘ D-DRUGS
- O C-COMPUTER

VICTIM INFORMED OF CRIME PREVENTION SERVICES? Y N O O

DOES VICTIM REQUEST ADDITIONAL CRIME ... Y N

PO-14B (5/89) CLEARANCE REPORT
MILWAUKEE POLICE DEPARTMENT

PAGE 1 of 1

INCIDENT # M-2491

INCIDENT INFORMATION

INCIDENT	HOMICIDE
VICTIM	TUOMI, STEVEN W.
VICTIM'S ADDRESS	1315 N. Cass St.

DATE OF INCIDENT	DATE OF REPORT	REP COM#
Nov.-1987	08-11-91	

LOCATION OF INCIDENT (Address)
2308 W. Wisconsin Ave.

DIST. 3

REPORTED BY
Same

PROPERTY

Property Codes ---LIST CODE FOR EACH ITEM OF PROPERTY IN "CODE #" COLUMN.

01-AIRCRAFT	09-CREDIT CARDS	15-HEAVY EQUIPMENT
02-ALCOHOL	10-DRUGS/NARCOTICS	16-HOUSEHOLD GOODS
04-BICYCLES	11-DRUG/NARC EQUIP	17-JEWELRY/PREC METAL
06-CLOTHES/FURS	12-FARM EQUIPMENT	18-LIVESTOCK
07-COMPUTER WARES	13-FIREARMS	19-MERCHANDISE
08-CONSUMABLES	14-GAMBLING EQUIP	20-MONEY

21-NEGOTIABLE INSTRMENT	27-RECORD/AUDIO VISUAL
22-NONNEGOT INSTRMENT	29-STRUCT-SINGLE DWL
23-OFFICE EQUIPMENT	30-STRUCT-OTHER DWL
77-OTHER	31-STRUCT-OTHER COMM
25-PURSE/BAG/WALLET	32-STRUCT-INDUST MFG
26-RADIO/TV/VCR	33-STRUCT-PUBLIC

34-STRUCT-STORAGE
35-STRUCT-OTHER
36-TOOLS
38-VEH/PART/ACC
39-WATERCRAFT
99-

RECOVERED

QUAN	TYPE OF PROPERTY	DESCRIPTION	SERIAL#	INVENTORY#	CODE#	VALUE

RELATED INCIDENT #'s M-2472 thru M-2488
EVIDENCE INVENTORY #'s (See File-M-2472)
ADDED PROPERTY ON ATTACHED PO-14 ☐
TOTAL VALUE RECOVERED PROPRTY $

WEAPON

USE FOR WEAPONS IN POSSESSION OF PRISONER AT TIME OF ARREST--CHECK ALL APPLICABLE ITEMS

1 2	1 2	1 2	1 2	1 2	1 2
O O ALTERED STOCK	O O CHROME/NICKEL	O O HANDGUN	O O OTHER	O O REVOLVER	O O SHOTGUN
O O AUTOMATIC	O O DOUBLE BBL	O O IMPLIED WEAPON	O O OTHER FIREARM	O O RIFLE	O O SIMULATED WEAPON
O O BOLT ACTION	O O DRUG/NARCOTIC	O O KNIFE/CUTTING INSTR	O O PERSONAL WEAPON	O O SAWED OFF	O O SINGLE BBL
O O BLUE STEEL	O O EXPLOSIVES	O O LIQUID GAS	O O POISON	O O SEMI AUTO	O O THROWN OBJECT
O O BLUNT OBJECT	O O FIRE/INCINDIARY	O O MOTOR VEHICLE	O O PUMP ACTION	O O SHORT/SNUB BBL	O O UNKNOWN

ARRESTEE NUMBER ONE

ARRESTED #1 LAST NAME	FIRST	MID	RACE	SEX	DATE OF BIRTH	AGE	ETHNIC ORIG
DAHMER,	JEFFREY	LIONEL	W	M	05-21-60	31	O HISP / ☒ NON-HISP

ADDRESS	CITY	STATE	HEIGHT	WEIGHT	BUILD	HAIR	EYES
924 N. 25th St., Apt. 213	Milw.	Wi.	6'	175	Med.	Brn.	

ALIAS

SCARS, MARKS, MOLES, DEFORMITIES, AMPUTATIONS, FACIAL HAIR, SKINTONE, TATTOOS, PECILIARITIES, ETC.

I.D. DIV #	SOC SEC #	ADDED WEAPON INFO ARRESTED #1
#227501	348-60-5777	

RESIDENT Y N OF COUNTY? ☒	GANG RELATED? O O DRUG RELATED? O O	LOCATION OF ARREST 924 N. 25th, Apt. 213	DATE/TIME OF ARREST 07-22-91 2356	TYPE OF ARREST O ORDERED IN/CITED O W/WARR/SUSP CARD O ALL OTHER ARRESTS

CHARGES
FIRST DEGREE INTENTIONAL HOMICIDE

POSSESSED SUSPECTED DRUGS AT TIME OF ARREST? Y N ☐ ☐

ARRESTEE NUMBER TWO

ARRESTED #2 LAST NAME	FIRST	MID	RACE	SEX	DATE OF BIRTH	AGE	ETHNIC ORIG
							O HISP / O NON-HISP

ADDRESS	CITY	STATE	HEIGHT	WEIGHT	BUILD	HAIR	EYES

ALIAS

SCARS, MARKS, MOLES, DEFORMITIES, AMPUTATIONS, FACIAL HAIR, SKINTONE, TATTOOS, PECULIARITIES, ETC.

I.D. DIV #	SOC SEC #	ADDED WEAPON INFO ARRESTED #1
		ADD

RESIDENT Y N OF COUNTY? ☐	GANG RELATED? O O DRUG RELATED? O O	LOCATION OF ARREST	DATE/TIME OF ARREST	TYPE OF ARREST O ORDERED IN/CITED O W/WARR/SUSP CARD O ALL OTHER ARRESTS

CHARGES
M-2472 SEC - 1 / PAGE 26

POSSESSED SUSPECTED DRUGS AT TIME OF ARREST? Y N ☐ ☐

VEH

VEH. USED	YEAR	MAKE	MODEL	TYPE	COLOR	LICENSE #	STATE	EXP	TYPE	V.I.N. #

REPORTING OFFICER	PAYROLL#	LOC#	ASSISTING OFFICER	SUPERVISOR	TOTAL

During the course of investigation on 8-5-91 the suspect Jeffrey DAHMER made positive identification of the photograph of one Steven W. TUOMI, w/m, 29 yoa, dob 12-19-62, our I.D. #216020, as being one of his, (DAHMER'S) victims whom he, DAHMER, states that during the month of November in 1987 while at the Ambassador Hotel, 2308 W. Wisconsin Ave., that he, DAHMER, did in fact cause the death of Steven W. TUOMI by striking him in the chest with his fist. The suspect DAHMER further states that prior to striking the victim in the chest that he, DAHMER, had drugged the victim with a prescription type drug. Suspect DAHMER further states that the victim was then placed in a large suitcase that he, DAHMER, had purchased within the Grand Avenue Mall and that he, DAHMER, then proceeded to the residence of his grandmother via taxi where the suspect DAHMER states that he dismembered the body of Steven W. TUOMI, w/m, 29 yoa, dob 12-19-62, and disposed of the remains.

Report dictated by Detective KENNETH MCHENRY.

KM:rd 8-11-91

REVIEWING D.A. ADA CAROL WHITE	P.O./DET. ASSIGNED	COURT CASE NUMBER
FINAL CHARGE	DISPOSITION/DATE	VICTIM NOTIFIED BY

INCIDENT STATUS	Ø CLEARED BY ARREST 18 OR OVER O PARTIAL CLEARANCE BY ARREST O UNFOUNDED/BASELESS O NO PROSECUTION DESIRED	O PROPERTY RECOVERED O WARRANT REFUSED	O ARREST UNDER 18 O A. Detained at MCCC O B. Order in to MCCC DATE:_____ O WAIVED AS AN ADULT

CLEARED EXCEPTNLLY	---- C.I.B. ADMINISTRATIVE USE ONLY ---- O A. Death of Offender O C. Extradition Denied O B. Prosecution Declined O D. Refused to Co-operate	O E. Juvenile, no custody O F. Not Applicable

JUSTIFIABLE HOMICIDE	O A. SUSP ATTCKD PO AND SAME PO KILLED SUSP O B. SUSP ATTCKD PO AND OTHER PO KILLED SUSP O C. SUSP ATTCKD CIVILIAN O D. SUSP ATTEMPTED FLIGHT FROM CRIME	O E. SUSP KILLED IN COMMISSION OF CRIME O F. SUSP RESISTED ARREST O G. UNABLE TO DETERMINE/NOT ENOUGH INFORMATION

JUVENILE ☐ ARREST REPORT ☐ CIB ☒	SERV # 9-8-8C	B OF I NUMBER 227501								

FAMILY ID #	FAMILY CASE #		JUVENILE #		ACTIVE CASE #			

LAST	FIRST	MIDDLE	D.O.B	AGE	JUV	SEX	RACE	HISP	MARITAL
DAHMER	JEFFREY	LIONEL	5-21-60	31	Y (N)	(M) F	(W) B-I-A	Y (N)	M (S) D W SEP

ADDRESS 924 N. 25ᵗʰ #213	CITY MILWAUKEE	STATE WI	ZIP 53208	TELE.

A.K.A.

	OCCUPATION MIXER

ARREST DATE 07-22-91	TIME 11:SOP		ADDRESS OF ARREST 924 N. 25ᵗʰ #213		ARREST DIST. 3

DRIVER LICENSE NO. NOT ON FILE	VEH. COLOR	VEH. YR.	MAKE	MODEL	STATE	EXP.YR.	LICENSE NO.	TYPE	VIN. N

WEAPON TYPE	SERIAL NO.	WEAPON MFG.	PROBATION (Y) N	PAROLE Y (N)	EVIDENCE (Y) N

ACCOMPLICE/OTHER NAME: 940.125 Q)   ACCOMPL REFERRED TO COURT Y-N

VICTIM/COMPLAINANT NAME TRACY M. EDWARDS B/M	PHONE NO.	D.O.B. 6

ADDRESS 1516 W KILBOURN	CITY MILW	STATE WI	ZIP 53

CHARGE	STATUTE NO./ORD. NO.	WARR.# / CIT.#	OFFENSE REPORT
HOMICIDE 10(CTS)	940.01		
ATT HOMICIDE	939.32 940.01		

VOP

ARRESTING OFFICER SIGNATURE P.O. Rory Mueller	PAYROLL NO. 50074	LOC.CD. 32	ASSISTING OFFICERS PAYROLL NUMBERS: 46038, 34907, 38281 32893

OFFICER TO COURT: NAME DET MURPHY	SEARCHED AT CVCAD BY Freske	PAYROLL NO. 34905	PRISONER PROPERTY INVENTORY NO. NONE

TRANSPORT - TO 93R	TRANSPORT - BY	PAYROLL NO. 34907	LOC. CD. 33	DATE 7-23-91	TIME 12:50 AM

WANTED CHECKED BY: CHILDS	PAYROLL NO. 57477	CK-DATE 7-23-91	CK-TIME 1212	INFORMATION RECEIVED NEG

MED HISTORY CHECKED BY: " "	PAYROLL NO. "	MED-DATE "	MED-TIME "	INFORMATION RECEIVED NEG

SEARCHED BY: GLODOWSKI	PAYROLL NO. 38281	PROPERTY INVENTORY NO.	DATE REC. JAIL	IN-TIME	OUT-TIME	CELL NUMBER

ARRESTEE DESCRIP.	HT. 6'	WT. 175	BLD.	COMPL.	EYES	HAIR	GLASSES YES	TEETH	MUST/BEARD	CHIN	HANDED (R) L	MARKS-SCARS	TATTOO NONE	DEFORM/AMPUTEE

CITY	STATE	EMP/SCHOOL NAME	ADDRESS

MILITARY (Y) N	BRANCH ARMY 3yr	E H R	NAME: LAST UNEMPLOY	FIRST	MIDDLE	SOC. SEC. NO. 348-60-5337

ADDRESS	EMP-PHONE

FINAL CHARGE Homicide 1° Int. Homicide	STATUTE/ORD.# 940.01(1)	DISPOSITION/ADJ. DATE issued 7-25-91	DISP. DATE 7-25-91	COURT-CASE NUMBER
	to be issued 8-6-91			

PHOTO TAKEN

ADMINISTRATIVE RELEASE BY:	DATE:	TIME:	RIGHT INDEX FINGER PRINT

BAIL/BOND 31,000,000 Cash	DATE 7-24-91	TIME 3:27	SET BY:	JUL 23 1990

COMMUNICATION TO:	AUTHORITY PAY NO.	C-DATE	C-TIME

SUPERVISOR APPROVAL	FUGITIVE RECEIVED BY X	DEPT MPD	DATE 7-25-91

SUPERVISOR NOTIFYING C.I.B.	PAYROLL NO.	D-DATE	D-TIME

SUPERVISOR NOTIFIED 2472	SEC 5	PAGE 1	

PARENT NOTIFIED	DATE	TIME

18

DETAILS OF ARREST (INCLUDE ELEMENTS OF THE CRIME(S) AND PROBABLE CAUSE STATEMENT) ~~ON FAGE JEFFREY DITHMEIS BROUGHT~~ TRACY EDWARDS TO HIS APARTMENT. WHILE THERE, JEFF GOT (1) HANDCUFF ON TRACY'S WRIST, THREATENED HIM WITH A KNIFE AND WHEN TRACY ASKED TO GO INTO THE BATHROOM FOR A TISSUE, TRACY FLED OUT OF THE DOOR AND FLAGGED DOWN A PASSING POLICE SQUAD. OFFICERS WENT BACK TO THE APARTMENT, QUESTIONED JEFFREY, SAW PHOTO'S IN WHICH THERE WERE MUTILATED HUMAN'S AND FOUND A HUMAN HEAD IN THE REFRIGATOR.

MAGISTRATE'S SIGNATURE: _JUDGE_ DATE 7-24-91 TIME 3.26 PROBABLE CAUSE FOUND ☒ YES ☐ NO

PARENT OR GUARDIAN — MOTHER LAST NAME | FIRST | ADDRESS | RES. PHONE | BUS. PHONE

FATHER LAST NAME | FIRST | ADDRESS | RES. PHONE | BUS. PHONE

Provide Pedigree information for subjects Brothers, Sisters, Spouse, Children and other Relatives. Include Age and Address data.

PROPERTY DAMAGE Y -(N) | PROPERTY LOSS Y -(N) | ESTIMATED AMOUNT $ (ATTACH ITEMIZED LIST IF APPLICABLE) | PERSONAL INJURY OF VICTIM (Y) N | MEDICAL TREATMENT

ADVISED OF MIRANDA WARNING

NAME | RANK | PAYROLL#

WITNESSED BY:

NAME | RANK | PAYROLL#

STATEMENT OF PRISONER: _____

INTERVIEWING OFFICER TO FURNISH: Name, Rank, Payroll Number.   Date and Time of Interview.

OFFICER TO COURT | OFF GROUP | SCHEDULED VACATION PERIODS

Dahmer's Early Life

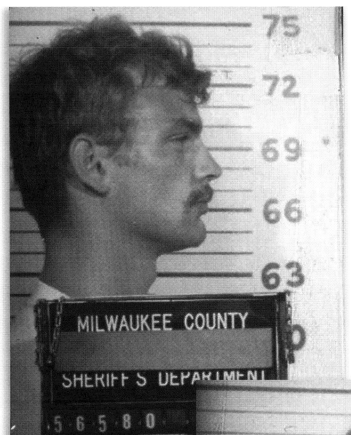

EARLY MUGSHOT

PA-45 - A
NAME: DAHMER (LAST) JEFFERY (FIRST) LIONEL (MIDDLE) 5-21-60 (D.O.B.) CIB FILE #

ARREST DATE AND TIME: CHARGE: STATUTE NO./ORD.NO.

STATEMENT OF PRISONER CONTINUED:

SUB STATES THAT HE IS 31 Y.O.A. + WAS BORN IN MILWAUKEE. HE MOVED TO BIERFIELD OHIO WHEN HE WAS 6 + WAS RAISED THERE SUB. ATTENDED + GRADUATED FROM REVERE HIGH SCHOOL. STATES HE SPENT 3 YRS IN THE ARMY + MOVED BACK TO MILWAUKEE WHEN HE WAS 22. SUB SUB. FATHER LIVES PENNSYLVANNIA + HIS MOTHER LIVES IN CALIFORNIA. SUB HAS ONE BROTHER 26 LIVING IN CINCINNATI + A GRANDMOTHER LIVING IN M.W. SUB. WAS OF THE PROTESTANT FAITH GROWING UP BUT NOW CONSIDERS HIMSELF ATHEIST. ADMITS PRIOR ARRESTS + STATES HE IS ON PROBATION CURRENTLY FOR TAKING PICTURES OF A MINOR.

SUB STATES THAT HE HAS BEEN ADVISED OF HIS CONSTITUTIONAL RIGHTS + THAT HE FULLY UNDERSTANDS THEM + HE FREELY WISHES TO MAKE THE FOLLOWING STATEMENT.

SUB STATES WHEN HE WAS 18 Y.O.A. IN BIERFIELD OHIO HE PICKED UP A HITCHHIKER A W/M ABOUT 19 Y.O.A. + HE TOOK HIM HOME + HAD SEX WITH HIM STATES THEY WERE DRINKING BEER + WERE INTOXICATED. THEY GOT INTO A PHYSI FIGHT + DURING IT SUB. STRIKES THE HITCH-HIKER WITH A BARBELL. STATES HE TOOK THE BODY INTO THE WOODS BY HIS HOUSE + LEFT IT THERE TO DE-COMPOSE FOR ABOUT 2 WEEKS. STATES HE RETURNED WITH A SLEDGE HAMMER + BROKE THE BONES + SCATTERED THEM ABOUT THE WOODS.

SUB STATES HE MOVED TO MILWAUKEE AFTER A 3 YR TOUR IN THE ARMY + 1 YR STAY IN MIAMI FLA. WHERE NOTHING HAPPENED. SUB. MOVED IN W/ HIS GRANDMOTHER AT 2357 S. 57. STATES THAT WHEN HE WAS ABOUT 25 HE PICKED UP A W/M 25 AT THE "219" BAR. STATES THEY GOT A ROOM AT THE "AMBASSADOR HOTEL" STATES HE GOT VERY DRUNK + PASSED OUT. WHEN HE WOKE UP THE GUY WAS DEAD WITH BLOOD COMING FROM HIS MOUTH. SUB. STATES HE WENT TO THE MALL + BOUGHT A LARGE SUITCASE + STUFF THE DEAD BODY INTO IT. SUB. CALLED A CAB + PLACED THE SUITCASE IN IT + WENT BACK TO 2357 S. 57. HE STATES THAT HE TOOK THE BODY DOWN HIS BASEMENT NEAR A FLOOR DRAIN + USED A KNIFE TO CUT THE FLESH OF THE BODY + THEN DISMEMBER THE BODY. PLACE THE VARIOUS PARTS INTO PLASTIC BAGS + THREW THEM IN THE TRASH. SUB. FEELS THIS OCCURRED IN + DURING THE SUMMER. SUB STATES THAT THERE HAVE BEEN MANY TIMES THAT HE HAS HAD SEX WITH MEN WITH NO VIOLENCE. SUB STATES ABOUT TWO MO-

INTERVIEWING OFFICER TO FURNISH: Name, Rank, Payroll Number,   Date and Time of Interview.

SEC. 5 PAGE 2

PA-45 A

NAME.   LAST   FIRST   MIDDLE   DOB   CIB FILE #

ARREST DATE AND TIME: CHARGE: STATUTE NO./ORD.NO.

STATEMENT OF PRISONER CONTINUED:

Later he met a H/m 18 at the "219" about 1°/am. They went back to his grandmas place + had sex with him + put a sleeping pill in his drink. He states when the guy fell asleep he strangled him with his hands. States he took the body down the basement by the drain + used a knife to dismember him + a sledge hammer to break up the bones then placed them in plastic garbage bags + threw them in the trash. States about a month later he met a black + white M/male 20 at "La Cage" + took him back to grandmas where he had sex + used sleeping pills. When he was asleep he strangled him + then dismembered the body + disposed of him in the same manner as before.

Sub states a year went by + he met a H/m 19 at "219" + returned with him to grandmas where he again had sex used sleeping pills + strangled him + again dismembered + disposed of the body in the same way. Sub states he moved to 808 N. 24 + lived there for a year + was arrested 1 time for taking pictures of a child. After 1 yr of work release at the House of Correction he moved back to grandmas + after about 6 months he moved to 924 N. 25 #213. Sub states in the winter of 89 he met a B/m 24 in front of the book store on 27th + took him to his apartment where he took pictures of him in various sexual poses + had sex with him + put sleeping pills in coffee + rum. When the B/m fell asleep he stabbed him with a large hunting knife w/4" blade + a black handle. He stabbed him in the neck. After the guy was dead he put the body in the bath tub + dismembered him. Sub states he used a plastic trash container + put the bones in it with hydrochloric acid for 3 days until they were mushy + then he flushed it down the toilet. The flesh he filled from the body + put in trash bags + threw out. Sub states he also started with the 3rd victim, boiled the head in a cleaning solution + kept the skulls. He kept the skulls in the closet. All I.D. + jewelry of the victims was cut up + thrown out.

Sub states about 2 months later he met a B/m 20 around North Ave. + Water + walked home with him + again had sex used sleeping pills

INTERVIEWING OFFICER TO FURNISH: Name, Rank, Payroll Number,   Date and Time of Interview.

23

PA-45 A

NAME ___ LAST ___ FIRST ___ MIDDLE ___ DOB ___ CIB FILE #

ARREST DATE AND TIME: ___ CHARGE: ___ STATUTE NO./ORD.NO.

STATEMENT OF PRISONER CONTINUED:

IN A COFFEE (ADDLE) + STRANGLED HIM. HE THEN DISMEMBERED THE BODY + DISPOSED OF HIM IN THE SAME MANNER AS BEFORE. SUB STATES HE BEGAN GETTING QUICKER AT CUTTING UP THE BODIES. SUB STATES ABOUT 1 MONTH LATER HE MET A TALL B/M 25 AT "CLUB 219" + TOOK A TAXI HOME WITH HIM + REPEATED THE SAME SCENARIO WITH HIM BUT HE DIDN'T BOIL + KEPT HIS HEAD. SUB STATES ABOUT 2 MNTHS LATER HE MET A B/M 20 WHILE IN CHICAGO + RIDE BACK TO MILW BY GREYHOUND. HE STATES BEFORE THIS HE MET A CHINESE MALE 15 AT THE GRAND AVE MALL AROUND MAY OR JUNE + TOOK A BUS BACK TO HIS AP. IT WAS DURING THE DAY (AFTERNOON) HE POSED FOR POLAROID PHOTOS + THEN HE GAVE HIM SLEEPING PILLS IN THE COFFEE-RUM DRINK AFTER HE PASSED OUT HE STRANGLED HIM + DISMEM-BERED + DISPOSED OF THEM (THE BODY PARTS) IN THE SAME WAY AS BEFORE. SUB STATES THAT THE BODY PARTS GAVE OFF AN AWFUL SMELL IN THE TRASH BUT NO ONE EVER DID ANYTHING SO HE JUST KEPT FOLLOWING HIS USUAL PROCEDURE OF DISPOSAL. RE: THE B/M FROM CHICAGO HE STATES THAT HE REPEATED HIS USUAL ACTIONS WITH HIM. RE: THE HEAD IN THE REFRIGERATOR. HE STATES HE MET HIM A B/M 25 AT 27 + WIS. + TOOK HIM HOME + REPEATED THE SAME. HE STATES ABOUT 1 MONTH AGO HE BOUGHT A 57 GALLON INDUSTRIAL DRUM + BEGAN PLACING BODY PARTS IN IT. SUB STATES ON ABOUT 7-19-91 HE MET A W/M 25 NEAR MARQUETTE + TOOK HIM HOME HAD SEX GAVE HIM SLEEPING PILLS IN THE COFFEE-RUM DRINK STRANGLED HIM + KILLED HIM IN THE BATH TUB, DISMEMBERED HIS + PLACED THEM IN THE INDUSTRIAL DRUM.

RE: THE CHINESE GUY SUB STATES THAT AFTER GIVING HIM SLEEPING PILLS HE FELL ASLEEP + HE (SUB) WENT TO A BAR ON 27 + HE SAW THIS CHINESE GUY RUNNING DOWN THE STREET NAKED THE POLICE SAW HIM + STOPPED HIM + HE WASN'T SPEAKING ENGLISH SO HE TALKED W/ POLICE + SAID THAT HE WAS A FRIEND + WAS STAYING WITH HIM. HE TOOK HIM BACK TO HIS APT. + GAVE HIM SOME MORE COFFEE-RUM DRINK W/ PILLS IN IT + AFTER HE FELL ASLEEP AGAIN HE STRANGLED HIM, DISMEMBERED + DISPOSED OF HIM IN THE USUAL WAY. SUB STATES HE THEN BOILED HIS HEAD. HE STATES IT TAKES ABOUT AN HOUR TO BOIL A HEAD. RE: HIS LAST VICTIM HE

INTERVIEWING OFFICER TO FURNISH. Name, Rank, Payroll Number. Date and Time of Interview.

2 4 ... SEC. 3 PAGE 4

PA-45 A

NAME:	LAST	FIRST	MIDDLE	D.O.B.	CIB FILE #

ARREST DATE AND TIME: CHARGE: STATUTE NO./ORD.NO.

STATEMENT OF PRISONER CONTINUED:

STATES THAT HIS I.D. CAN BE FOUND IN THE BEDROOM OF HIS APT. RE° 7-23-91. SUB. STATES HE MET A B/M 25 AT THE MALL ON WIS. AVE. HE OFFERED HIM $20°° IN CASH TO LET HIM TAKE SOME NUDE PICTURES OF HIM. ONCE AT HIS APT. THEY DRANK RUM & HE THE SUB. GOT INTOXICATED. SUB. STATES THAT HE TRIED TO PUT HANDCU ON THE VICTIM & HE RAN OUT & GOT POLICE. SUB. STATES THAT HE'S NOT SURE WHAT HAPPENED NEXT BECAUSE HE WAS DRUNK. RE° THE HANDCUFFS THAT HE WOULD ASK TO TAKE A BONDAGE PICTURE OF HIS VICTIM WITH CUFFS ON & THATS HOW HE WOULD GET THEM CUFFED.

SUB. STATES THAT THERE IS AN I.D. FROM THE B/M HE MET AN 27 & WISCONSIN IN HIS WALLET. SUB. STATES THAT ALL HIS VICTIMS KNEW THAT HOMOSEXUAL ACTIVITY WAS THE IDEA & POSSIBLY PICTURES.

SUB. STATES THAT ALL THAT IS WRITTEN HERE IS THE TRUTH & HE GAVE THIS STATEMENT FREELY TO MAKE A CLEAN SWEEP OF HIS LIFE & THE MATTERS THAT HAVE HAPPENED

Jeff Dahmer

DET. Patrick Kennedy

Det. Dennis Murphy

INTERVIEWING OFFICER TO FURNISH: Name, Rank, Payroll Number,   Date and Time of Interview.

2462, SEC 5 PAGE 5

25

DOC-212 (Rev. 08/90)

(copy)

Wisconsin Statute
Sections 48.22, 57.06 & 973.10(
Administrative Ru
Chapter DOC 328.

ORDER TO DETAIN

DATE: 7-23-91

TO: Milw Co Sheriff / Police

Pursuant to the authority by Statute and Administrative Rule of the Department of Corrections, you are hereby directed to hold in custody the below-named:

Re: DAhmer, Jeffry _____ (Client's Name) Client Number: 177252

Conviction: ☑ Felony ☐ Misdemeanor Date of Birth: 5-21-60

The above-named was convicted on ___1-30-90___ in the

Circuit Court of ___℥ᶜ Milwaukee___ County of the charge(s)

2ᶜ Sex assault enticing child for immoral purpose (Offense and Statute Number)

and is now on probation / parole supervision, or is a Wisconsin State Prison inmate.

The above-named is to be held in your custody until further instructions are received from the undersigned or a duly authorized representative of the Department of Corrections.

NAME Michele Mitchem TITLE Probation agent

ADDRESS for 30908 TELEPHONE # ( )

Behavior or violation resulting in custody: (State whether alleged behavior constitutes a violation of law or a violation of the rules or conditions of supervision)

Homicide

SEC 5 , PAGE 6

DISTRIBUTION: Original - Law Enforcement Agency; Copy - Supervisor; Copy - Case File

26

NAME   DAHMER   JEFFREY   LIONEL

DESC   HGT   WGT   BUILD   HAIR   EYES
       6-00   175   SLENDER   BLN   BLU

       FBI   CTB   OTHER   PHOTO
       1AA5ABAAB   ZAA604

SMT   DOB

IDENTIFICATION DIVISION   CRIMINAL INVESTIGATION BUREAU

MPD CHARGES   WT/CK BY PA. CHILDS 57477

RECORD   YES   DATE 7-23-91   TIME 12.17AM

CHECKED AT R OF I BY   SUSPECT neg.

   BARTOLOTTA KATHLEEN   MO neg

REQUESTED BY OFFICER   OH Above

                                   OTHER

                          Subject not on file.
                            No warrant.
                        probation state 94 0 225 0

27

PREPARED ON 7/23/91   MILWAUKEE POLICE DEPARTMENT
        AT 08 13   IDENTIFICATION DIVISION
REQUEST #1

                    NAME   DAHMER   JEFFREY   LIONEL

                    DOB   05/21/60   AGE 31   RACE W   SEX M

                    FPC # 14A5A9A08   OHR # 0000022750
                                                SID # 36460A
      ALIAS

....
      AGENCY   DATE   CHARGE   DISPOSITION
....

        FOR LAW ENFORCEMENT PURPOSES ONLY

        09/08/86   1 & 1 AMENDED TO DISORDERLY
                                            1 YR PROB
        09/08/86   INDECENT EXP

        09/27/88   SEXUAL EXPLOITATION OF CHILD
                                            5YRS DET CONSEC STAY.
                                            5YRS PROB
        09/27/88   SEX ASSAULT SECOND DEGREE
                                            5YRS DET STAY 5YR PROB
                                            1ST YR HOEC HUBER

        REQUESTOR 50674

....

        EXTENT OF RECORD CHECK DEPENDENT ON INFORMATION SUPPLIED BY REQUEST
        ENTRIES PRECEDED BY AN ASTERISK (*) REPRESENT INFORMATION FURNISHED
        TO THIS DEPARTMENT BY THE FBI, CIB, OR OTHER GOVERNMENTAL AGENCIES
        THESE ENTRIES ARE NOT SUPPORTED BY FINGERPRINTS IN THE FILES OF THE
        MILWAUKEE POLICE DEPARTMENT.   IF FURTHER EXPLANATION OF INFORMATION
        IS DESIRED, COMMUNICATE WITH CONTRIBUTING AGENCY

                                28

```
IZS.Q4.1:DAHMER/JEFFREY/L.2:M/W.3:P8/21/60.
+NAMMMPWLI.LAHMER/JEFFREY
+NAMMMPWLI.DAHMER/JEFFREY
+LAMMMPWLI.PAMMER/JEFFREY
```

REASONS FOR DELETIONS OF PORTIONS OF THIS REPORT

#41 Pursuant to a formal agreement between the
     Milwaukee Police Department and the Wisconsin
     Department of Justice, Division of Law Enforce-
     ment Services, access by the Milwaukee Police
     Department to Crime Information Bureau or
     National Crime Information Center records is
     specifically conditioned to the Milwaukee
     Police Department limiting access to the infor-
     mation obtained pursuant to this agreement only
     to those individuals and agencies who are
     authorized to receive criminal history record
     information. Under no circumstances shall such
     information be provided to non-criminal justice
     agencies except as authorized by law. See also
     Sec. 905.09, Wisconsin Statutes.

3 Pages

29

IWS.QW.1:DAHMER/JEFFREY/L.2:M/W.3:05/21/60.
+NAMM*MWD1.DAHMER/JEFFREY
+NAM*MWD1.DAHMER/JEFFREY
+NAMA*MWD1.DAHMER/JEFFREY

IWS./S99S 1055   WIMPD0058
TIME   30994   10 07/23/91 00:17 01 CF 01
DOT   NCIC CIB
FIELD EDIT SUCCESSFUL
DAHMER,JEFFREY/L
05211960

*MWD1.
NO RECORD FO ND FOR DAHMER   JEFFREY   ON MOVING FILE

*MWD1.
NO RECORD FO ND FOR DAHMER   JEFFREY   ON MISDEMEANOR FILE

IWS./0473 10 5   WIMPD0058
NCIC   3099   11 07/23/91 00:17 01 OF 01

NO NCIC WANT DOB/052160 NAM/DAHMER, JEFFREY L SEX/M RAC/W

IWS./0473 10 5   WIMPD0058
CIB   3099   12 07/23/91 00:17 01 OF 01
NO HITS FROM THE CIB FILES
DAHMER JEFFR Y/L
05211960

IWS./0473 10 5   WIMPD0058
DOT   3099   13 07/23/91 00:17 01 OF 01

DE/JEFFREY/L DAHMER/M/052160   07/23/91 00.17AM CT
SUBJECT NOT N FILE, CHECK YCUR DATA
(PAGE 1 -   ND)

                         SEC   8

*MWD1.

| FO15-B 5-89 SUPPLEMENT REPORT MILWAUKEE POLICE DEPARTMENT | O INCIDENT SUPPLEMENT O ACCIDENT SUPPLEMENT O JUVENILE SUPPLEMENT | PAGE 1 of 5 | DATE OF REPORT 7-23-91 | INCIDENT/ACCIDENT # M-2472-2481 | |

| INCIDENT INFORMATION | INCIDENT HOMICIDE | | DATE OF INCIDENT/ACCIDENT 7-23-91 | | REP CON # |
| | VICTIM LACY, Oliver nmn | | LOCATION OF INCIDENT/ACCIDENT (Address) 924 N. 25th St. | | DIST |

| JUVENILE LAST NAME | FIRST | MID | DATE OF BIRTH | O DETAINED O ORDERED TO MCCC O OTHER |

| QUAN | TYPE OF PROPERTY | DESCRIPTION | | SERIAL # | CODE # | VALUE |

On Tues., 7-23-91, I, Det. KENNEDY, on Squad 126, along with Det. Michael DUBIS, responded to 924 N. 25th St., #213, to investigate. Upon our arrival, we were met by Squads 31-P.O. RAUTH and MUELLER, who state that at approximately 11:25PM, they were flagged down by an individual who had a handcuff on and stated that a man had threatened him with a knife in Apt. #213 at the apartment building 924 N. 25th St. They state that at this time, they proceeded to that apartment and upon knocking on the door, they were allowed to enter the suspect's dwelling and began to question him. During questioning, they state they observed several polaroid photographs which showed mutilation of human bodies and human heads. They state at this time they placed the individual under arrest for the attempted homicide regarding the individual, Tracy EDWARDS, who flagged them down previously and called for the CIB.

At this time I rode along with the suspect, Jeffrey L. DAHMER in Squad 93, down to the CIB. Once at the CIB, I advised Jeffrey L. DAHMER of his constitutional rights and he stated that he fully understood them and that he wished to freely make a statement regarding the incident. At this time Mr. DAHMER states that he is 31 years of age, born in Milwaukee, WI. He states he moved to Richfield, Ohio, when he was about 6 years old and he was raised there and attended and graduated from Revere High School. He states he spent three years in the army after graduation and moved back to Milwaukee when he was approximately 23 or so years old. The subject states he has a father who lives in Pennsylvania and a mother who lives in California. He states he has one brother, 26, living in Cincinnati, and his grandmother on his father's side lives in Milwaukee. Subject states he was raised in the Protestant faith as he was growing up, but he now considers himself to be an atheist. He admitted that he had been arrested in the past and states he is currently on probation for taking polaroid pictures of a minor. Subject states that when he was 18 years of age and living in Richfield, Ohio, he picked up a hitch-hiker whom he described as a white male about 19 years of age. He states he took him home and had homosexual sex with him and states they were drinking beer and became intoxicated. He states they got into a physical fight because the 19-year old individual tried to leave and that during the fight, he states he struck the hitchhiker with a barbel. He states that the blow of the barbel caused the death of the hitchhiker, and at this time he took

| REPORTING OFFICER ✗ 4 7 2 / SEC 5 / PAGE 9 | PAYROLL # | LOC CODE | SUPERVISOR SIGNATURE |

| INCIDENT INFORMATION | INCIDENT HOMICIDE | | DATE OF INCIDENT/ACCIDENT 7-23-91 | | REP CON # |
| VICTIM LACY, Oliver nmn | | LOCATION OF INCIDENT/ACCIDENT (Address) 924 N. 25th St. | | DIST |

| JUVENILE LAST NAME | FIRST | MID | DATE OF BIRTH | O DETAINED O ORDERED TO MCCC O OTHER |

| QUAN | TYPE OF PROPERTY | DESCRIPTION | | SERIAL # | CODE # | VALUE |

the body out into a wooded area by his house and left it there to decompose for about two weeks. He states he returned with a sledge hammer at this time and used it to break the bones and then he scattered them about the woods. The subject states he moved to Milwaukee after a 3-year tour in the army and a 1-year stay in Miami, Florida, where according to the subject, nothing of this nature happened. Subject states he moved in with his grandmother at 2357 S. 57th St. when he returned to Milwaukee, and he states that when he was about 25 years of age and living in Milwaukee, he picked up a white male, approximately 25 years of age at the 219 Tavern. He states they got a room at the Ambassador Hotel and they got very drunk and passed out. Subject states when he woke up the guy was dead and had blood coming from his mouth. He states he went to the mall and bought a large suitcase and stuck the dead body into it. He states he called a cab and placed the suitcase in it and went back to 2357 S. 57th St. He states that he took the dead body down his basement near a floor drain and used a knife to cut the flesh off the body and then dismembered the body, placed the various parts into plastic bags and then threw them into the trash. The subject feels this occurred in 1984, during the summer. He indicates that there had been many times that he has had sex with men where no violence was involved and states about two months after this incident, he met a hispanic male, about 18 years of age, also at the 219 Tavern, at about 1:00AM. They went back to his grandmother's place and had sex with him, and put sleeping pills in his drink. He states when the guy fell asleep, he strangled him with his hands and took the body down the basement by the drain and used a knife to dismember him, and a sledge hammer to break up the bones, and then placed them in plastic bags and threw them in the trash. He goes on to state, about a month later, he met a black and white mixed male, about 20 years of age, and the Lacage, a tavern on National Avenue, and took him back to his grandmother's house where he had sex and used sleeping pills with him. He states when he was asleep, he strangled him and then dismembered his body and disposed of him in the same manner as before. The subject states a year went by and he met a hispanic male, about 19 years of age at the 219 Club and returned with him to his grandmother's house where he again had sex, used sleeping pills and strangled him, and again dismembered and disposed of the body in the same way. Subject states he moved to 808 N. 24th St. and lived there for a year, and was arrested one time for taking pictures of a minor. After one year of work release

| REPORTING OFFICER 2472 SEC | 5 | PAYROLL # PAGE 10 | LOC CODE | SUPERVISOR SIGNATURE |

32

| INCIDENT INFORMATION | INCIDENT HOMICIDE | | DATE OF INCIDENT/ACCIDENT 7-23-91 | | REP COM # |
| | VICTIM LACY, Oliver nmn | | LOCATION OF INCIDENT/ACCIDENT (Address) 924 N. 25th St. | | DIST |

| JUVENILE LAST NAME | FIRST | MID | DATE OF BIRTH | O DETAINED
O ORDERED TO MCCC
O OTHER |
| QUAN | TYPE OF PROPERTY | DESCRIPTION | SERIAL # | CODE # | VALUE |

from the House of Correction, he moved back to his grandmother's house and lived there for approximately six months. At this time he moved to 924 N. 25th St., #213. Subject states in the winter of 1989, he met a black male, about 24 years of age, in front of the bookstore on 27th St., and took him to his apartment where he took pictures of him in various sexual poses, and had sex with him, and put sleeping pills in a coffee and rum drink, which he gave to the black male. When the black male fell asleep, he stabbed him with a large hunting knife which he described as having a 6" blade, and a black handle. He stabbed him in the neck. After the guy was dead, he put the body in the bathtub and dismembered him. He states he used the knife to dismember him. The subject states he used a plastic trash container or garbage can, and put the bones in it with hydrochloric acid and let them sit for about three days until they turn to a mushy substance, and then he flashed them down the toilet. The flesh that he filleted from the body he put into trash bags and threw them out. The subject states he also, starting with the 3rd victim, boiled the heads in a cleaning solution, and kept the skulls. He kept the skulls in the closet. All identification and jewelry of the victims, he states he cut up and threw out in the garbage. The subject states about two months later, he met a black male, about 20 years of age, around Wisconsin and Water, and walked home with him, and again had sex, used sleeping pills which was placed in a coffee mixture, and strangled him. He then dismembered the body and disposed of him in the same manner as before. Subject states he began getting quicker at cutting up the bodies. The subjects states about one month later, he metl a tall black male, about 26 years of age at Ciest La Vie and they took a taxi home to his apartment and he repeated the same scenario with him, but he did not boil and keep his head. The subject states this was due to time constrains. Subject states about 6 months later, he met a black male, about 20 years age while in Chicago, and rode back to Milwaukee by Greyhound bus. He states before this, he met a Chinese male, about 15 years of age at the Grand Avenue Mall, this was around May or early June. He states they took a bus back to his apartment. It was during the day or the afternoon. He states the Chinese posed for polaroid photos and then he gave him sleeping pills in the coffee rum drink. After he passed out, he strangled him and dismembered and disposed of his body parts in the same way as before. The subject states that the body parts gave off an awful smell in the trash, but no ever did anything, so he just kept following his usual procedure o

| REPORTING OFFICER 2472 SEC 5 / PAGE 11 | PAYROLL # | LOC CODE | SUPERVISOR SIGNATURE |

INCIDENT INFORMATION	INCIDENT HOMICIDE		DATE OF INCIDENT/ACCIDENT 7-23-91		REP CON 1
	VICTIM LACY, Oliver nmn		LOCATION OF INCIDENT/ACCIDENT (Address) 924 N. 25th St.		DIST
JUVENILE LAST NAME	FIRST	MID	DATE OF BIRTH	O DETAINED O ORDERED TO MCCC O OTHER	
QUAN	TYPE OF PROPERTY	DESCRIPTION		SERIAL #	CODE #	VALUE

disposal. Regarding the black male from Chicago, he states that he repeated his usual actions with him. Regarding the head in refrigerator, he states he met him, a black male, about 25 years of age, at 27th and Wisconsin, and took him home and repeated the same actions with him. He states about one month ago, he bought a 57 gallon industrial drum and began placing body parts in it. Subject states on about 7-19-91, he met a white male, about 25 years of age near Marquette University, and took him home, had sex with him, gave him sleeping pills in the coffer rum drink, strangled him, and filleted him in the bathtub, dismembered him and placed the body parts in the industrial drum. Regarding the Chinese male, the subject states that after giving him sleeping pills, he fell asleep, and he, the subject, went to a bar on 27th St. He states that as he left the bar, he saw the Chinese guy running down the street naked and the police saw him and stopped him, and he was not speaking any English so he talked with police and said that he was a friend of his and that he was staying with him. At this time he took the Chinese guy back to his apartment and gave him some more coffee and rum solution with the sleeping pills in it, and after he fell asleep again, he strangled him, dismembered him, and disposed of him in the usual way. He then boiled his head. He states it takes about an hour to boil a head. Regarding his last victim, he states that his I.D. can be found in the bedroom of his apartment.

Regarding 7-23-91, the subject states he met a black male, about 25 years of age, at the mall on Wisconsin Avenue. He states he offered him $20 in cash to let him take some nude pictures of him. Once at his apartment, they drank rum, and he, the subject, got intoxicated. Subject states that he tried to put handcuffs on the victim and the victim ran out and got the police. Subject states he is not sure what happened next because he was drunk. Regarding the handcuffs, he would ask his victims if they would allow him to take a bondage picture with the handcuffs on and that is how he would get them handcuffed. The subject states there is an I.D. from the male he met on 27th and Wisconsin in his wallet. The subject states that all his victims knew that homosexual activity was the idea, and possibly, pictures.

At this time, after the subject gave me this statement verbally, I advised him that I would like to write it down verbatim on paper, however, before I did so, I would

| REPORTING OFFICER 2472, SEC. 5, PAGE 12 | PAYROLL # | LOC CODE | SUPERVISOR SIGNATURE Det Lt Raymond R Such |

P015-8 5-89 SUPPLEMENT REPORT MILWAUKEE POLICE DEPARTMENT | O INCIDENT SUPPLEMENT O ACCIDENT SUPPLEMENT O JUVENILE SUPPLEMENT | PAGE 5 of 6 | DATE OF REPORT 7-23-91 | INCIDENT/ACCIDENT # M-2472-2481

INCIDENT INFORMATION

INCIDENT: HOMICIDE | DATE OF INCIDENT/ACCIDENT: 7-23-91 | REP CON #

VICTIM: LACY, Oliver nmn | LOCATION OF INCIDENT/ACCIDENT (Address): 924 N. 25th St. | DIST

LAST NAME | FIRST | MID | DATE OF BIRTH | O DETAINED O ORDERED TO HCCC O OTHER

TYPE OF PROPERTY | DESCRIPTION | SERIAL # | CODE # | VALUE

181 pages to the confession

This is portion of the confession (only).

...d and that he wished to cooperate, and at this time, I went and got Det. Dennis ...o entered the room, and together, we reiterated his constitutional rights which ... he understood and that he wished to waive them in order to help us with this ...ation. It was during this time that a 4-page confession was written out by Det. KENNEDY and read back to the subject who also read it and then stated that it ...rate and true, and then he signed it, Jeffrey DAHMER. He also initialed each page ...-page confession.

It should be noted that during the entire time that I spoke with the subject, Jeffrey DAHMER, he was given numerous cigarettes, 4-5 cups of coffee, two glasses of water, and two cans of coca-cola soda pop. He was also allowed to use the bathroom upon request. This entire interview and confession started at approximately 1:30AM and finished at approximately 7:15AM. After the confession was completely written out, read over, and signed by the subject, he was asked if there is anything that he would like to do, or that if he was hungry. He stated that he was not hungry and probably will not be hungry for a long time, however, he would like to just sit and talk about the offenses a little bit more. The conversation which followed at this time has been recorded by Det. Dennis MURPHY, and he will file a detailed supplementary regarding what was said during this interview.

Report per Det. Patrick KENNEDY.

PK/rqg 7-23-91

2472 - / SEC 5 / PAGE 13

REPORTING OFFICER	PAYROLL #	LOC CODE	SUPERVISOR SIGNATURE
Patrick KENNEDY - Det.	48171	93	Det. Lt. Raymond J. Sucik

INCIDENT INFORMATION	INCIDENT HOMICIDE		DATE OF INCIDENT/ACCIDENT		REP COM #
	VICTIM LACY, Oliver		LOCATION OF INCIDENT/ACCIDENT (Address) 924 North 25th St., #215		DIST

JUVENILE LAST NAME	FIRST	MID	DATE OF BIRTH	O DETAINED O ORDERED TO MCCC O OTHER

QUAN	TYPE OF PROPERTY	DESCRIPTION	SERIAL #	CODE #	VALUE

On Tue., 7-23-91, after obtaining the signed confession from the suspect, Jeffrey L. DAHMER, W/M, DOB; 5-21-60, he requested that we just sit in the interview room (#411) and talk with him, so he can have a couple of cigarettes, some coffee, and think as to what had occurred. We, Det. Dennis MURPHY and Patrick KENNEDY, then talked with Jeffrey DAHMER regarding his family and he stated his mother and father are divorced. His mother, Joyce FLINT, is presently living in Northern California somewhere and his father, Lionel DAHMER, is presently living in Pennsylvania and works for the Pittsburgh Paint and Glass Co. A further check and that phone number there is (412-325-51523) and a home number of (216-666-8323). Jeffrey stated he has not seen either parent for quite some time and he believes that the last time he saw his father was in 1979. He also stated he has a brother in Cincinnati, but he has not seen him for quite a while.

We then questioned him regarding his address at the time that these homicides first occurred when he was 18 years old and he stated that his home town was Bath, Ohio, and that while he was there, he picked up a hitchhiker in Bath, Ohio, across from the fire house and took him to his house at 4480 West Bath Rd., in Bath, Ohio. He stated they had sex, got into an argument and he killed this individual by hitting him with a bar bell. He stated after this occurred, he cut him up, put him in garbage bags and threw the bags in the woods behind his house, to the west, and left him there for about two weeks. He stated after two weeks, he went to the woods with his sledgehammer and broke the bones up into little pieces and scattered them about the woods.

He stated that after this he joined the Army, in 1979. He was subsequently discharged in March of 1981. He stated that after he was discharged, he lived in Miami, Florida, for approximately one year. He then moved back to Bath, Ohio, for four months. Then in about June or July of 1982, he moved in with his grandmother at 2357 South 57th St. He stated that from the first homicide through all this time, he was not involved in any other homicides.

Regarding any activities as to why he had kept some body parts of the victims or whether or not he had consumed any of the body parts, he stated the only time he ever did consume any body parts, was one time and it was the biceps (he pointed to his right biceps) of the black male whom he had met on 27th and Wisconsin. He stated the reason he

REPORTING OFFICER 2472, SEC 5, PAGE 14	PAYROLL #	LOC CODE	SUPERVISOR SIGNATURE

INCIDENT	HOMICIDE		DATE OF INCIDENT/ACCIDENT		REP CON
INFORMATION	VICTIM LACY, Oliver		LOCATION OF INCIDENT/ACCIDENT (Address) 924 North 25th St.		DIS
JUVENILE LAST NAME	FIRST	MID	DATE OF BIRTH	O DETAINED O ORDERED TO HCCC O OTHER	

QUAN	TYPE OF PROPERTY	DESCRIPTION				SERIAL #	CODE #	VALUE

consumed this biceps was because it was big and he wanted to try it. He then stated he
didn't want to talk about it any more. He also stated he would masturbate in front of the
body parts and skulls he had collected because it brought back memories of the victim. He
stated he would put these body parts in formaldehyde and he would boil the skulls to get
rid of the skin. He stated he also spray painted several of the skulls. (This will be
reflected on a spearate supplementary report.)

He stated of all the victims he killed, which he believed to be in the vicinity of
possibly 15, he did keep three skulls. He stated one of the skulls was from the victim
in Ohio and then there were two others of black males. He stated he put these two skulls
in acid and got rid of them that way. He stated the total length of time that this
occurred was for about six years he believed. He stated the type of pills he used to put
the victims to sleep prior to him strangling them, were sleeping pills which he had
obtained from a Dr. HONG. He stated the reason that he killed these homosexuals and he
stated they all were homosexuals, was because he wanted to be with them. He stated he
kept the skulls of the good looking ones because he didn't want to loose them. He also
stated that he felt he could hang on to them if he would in fact kill them and keep their
skulls. He stated the last three skulls that were in the refrigerator and not boiled,
belonged to his last three victims.

At this time Mr. DAHMER stated he was tired and he wished to get some rest. He was
then taken to the City Jail.

Report per Det. Dennis MURPHY.

DM/lh   7-23-91

2472 SEC 5 / PAGE 15

REPORTING OFFICER Det. D. MURPHY	PAYROLL # 32983 91	LOC CODE	SUPERVISOR SIGNATURE

INCIDENT INFORMATION	INCIDENT HOMICIDE (STABBING)		DATE OF INCIDENT/ACCIDENT 07-23-91		REP CON
	VICTIM LACY, Oliver		LOCATION OF INCIDENT/ACCIDENT (Address) 924 North 25th Street, Apt. 213		DIS

JUVENILE LAST NAME	FIRST	MID	DATE OF BIRTH	O DETAINED O ORDERED TO MCCC O OTHER

QUAN	TYPE OF PROPERTY	DESCRIPTION	SERIAL #	CODE #	VALUE

On Tuesday, 07-23-91, I, Detective KENNEDY, of Squad 126, while investigating the above incident and filing reports down on the 4th fl., of the CIB, was given a message, by the head jailer in LUCAD, that the suspect in this offense, one Jeffrey DAHMER, had requested to speak with me again.

At this time I proceeded to the 5th fl., LUCAD lock up, where I went to the cell, where DAHMER, the suspect was sitting. At this time I asked if he had in fact requested to see me again, and he stated "yes I did". At this time myself and Det. Dennis MURPHY, escorted DAHMER back down to the 4th floor, CIB, to an interview room, where we conducted the following investigation. At this time DAHMER stated that he wish to talk to us about an additional two Homicides that he forgot to mention in the original interview. This information was given to Det. MURPHY, and he will file a separate detailed supplement regarding this.

Also during this interview I asked DAHMER what substance was sprayed on some of the skulls, which were found in his apartment, as the Medical Examiners stated there appeared to be a paint like substance on three of the skulls. To this DAHMER stated he had gone to the Pallette Shop, which is an Art Store, located on South Water St. He states at the store he purchased some enamel spray paint, type of color being fake granite. When asked why he used this spray paint on the skulls, he stated he sprayed them in order to give them an artificial look, in case someone would see them, they would feel they were not real. Upon asking him which skulls he did spray, he stated the black male which he met on 27th St., was one of the skulls, the mixed mulatto male which he met at LaCage, on West National, was the 2nd skull sprayed and a black male prostitute which he picked up in front of 219 S. 2nd was the 3rd skull he sprayed. At this time I also questioned DAHMER, regarding the numerous boxes of Soilex, which is a cleansing powder that was found in his apartment. To this he stated that he used the Soilex, along with a water solution to boil the heads which he had decapitated from his victims. He stated the Soilex would effectively boil off the skin and hair from the skulls, in about an hours time. He also stated one of the torsos that he had taken from a victim, he had also boiled in a large kettel, which he kept in the Soilex. At this time I also questioned DAHMER regarding the Homicide investigation of Dean VAUGHN, who also resided at 924 N. 25th St., on the 3rd

38

PO15-B 5-89 SUPPLEMENT REPORT
MILWAUKEE POLICE DEPARTMENT
O INCIDENT SUPPLEMENT
O ACCIDENT SUPPLEMENT
O JUVENILE SUPPLEMENT
PAGE 2 of 2   DATE OF REPORT 07-23-91   INCIDENT/ACCIDENT 91-51767 (M2472/M248

	INCIDENT	HOMICIDE (STABBING)			DATE OF INCIDENT/ACCIDENT 07-23-91		REP COM #
INCIDENT INFORMATION	VICTIM	LACY, Oliver			LOCATION OF INCIDENT/ACCIDENT (Address) 924 North 25th Street		DIST

JUVENILE LAST NAME	FIRST	MID	DATE OF BIRTH	O DETAINED O ORDERED TO MCCC O OTHER

QUAN	TYPE OF PROPERTY	DESCRIPTION	SERIAL #	CODE #	VALUE

floor. To this DAHMER stated that he recalled several months ago, a Detective coming to his apartment to question him regarding the Dean VAUGHN Homicide. He states, he in no way had anything to do with this. He states when the Detective came to his door, he felt that he was sure he was going to be apprehended for the numerous Homicides, which he has already admitted to. However, when the Detective began speaking of a black male, by the name of Dean VAUGHN, he was relieved, as he knew he had nothing to do with that and he told the Detective so. He states he had nothing to do with the VAUGHN Homicide and since he has already admitted to several other Homicides, he would not be afraid to admit if had participated in that offense. At this time there was one other question, which I asked DAHMER and that was pertaining to the fact, that numerous types of ether were found in his apartment, and to this he stated that he had brought the ether in an attempt to use it on some of his victims, after he had drugged them, to attempt to keep them in a sleep like state longer, however, he stated that the ether did not work very well and only made them slightly intoxicated or high, and didn't put them to sleep.

At this time my part of the interview of DAHMER was terminated.

Report dictated by: Detective Patrick KENNEDY

PK: hvs 07-23-91

2472 = SEC 5 / PAGE 17

REPORTING OFFICER	PAYROLL #	LOC CODE	SUPERVISOR SIGNATURE
Det. KENNEDY	48171	93	

INCIDENT INFORMATION	INCIDENT HOMICIDE			DATE OF INCIDENT/ACCIDENT		REP CON #
	VICTIM LACY, Oliver			LOCATION OF INCIDENT/ACCIDENT (Address) 924 North 25th St., #215		DIST 3

JUVENILE LAST NAME	FIRST	MID	DATE OF BIRTH	O DETAINED O ORDERED TO MCCC O OTHER

QUAN	TYPE OF PROPERTY	DESCRIPTION	SERIAL #	CODE #	VALUE

On Tue., 7-23-91, *at 12:45 PM* we, Det. Dennis MURPHY and Patrick KENNEDY, were requested by the suspect to come to the jail so he could give us additional information regarding our investigation. We proceeded to that location, where Mr. Jeffrey DAHMER, was taken from the jail to the interview room at the CIB, where he stated that he had more information regarding other homicides. We advised Mr. DAHMER of his Miranda rights, which he stated he understood and he stated, "I've told you everything already. I have nothing to hide, so I might as well tell you about these ones I forgot."

He stated there was one more Hispanic male that he met in Chicago about two weeks ago, just after the 4th of July and he stated this Hispanic male was about 25 years old and he met him at Carol's, a gay bar on Wells St. He stated he and this Hispanic male then took a Greyhound back to Milwaukee and the Hispanic male stayed two days. He stated he does not recall his name, it may have been Tony, but he is not sure. He stated that after the first day, they had oral sex with each other and got along together.

On the second day the Hispanic male stated he was going to be leaving, at which time the defendant, Jeffrey, stated he did not want him to leave, so he gave him sleeping pills in the coffee in order to keep him there. He stated that after he passed out, he then strangled the Hispanic male and dismembered and put his head in the refrigerator. He stated he did not boil the head and when he would boil the heads, he would use "Soilex" to boil the heads. He stated he also had purchased a 57 gallon drum, in which he put the torsos of three of his victims. He stated he even sprayed some of the skulls with spray paint so they looked artificial. Mr. DAHMER stated he purchased the spray paint from an art shop on Water St.

I then questioned him regarding the torsos in the 57 gallon tank and he stated one was that of the Hispanic male from Carol's bar, one was from the black male on 27th St. and the third one was from the black male he met at the bus station in Chicago. I informed him there was a skeleton recovered in his apartment and he stated that was from the black male he met in front of the bookstore approximately one year ago.

Mr. DAHMER further stated he would cut off the penis and body parts, and put them in formaldehyde to perserve them and then look at them and masturbate for gratification. He further stated he had experimented with ether to put the people asleep, but it didn't

REPORTING OFFICER 2472	SEC 5	PAYROLL 8 PAGE 18	LOC CODE	SUPERVISOR SIGNATURE Lt. Raymond Guth

INCIDENT INFORMATION	INCIDENT	HOMICIDE		DATE OF INCIDENT/ACCIDENT		REP COM
	VICTIM	LACY, Oliver		LOCATION OF INCIDENT/ACCIDENT (Address) 924 North 25th St.		DIS
JUVENILE LAST NAME	FIRST	MID		DATE OF BIRTH	☐ DETAINED ☐ ORDERED TO MCCC ☐ OTHER	

QUAN	TYPE OF PROPERTY	DESCRIPTION			SERIAL #	CODE #	VALUE

work. Regarding the other six torsos that apparently are missing and that can not be accounted for by the amount of heads that were discovered in the apartment, he stated that these torsos had been placed in acid and were eaten away and then flushed down the toilet when they became "sludgy."

Mr. DAHMER then stated he remembers another victim, and this homicide occurred about five months ago and this was a black male about 20 years old who he met at 27th and Wisconsin. He stated he got this individual to pose for him, gave him a drink and then cut off his skin. He eventually put the skin in acid. He stated he skinned the entire body and then boiled the skull of this individual and subsequently disposed of the body in plastic bags after dimembering same. He stated that when he would strangle his victim, he used his hands and about four times he used a black strap, leather type, that he had bought for that specific purpose.

Regarding his activities upon joining the Army, he stated he joined in 1979, was discharged in March of 1981, stationed in Braunhold, Germany. He stated after that he went to Florida for a year, returned to Bath, Ohio, in March of 1982, and stayed for four months. He then returned to the residence of his grandmother at 2357 South 57th St. He stated he had originally said the killings started in 1984, but to the best of his recollection, he believes these killings started in 1987. Mr. DAHMER stated that this was all he could remember at this time and if he does recall any further information, he will contact either myself or Det. KENNEDY. He stated these are the only homicides he can recall being involved in at this time.

While questioning Mr. DAHMER regarding the sledgehammer he used to break up the bones of his victims while he was living at his grandmother's house, he stated the sledgehammer was kept in the garage and had a grey handle. I was subsequently informed by Det. FARMER that they recovered a sledgehammer in the garage and upon Det. FARMER returning to the CIB with the sledgehammer, it was shown to the defendant and upon viewing it, stated this is the sledgehammer he used to break up the bones of the victims at 2357 South 57th St. This sledgehammer will be placed on inventory by Det. FARMER.

Report per Det. Dennis MURPHY.

DM/lh   7-23-91 2 4 7 2 -SEC 5 / PAGE 1 9

REPORTING OFFICER Det. D. MURPHY	PAYROLL # 32983 91	LOC CODE	SUPERVISOR SIGNATURE	

| PO15-A 5-89 SUPPLEMENT REPORT
MILWAUKEE POLICE DEPARTMENT | ☒ INCIDENT SUPPLEMENT
○ ACCIDENT SUPPLEMENT
○ JUVENILE SUPPLEMENT | PAGE 1 of 1 | DATE OF REPORT
7-24-91 | INCIDENT/ACCIDENT # |

| INCIDENT INFORMATION | INCIDENT | | DATE OF INCIDENT/ACCIDENT | | REP CON |
| | VICTIM | | LOCATION OF INCIDENT/ACCIDENT (Address) | | DI: |

| JUVENILE LAST NAME | FIRST | MID | DATE OF BIRTH | ○ DETAINED
○ ORDERED TO MCCC
○ OTHER |
| QUAN | TYPE OF PROPERTY | DESCRIPTION | | SERIAL # | CODE # | VALUE |

On Wednesday, July 24, 1991, at 8:15 a.m., I, Captain Howard K. LINDSTEDT, LUCAD-Days, had occasion to personally inspect the "suicide watch" which had been previously established for the prisoner, Jeffrey L. DAHMER, W/M, 5-21-60, who was housed in cell "N-1" in the upper level of cells at LUCAD. At this particular time I spoke with P.O. Kevin ARMBRUSTER, District #3-Late, who was assigned to the watch, and I inquired as to the condition of the prisoner and the current status of the day shift relief officer. P.O. ARMBRUSTER replied that everything was alright and that there weren't any problems. I observed DAHMER who was awake and standing in cell "N-1." DAHMER walked towards the front of his cell and looked down at what appeared to be a small piece of paper which he held in his hand. He then stated that he wanted to talk to Detective Pat KENNEDY. I informed P.O. ARMBRUSTER, in DAHMER's presence, that I would notify the Criminal Investigation Bureau of DAHMER's request to speak with Detective KENNEDY and that I would also check on the status of the day shift relief officer, who was now fifteen minutes late. (P.O. ARMBRUSTER had mentioned that he was scheduled to make an 8:30 a.m. court appearance today.) I then walked out of the cellblock area and walked to the Sergeant-in-Charge's office where I notified Sgt. Rudolph BINTER of DAHMER's request. I instructed Sgt. BINTER to call "extension 302" and notify the "CIB" that DAHMER had made a request to speak to Detective Patrick KENNEDY.

| REPORTING OFFICER | PAYROLL #
29939 | LOC CODE
83 | SUPERVISOR SIGNATURE |

PO15-0 5-89 SUPPLEMENT REPORT MILWAUKEE POLICE DEPARTMENT	X INCIDENT SUPPLEMENT O ACCIDENT SUPPLEMENT O JUVENILE SUPPLEMENT	PAGE 1 of 2	DATE OF REPORT 07-24-91	INCIDENT/ACCIDENT # 91-51767	
INCIDENT INFORMATION	INCIDENT HOMICIDE		DATE OF INCIDENT/ACCIDENT 07-23-91		REP CON,#
	VICTIM LACY, Oliver		LOCATION OF INCIDENT/ACCIDENT (Address) 924 N. 25th St., #213		DIST
JUVENILE LAST NAME	FIRST	MID	DATE OF BIRTH	O DETAINED O ORDERED TO MCCC O OTHER	
QUAN	TYPE OF PROPERTY	DESCRIPTION		SERIAL #	CODE #	VALUE

On Wednesday, 7-24-91, I, Det. KENNEDY, Squad-126, along with Det. Dennis MURPHY, were requested at approximately 8:30A by the suspect in this offense, Jeffrey DAHMER, to speak with him.

At this time I proceeded to the 5th floor, LUCAD, where I infact asked the suspect, Jeffrey DAHMER, if he had requested to speak with me at which time he stated he did. I took him with me from the 5th floor down to an interview room at the CIB, where we again began to speak of the offense.

During this time Jeffrey DAHMER stated that he wished to speak slightly regarding earlier years of his life in Ohio.

At this time he states that he remembers his early family life as being one of extreme tension. He states the tension came from the relationship that existed at that time betweeen his mother and his father. He stated although he was not physically or sexually abused and he did not witness any physical abuse from his parents, he stated that they were "constantly at each others throats" and arguing. He states that his mother appeared to have some psychiatric problems and had infact suffered a nervous breakdown at one time during his early childhood. He states that she was on medication and had been seeing a doctor much of the time. He states that he was advised by relatives that his mother suffered severe Post-Partum Depression after he was born, and he took that as an indication that he was at least partially the problem for his parents bad marital state. He states that he believes his mother became depressed after his birth and never quite fully recovered, and thereby he states he felt a certain amount of guilt in regard to the bad marriage of his parents.

He states that when he was approximately 18-yoa., is when a divorce occurred between his mother and his father, and at this time his mother moved to Chippewa Falls, WI., and his father had been court ordered to stay out of the house and had moved to a motel which was several miles from the house. He states at this time his mother took his younger brother, who was approximately 6-years younger than him when she moved out and that he was left all alone at the house in Richfield, Ohio.

He states that it was at this time when he started to have strong feelings of being left all alone, and that it was at this time that he remembers having strong desires

REPORTING OFFICER 472, SEC 5, PAGE 2	PAYROLL #	LOC CODE	SUPERVISOR SIGNATURE Lieut. Raymond Smith

43

	INCIDENT HOMICIDE		DATE OF INCIDENT/ACCIDENT 07/23/91		REP COM
INCIDENT INFORMATION	VICTIM LACY, Oliver		LOCATION OF INCIDENT/ACCIDENT (Address)		DIST

JUVENILE LAST NAME	FIRST	MID	DATE OF BIRTH	☐ DETAINED ☐ ORDERED TO MCCC ☐ OTHER

QUAN	TYPE OF PROPERTY	DESCRIPTION	SERIAL #	CODE #	VALUE

of not wanting to have people leave him. He stated it was also at this time that he began hating to sleep alone at night. He further indicates that it was around this time in his life that he became familiar with alcohol, and that he immediately became a heavy drinker and abused alcohol on a regular basis. When he went into the Army, he indicates that his alcohol intake increased, and that he was actually released 6-months early from the Army because of abuses of alcohol. He states that he was a Field Medic while he was serving in the Armed Forces.

The suspect, Jeffrey DAHMER, states that he began having fantasies of killing people at the early age of 17 or 18. He states although these fantasies were fleeting, he feels that he had the fantasies to overcome the feelings he had of frustration and emptiness which he felt were in his life.

He states that after he moved to Milwaukee in 1981, the fantasies of killing people began to excite him and became more frequent.

Regarding his victims, he states that he received physical pleasure from being with the victims when they were alive and he would have preferred that the victims remained alive; however, he states that it was better to have them with him dead than to have them leave. He states that when he felt when they were to leave, that is when he would decide to kill them.

Regarding the fact that he stated that he had infact eaten the parts of one of his victims, he states that he feels that by eating parts of the victim, this was his way of keeping them with him even longer and making his victims part of himself.

At this time Jeffrey DAHMER answered other questions put to him by Det. MURPHY, and he will file a detailed supplementary regarding that part of this interview.

Report per: Det. Patrick KENNEDY.

PK/slb   7-24-91

4472, SEC 5 PAGE 22

REPORTING OFFICER DET. PATRICK KENNEDY	PAYROLL # 48171	LOC CODE 93	SUPERVISOR SIGNATURE

PO15-8 5-89 SUPPLEMENT REPORT MILWAUKEE POLICE DEPARTMENT	☒ INCIDENT SUPPLEMENT ☐ ACCIDENT SUPPLEMENT ☐ JUVENILE SUPPLEMENT	PAGE 1 of 3	DATE OF REPORT 07-24-91	INCIDENT/ACCIDENT # 91-51767 (M2472)	
INCIDENT INFORMATION	INCIDENT HOMICIDE		DATE OF INCIDENT/ACCIDENT 07-22-91		REP CON #
	VICTIM LACY, Oliver		LOCATION OF INCIDENT/ACCIDENT (Address) 924 N. 25th St., #213		DIST
JUVENILE LAST NAME	FIRST	MID	DATE OF BIRTH	☐ DETAINED ☐ ORDERED TO MCCC ☐ OTHER	
QUAN	TYPE OF PROPERTY	DESCRIPTION	SERIAL #	CODE #	VALUE

On Wednesday, 7-24-91, at approximately 8:30 A.M., I, along with Det. Patrick KENNEDY, were notified by the jail that the suspect in this offense, Jeffrey DAHMER, requested to speak to us regarding this investigation.

We proceeded to the County Jail where he was taken from the cell and conveyed Room #407 at the CIB, where he was re-interviewed by us. We informed Mr. DAHMER of his "Miranda Rights", and he stated he knows his rights, but he just wants to talk to us regarding this investigation.

We then talked to him regarding his childhood and family status and a supplementary report will be called in reflecting his statements to these questions.

We asked Jeffrey some additional questions regarding the first homicide that occurred in Bath, Ohio, and he stated that prior to that he had just started drinking when he was 17-years old. .He states his friends were straight that he knew of. He states he had a friend named Jeff SIX, and they all smoked marijuana in high school. He states that he did not know of any friends being gay, but that he, himself had homosexual tendencies and had never gone out with a girl or had sex with any females.

He states his first homicide which occurred, he believes around October of 1978, was of a white male hitchhiker, whom he describes as 18-yoa., 5'10" tall, skinny build, maybe 150 lbs., having straight brown collar length hair, not wearing glasses, clean shaven, and he believes he was not a homosexual. He states he didn't have sex with this individual, he just invited him in for a drink, and when the individual wanted to leave that's when he hit him with a "barbell" and subsequently disposed of the body behind his residence. He states he did burn his clothes and identification.

He again went through the various places that he lived, and after joining the Army in 1979 and being discharged in March of 1981, where he was a Field Medic in the Army he moved to Miami and left about October of 1981.

He states that he then went back to Bath, Ohio, and lived there until around December of 1981 or January of 1982.

He states he then moved to Milwaukee with his grandmother from about December of 1981 or January 1982 until 1988, when he moved to 808 N. 24th St. He states he remained

REPORTING OFFICER 2472 /-SEC 5 / PAGE 2 3	PAYROLL #	LOC CODE	SUPERVISOR SIGNATURE *[signature]*

45

Man confesses mass killings

Tells of drugging, strangling, dismembering victims

MILWAUKEE (AP) — The convicted child molester whose apartment held body parts of 11 men has confessed, saying he drugged and strangled the victims then dismembered them and boiled some of their skulls to preserve them, authorities said yesterday.

In an affidavit submitted in Milwaukee County Circuit Court, Police Lt. David Kane wrote that Jeffrey L. Dahmer, 31, told police he met his victims at taverns or shopping malls and lured them to his apartment for photographs.

"Dahmer further stated that he would drug these individuals and usually strangle them and then he would dismember the bodies, often boiling the heads to remove flesh so he could retain the skulls," the affidavit said.

"Mr. Dahmer further stated that he took Polaroid photographs of a number of these persons while they were still alive, after he had killed them, and of their heads and body parts after he had dismembered them," it said.

Circuit Judge Frank T. Crivello accepted the affidavit during a brief probable cause hearing and set bail at $1 million cash. No criminal charges were filed.

Dahmer, a former chocolate factory worker on probation for a 1988 sexual assault of a teen-age boy, did not appear in court. Prosecutors said they plan to file a criminal complaint charging him this afternoon.

One victim has been positively identified through fingerprints as Oliver Lacey, 23, of Chicago. Lacey was recently staying in Milwaukee with his parents, Deputy Inspector Vincent Partipilo said.

Earlier, Police Chief Philip Arreola confirmed that Dahmer was cooperating with investigators, but declined to address reports that Dahmer had confessed to the killings and cannibalism.

"As to the information I can release, for the most part the victims are male," he said. "We have no indication up to now that we have any female victims."

Dahmer's lawyer, Gerald Boyle, said Dahmer held himself responsible for the killings.

"I am told by authorities and by himself that he has made many statements that inculpate him," Boyle said.

Dahmer's apartment

Window

Window

Living Room

Bedroom

Bath

Dining Area

Hall

Refrigerator

Entrance

Closet

Hall

JAMES LANE LUNDE / Sentinel artist

Bodies appeared to have been dismembered in this one-bedroom apartment in the Oxford Plaza Apartments, 924 N. 25th St. The apartment was occupied by Jeffrey L. Dahmer, 31. Skulls were found in a file cabinet, a closet, a refrigerator and a freezer.

| INCIDENT INFORMATION | INCIDENT HOMICIDE | | DATE OF INCIDENT/ACCIDENT 07-22-91 | | REP CON # |
| | VICTIM LACY, Oliver | | LOCATION OF INCIDENT/ACCIDENT (Address) 924 N. 25th St. | | DIST |

| JUVENILE LAST NAME | FIRST | MID | DATE OF BIRTH | ☐ DETAINED ☐ ORDERED TO MCCC ☐ OTHER |

| QUAN | TYPE OF PROPERTY | DESCRIPTION | SERIAL # | CODE # | VALUE |

there 6-months to a year, and then moved to his present address of 924 N. 25th St.

He again states that there was no homicides occurring until the one at the Ambassador Hotel, he believes in 1984, where the individual died and he subsequently took him to his grandmother's residence at 2357 S. 57th St., and there dismembered the body and disposed of the body parts.

He goes on to relate, that there was three other homicides at his grandmother's location, and the rest were at his present address, 924 N. 25th St.

He states the reason there were no homicides from 1978 to 1984 was because he was busy with what he was doing. He said he was busy in the Army and after work he'd go out drinking with the guys, and then go to bed and get up and work. He states when he went to Florida he was too busy, and when he arrived in Milwaukee he was too busy until he discovered the gay bars. He further states that he did not have a homosexual relationship while he was in the Army or in Florida. He states the first experiences started after arriving in Milwaukee and going to the gay bars. He states that he would not maintain a relationship with the individuals whom he had sex with, and most of them were one night stands. He states he enjoyed the company of these individuals, but did not like to see them go.

After the murders started, he states that being with these other homosexuals gave him pleasure and he preferred them alive, but if they wanted to leave and he couldn't have them alive then he would have them dead and that's why he would dismember them and save either their skulls or other body parts. He states that the victim, whose right bicep he had eaten, was one that he cared for and the individual had big bicepts. He stated that he put Crisco on the bicept, softened it up with a meat tenderizer, and then fried it in a skillet. He states he also saved this individuals heart in the freezer, and a portion of an arm from the black male that he had met at a bookstore about 1-year ago. He states he did intend to consume these parts.

He also states that he had killed the individuals he had anal and oral sex with the victim's after death, but not all of them. He states that when he was in high school he had fantasized about killing someone, but it did not take effect until 1978, the first time, and then later on 1984, in Milwaukee.

We asked him why he just didn't have oral or anal sex with the individuals while

| REPORTING OFFICER 2472 SEC | 5 | PAYROLL # PAGE 24 | LOC CODE | SUPERVISOR SIGNATURE Lt. Raymond R. Swick |

| INCIDENT INFORMATION | INCIDENT HOMICIDE | | DATE OF INCIDENT/ACCIDENT 07/22/91 | | REP COM |
| | VICTIM LACY, Oliver | | LOCATION OF INCIDENT/ACCIDENT (Address) 924 N. 25th St. | | DIST |

| JUVENILE LAST NAME | FIRST | MID | DATE OF BIRTH | ☐ DETAINED ☐ ORDERED TO MCCC ☐ OTHER |

| QUAN | TYPE OF PROPERTY | DESCRIPTION | SERIAL # | CODE # | VALUE |

they were alive and let them go, and he stated because he didn't want to loose them and that the death and dismemberment led-to the excitement and gratification. We then asked him if he had ever talked to a psychiatrist, and he stated that he talked to a Dr. CROWLEY, who works for the Social Services a couple of times, possibly 2 or 3 times, in the past month or so. He states that Dr. CROWLEY had prescribed medication for him, but he states he didn't get any because he felt he didn't need it.

He also states that he was fired from his job on July 7, 1991, and he had known the week prior that he was going to get fired and he feels this is the reason why the killings escalated because he was alone at night and did not want to be alone. He had no company and felt that these individuals would keep him company.

We were then informed by Det. Lt. David KANE that his attorney, Wendy PATRICKUS, had arrived with a psychiatrist by the name of Dr. SMAIL. Dr. SMAIL did infact interview the suspect, and when he finished the interview he informed us that the suspect wanted to talk to detectives and get cigarettes and coffee.

We then asked Mr. DAHMER if he would be willing to view the photos that he had taken; namely, the Polaroids that were recovered in his apartment and to try to identify the victims for us, and he stated that he would, and he would look at any other photos we had available of any of the alleged victims and try to make identification for us. He also stated that he will try to remember any physical descriptions of the victims to help us discover their identity.

We then informed Mr. DAHMER of the Probable Cause Hearing which would be taking effect this afternoon, and he stated that he would like to talk to us after that hearing.

Report per: Det. Dennis MURPHY.

DM/slb   7-24-91

2472 / SEC. 5 / PAGE 25

| REPORTING OFFICER DET. DENNIS MURPHY | PAYROLL # 32893 91 | LOC CODE | SUPERVISOR SIGNATURE Act. Lt. Raymond R Smith |

INCIDENT INFORMATION	INCIDENT HOMICIDE (STABBING)		DATE OF INCIDENT/ACCIDENT 07-23-91		REP CON
	VICTIM LACY, Oliver		LOCATION OF INCIDENT/ACCIDENT (Address) 924 N. 25th Street #213		DIST 3

JUVENILE LAST NAME	FIRST	MID	DATE OF BIRTH	☐ DETAINED ☐ ORDERED TO MCCC ☐ OTHER

QUAN	TYPE OF PROPERTY	DESCRIPTION	SERIAL #	CODE #	VALUE

On Wednesday, 07-24-91, we took the suspect, Jeffrey DAHMER, from his cell and conveyed him to the CIB where he met with his attorney Gerald BOYLE and his assistant, Wendy PATRICKUS. At that time he signed a consent form to talk with us regarding this investigation on anything related to the Wisconsin Homicides.

At approximately 4:20 P.M. we sat with Jeffrey in room 407 of the Detective Bureau and gave him cigarettes, coffee and soda and questioned him regarding the Polaroid photos that he had taken of the Homicide Victims in an attempt to make indentification of these individuals and to establish an order of the homicides and what had actually occurred. Mr. DAHMER stated that he would be glad to cooperate with us in any way.

We started with the first homicide committed in Milwaukee and he stated that it occurred in either November of 1984 or November of 1985 to the best of his recollection. He stated that he met this victim and they went to the Ambassador Hotel. He described this individual as a white male, 25 yrs, 5'6, 130 lbs, slim build, blonde hair, shoulder length straight, maybe parted in the middle, and clean shaven. He stated he was fair complected and had smooth skin and was possibly wearing jeans. He indicated that he went to the hotel with the individual, they were drinking and he gave him a drink which contained sleeping pills. When he awoke the subject was dead next to him and blood was coming from his mouth. He stated that he then put the subject in a suitcase and took a cab to his grandmother's house at 2357 S. 57th Street where he drained the blood, cut the body up and used a sledge hammer to break the bones. He stated that he then disposed of the body in plastic garbage bags.

He indicated that in January of 1985 or 1986 he met victim #2 in front of the 219 Club on 2nd Street. He stated that the victim was waiting for a bus which was heading towards the south side. He described this individual as a Hispanic male, 16 to 18, 6'0, 150lbs, slim build, dark straight short hair, clean shaven, possibly wearing a tshirt and tennis shoes.

He stated that when he met this individual and all of the victims he would approach them and ask them if they would like to make money by posing for him in the nude, viewing videos and coming for a drink at his residence. He related that he would offer various amounts of money to these individuals. He stated that each individual accepted his offer and would go with him to his residence. He indicated that the second victim went to his grandmother's house at 2357 S. 57th Street with him by taking the

REPORTING OFFICER 2472, SEC 5	PAYROLL PAGE 26	LOC CODE	SUPERVISOR SIGNATURE

	INCIDENT	HOMICIDE (STABBING)	DATE OF INCIDENT/ACCIDENT 07-23-91		REP CON #
INCIDENT INFORMATION	VICTIM	LACY, Oliver	LOCATION OF INCIDENT/ACCIDENT (Address) 924 N. 25th Street #213		DIST 3

JUVENILE LAST NAME	FIRST	MID	DATE OF BIRTH	O DETAINED O ORDERED TO MCCC O OTHER

QUAN	TYPE OF PROPERTY	DESCRIPTION	SERIAL #	VALUE

subsequently had sex and then gave the victim the sleeping

potion, killed him by strangulation and then smashed the bones with the sledge hammer and disposed of the bones. He stated that he did not keep anything from this individual nor did he keep anything from the first victim.

The third victim he met about two months later, probably March of 1985 or 1986. He stated that he met another Hispanic male in the Phoenix Bar located on 2nd Street near the 219 Club. He related that this individual was a Hispanic male, 19 to 21 yrs, 5'8", 130 lbs, slim build, light brown complexion, having straight short black hair, clean shaven, and smooth skin. He was wearing a long knee length brownish vinyl coat.

He stated he asked this individual to come to his residence to look at videos, take photos or engage in sex. He stated that this victim did accompany him to his grandmother's house where he had oral sex with him. He then proceeded to drug this individual so he slept. He subsequently killed him, dismembered the body and disposed of it. He related that he did not keep any body parts from this victim.

The fourth victim, whom he stated he met sometime in 1987, but is not sure because it could have been when he was at his grandmother's house the second time in 1989. He was not sure of his dates, but he stated that he did meet this individual at LaCage at closing time. Upon viewing a photo of Anthony SEARS, DOB 01-28-65, he stated that this is the individual that he believes he met at LaCage. He described this victim as a black male, 21 to 22yrs, 5'9, 150lbs, slim to medium build, light complexion, having short curly hair and a small ponytail in back with a rubber band. He stated that he was wearing jeans.

He stated that he and this individual that he identified as Anthony SEARS through a (FRIEND OF SEARS) photo of Anthony SEARS, got into his friend's auto and his friend drove him to his grandmother's house. He described the auto as a large beat up older model, dark blue.

He indicated that after arriving at the residence he used the same ploy to get the individual to come with him. He related that when they got there, they engaged in sex, that put him to sleep he gave him the drink and subsequently killed him and dismembered the body. He indicated that this is the first one where he kept anything of the individual. He stated that he kept the victim's skull which he boiled to remove all the skin, he kept the scalp with the small ponytail because he liked it and he kept the genitals of this person. He stated that at the time of his arrest it was in the black metal cabinet. He also stated to preserve the skull and genitals he had called the hardware store and

REPORTING OFFICER 2472 / SEC 5 / PAGE 27	PAYROLL #	LOC CODE	SUPERVISOR SIGNATURE Det.Lt. Raymond Such

51

PO15-B 5-89 SUPPLEMENT REPORT MILWAUKEE POLICE DEPARTMENT	O INCIDENT SUPPLEMENT O ACCIDENT SUPPLEMENT O JUVENILE SUPPLEMENT	PAGE 3	DATE OF REPORT 07-24-91	INCIDENT/ACCIDENT # 91-51767/M2472-M2481	
INCIDENT INFORMATION	INCIDENT HOMICIDE (STABBING)		DATE OF INCIDENT/ACCIDENT 07-23-91		REP CON #
	VICTIM LACY, Oliver		LOCATION OF INCIDENT/ACCIDENT (Address) 924 N. 25th Street #213		DIST 3
JUVENILE LAST NAME	FIRST	MID	DATE OF BIRTH	O DETAINED O ORDERED TO HCCC O OTHER	
QUAN	TYPE OF PROPERTY	DESCRIPTION		SERIAL #	CODE # VALUE

asked what would dry out a rabbit skin and they recommended acetone which he used to dry out the scalp and genital area. He stated the reason he kept the scalp was because he liked it. He also stated that the skull he kept he painted.

The fifth victim was two months after he moved into his apartment at 924 N. 25th Street which he figures was in 1990. He stated that this individual was the first one he also took photos of. We showed him a photo album which contained 15 photos of a black male in various positions and he identified this individual as the person he met in the 219 Club area and offered him the same line as to come to be photographed, to have a drink and look at dirty videos. He indicated that this victim agreed and took him to 924 N. 25th Street #213 and there he drugged him and subsequently killed him by strangulation. After removing his clothes he saw the tattoo "Cash D" on his chest with pitchforks going up above the name "Cash." The photographs in the album depict this openly. He described this individual as a black male, 22 yrs, 5'8 to 5'9, 140 lbs, curly black hair with a slight mustache. The photo also depicts this. He stated that after "Cash D" had died he had oral sex on him.

The next individual, victim #6, was met at the Phoenix on 2nd St. and he again approached this individual with the same line as to having to pose for photos and having to view videos and drink. He describes this individual as a black male, about 24, 6'2", 170 lbs., medium build, dark skin, prematurely bald, close cut hair, clean shaven, and he said he used to be with the Milwaukee Ballet. He states that he had oral sex with this individual and then killed him by the same procedure, drugging him until he slept, strangling him, and then dismembering him. He states he did not keep anything from this individual. Upon viewing a photograph of a missing person, he identified victim #6 being SMITH, Edward Warren-M/B, B of I #244654. He states that this photo does look like the individual he picked up and states he did not keep any body parts.

Regarding victim #5, Cash D, he states he did keep this individual's skull and painted it after it had dried out.

He then continued on with victim #7 who he stated he met in front of the book store in the 800 block of N. 27th St. He states this occurred in the summer of 1990 and he describes him as a black male, 24, 6', 160 lbs., medium build, medium complexion, chin whiskers, short black hair, and states he approached him with the same line, had sex, and then drugged him and killed him by cutting his throat. He states after taking

INCIDENT	HOMICIDE (STABBING)	DATE OF INCIDENT/ACCIDENT 07-23-91	REP CON #
VICTIM	LACY, Oliver	LOCATION OF INCIDENT/ACCIDENT (Address) 924 N. 25th Street #213	DIST 3

JUVENILE LAST NAME	FIRST	MID	DATE OF BIRTH	O DETAINED / O ORDERED TO MCCC / O OTHER

QUAN	TYPE OF PROPERTY	DESCRIPTION	SERIAL #	CODE #	VALUE

photos of this individual, he dismembered him, disposed of the body parts except for his bicep which he kept in the freezer and his skull which he painted after the skin was removed and it had dried. *Also states he kept the entire skeleton and bleached it.*

He states he met victim #8 at 2nd and Wisconsin by the bank about two months after victim #7. He states that this individual was a black male, about 20, 5'9", 150 lbs., slim build, medium to dark complexion, short black hair, and they walked to his residence up Wisconsin Ave. He states he approached him with the same line and when they got to his apartment they drank and talked but didn't have any sex because he wasn't his type. He states that he killed him because he had already given this individual the potion and after doing that he did not want sex with him and he thought this individual would wake up and be pissed off at him so he killed him. He states he did not keep anything from this individual after he dismembered him because he wans't his type.

He continues on that he met victim #9 in February of 1991 and the subject was waiting for a bus by Marquette. He states this occurred about four months after meeting victim #8. He describes this individual as a black male, 18, 6', 140 lbs., slim build, medium complexion, with a 3" perm and a thin mustache. He states he approached him with the same offer and when the guy agreed to accompany him to his apartment, subsequently gave him the drinking potion, had oral sex, and then killed him by strangulation. He stated that he used the strap to strangle him this time and that the subject was wearing an earring. He states he kept the skull of this individual, the hands, and the genitals. Upon viewing a family photograph which was submitted by one of the relatives, this individual was identified as being Curtis STAUGHTER-M/B, dob-4/16/73, B of I #231279.

He continued on that he met victim #10 in March of 1991 on the corner of 27th and Kilbourn. He described him as a black male, 25, 5'9" to 5'10", 150 lbs., short black hair, medium build, and medium complexion. He stated that he went throught the same procedure in meeting this individual and the same offers and upon getting him to his residence, he subsequently drank the potion where he strangled him and had oral sex with the victim after his death. Mr. DAHMER viewed the B of I photo #220831 of a Errol LINDSEY-M/B, dob-3/3/72 and states he believes is the same individual whom he identified as victim #10. He states he also saved this individual's skull.

He then continued on and stated that he met victim #11 in front of 219 Bar on 2nd

REPORTING OFFICER 2472	SEC 5 / PAGE 29	PAYROLL	LOC CODE	SUPERVISOR SIGNATURE

INCIDENT INFORMATION	INCIDENT HOMICIDE (STABBING)		DATE OF INCIDENT/ACCIDENT 07-23-91		REP CON #
	VICTIM LACY, Oliver		LOCATION OF INCIDENT/ACCIDENT (Address) 924 N. 25th Street #213		DIST 3

JUVENILE LAST NAME	FIRST	MID	DATE OF BIRTH	O DETAINED O ORDERED TO MCCC O OTHER

QUAN	TYPE OF PROPERTY	DESCRIPTION	SERIAL #	CODE #	VALUE

St. around May of 1991 and this individual was deaf and dumb. He states this individual's friends drove him to 23rd and Wells and they were a white female and a heavyset white male and they were also deaf mutes. He states that he communicated with this individual by writing and that he felt this individual could read lips partially. He states he offered this individual $50.00 to come over to take photos, to view videos, but it was not known if he had sex. He states that he gave this individual the drinking potion, passed out, and when he woke up he was dead. He states he continued through the same procedure as to drain the body of blood, dismembered it, and dispose of it and that he did keep this individual's skull. He then viewed a Wisconsin Driver's License with the photo of Tony A. HUGHES-M/B, dob-8/26/59, described as 6', 150 lbs., and lives at 1019 Coby St., Madison, WI, and upon viewing this photo, he states that is the deaf mute that he had met at the bar and took to his house and subsequently killed. He identified him as victim #11. HUGHES I.D. WAS FOUND IN THE VICTIMS APT.

He stated he then met victim #12 in Late May in front of the Grand Ave. Mall. He states that he went through the same procedure of offering money to have photos taken and he describes this individual as being a Oriental male, about 14, but whom he thought at first was 17 or 18, 5'5", 120 lbs., slim build, having dark hair. He states that him and this male took the bus back to his residence and this individual posed for two photos while he was alive and then he gave him the drink mixture which contained a sleeping potion. He states they were watching videos and this individual passed out. He states he then had oral sex with him and then went to the bar to get some beer because he ran out of beer. He states while he was walking back from the bar which was located on 27th just north of Kilbourn, called the Gare Bear Bar, he saw the Oriental male staggering down the street. He states he went up to him and the police stopped him. He states that when he told the police that he was a friend of this individual and that he had gotten drunk and done it before. The police escorted them back to his apartment and he stated he would take care of him because he is his friend. He states he then went into the apartment and subsequently killed this individual in the same way as he killed the others by strangulation and after this he had oral sex on the victim. He states he then took more photographs and dismembered the body keeping the skull. He also states that he had anal sex with the victim after death. After viewing the photographs of the victim that he took, this was the same individual that had run down the street and was

REPORTING OFFICER SEC 5 / PAGE 3 0	PAYROLL #	LOC CODE	SUPERVISOR SIGNATURE

INCIDENT INFORMATION	INCIDENT HOMICIDE (STABBING)		DATE OF INCIDENT 07-23-91		REP CCN #
	VICTIM LACY, Oliver		LOCATION OF INCIDENT/ACCIDENT (Address) 924 N. 25th Street #213		DIST 3

JUVENILE LAST NAME	FIRST	MID	DATE OF BIRTH	O DETAINED O ORDERED TO MCCC O OTHER

QUAN	TYPE OF PROPERTY	DESCRIPTION	SERIAL #	CODE #	VALUE

stopped by the police. A check of the records revealed that this individual has been identified as SINTHASOMPHONE, Konerak-M/Oriental, dob-12/2/76 of 2634 N. 56th St. He has been missing since May 26, 1991. *He states that kept the victim's skull*

٭ 13 The next individual, he met at a Chicago bus station after the Gay Pride Parade on June 30th in Chicago. He describes this individual as a black male, 22, 5'8", 140 lbs., medium build, dark complexion, having a high top fade cut on the left side. He states he met this individual and went through the same procedure to offer him money to pose nude and view *videos*. He states this individual and himself took a Greyhound back to the city and then took a City Vet Cab to his residence. He states he usually does use City Vet Cab. He states that they were playing with each other but they had no sex. He states he gave him the drink and when he subsequently passed out, he then used the strap to kill him. He states that he did not have sex with this individual but he did dismembered him, kept his head, and put it in the freezer. He said the body was put in the 57 gallon barrel that he had in his residence. A print was obtained from this individual and it was identified as being, possibly from a Donald MONTRELL-dob-7/3/70. This individual is from Chicago and a photo was sent from Chicago to Milwaukee which depicted a picture of this individual photographed on May 3, 1990. This photo was shown to the individual, Jeffery DAHMER, and he stated it looks like the guy but he cannot be sure because the photo is old. Upon viewing this photo, it appears that the nose and lips and eyes are this individual and it is, in fact, the individual Donald MONTRELL.

We then continued on with the photographs he had taken and the 14th victim he states he also met in Chicago at Carol's Gay Bar after the 4th of July, possibly the 5th of 6th of July. He states he stayed at the bar until about 4:30 A.M. and then left with this individual because he made the same deal to him to come to Milwaukee to view *videos* and pose for him. He states that they took the Greyhound bus from Chicago to Milwaukee and that they then took a cab to his residence. He describes this individual as possibly a Puerto Rican male, 23 to 24, 5'10", 140 lbs., slim build, light to medium complected, short black hair, and thin mustache. He states that this individual was half Puerto Rican and half Jewish. He also states that this individual stayed for two days and they had oral sex together the first day. He states on the second day this individual wanted to leave at which time he decided he did not want him to leave so he gave him the drink with the sleeping potion in it and when he fell asleep he states he

INCIDENT INFORMATION	INCIDENT HOMICIDE (STABBING)		DATE OF INCIDENT/ACCIDENT 07-23-91		REP CON #
	VICTIM LACY, Oliver		LOCATION OF INCIDENT/ACCIDENT (Address) 924 N. 25th Street #213		DIST 3

JUVENILE LAST NAME	FIRST	MID	DATE OF BIRTH	O DETAINED O ORDERED TO MCCC O OTHER

QUAN	TYPE OF PROPERTY	DESCRIPTION	SERIAL #	CODE #	VALUE

killed him the same way he did the others, took the photos of him, dismembered him, took more photos, and then kept his head in the freezer. We had obtained a name as possibly being that of Jerimiah WEINBERGER due to the fact that there was a missing report from Chicago and a photo was brought to Milwaukee by Chicago Detectives and upon viewing this photo he identified it as victim #14. The photo is that of Jerimiah WEINBERGER-Puerto Rican male, dob-9/26/67 of 3404 N. Halstead, Chicago, Illinois, phone #929-2478. He states that after he killed him, he put his head in the freezer and put his body in the same 57 gallon drum in his apartment.

He then went on to identify victim #15 whom he states he met on 27th St. between State and Kilbourn a week prior to being caught and he states this was his second to last victim. He identified this individual as a black male, 24, 5'7", 160 to 170 lbs., having short hair, muscular build, and he states that his ID was in his wallet. A check revealed that this individual has been identified as Oliver LACY-M/B, dob-6/23/67 of 3237 N. 24th Place, and showed this photograph to the suspect and he stated that this is, in fact, the individual who was his 15th victim and the second to last to die. He states he met him on 27th St. and he asked him where he was going and this individual stated he was going to his cousin's house. He then went through the same procedure as to invite him over to his residence to pose for photos and he stated that this guy was a body builder and a model and he agreed to come along. He states he was wearing a white shirt, blue jeans, and some type of leather shoes. He states when they arrived at his residence they removed their clothes and were doing body rubs when he gave him the drink and when the individual fell asleep he proceeded to strangle him, killing him, and then having anal sex after death. He states he put this individual's head in the bottom of the refrigerator in a box and he kept his heart in the freezer to eat later. He states he did keep his right bicep which he subsequently fried on the skillet and ate part of it. He stated it tasted like beef. He stated the reason he kept this individual's identification because he wanted more pictures than he had taken of him in the various positions that he had placed him in.

Victim #16, whom he stated was his last victim, was identified by this suspect through an ID card that he had left in his apartment. This individual is identified as Joseph BRADEHOFT-M/W, dob-1/24/66 of 426 E. Spring, Lot 11, Greenville, Illinois, 62246. Mr. DAHMER states that he met him on Wisconsin Ave. near Marquette University and this

REPORTING OFFICER 2472	5	PAYROLL # 32	LOC CODE	SUPERVISOR SIGNATURE

| INCIDENT INFORMATION | INCIDENT HOMICIDE (STABBING) | | DATE OF INCIDENT/ACCIDENT 07-23-91 | | REP CON |
| | VICTIM LACY, Oliver | | LOCATION OF INCIDENT/ACCIDENT (Address) 924 N. 25th Street #213 | | 01 |

| JUVENILE LAST NAME | FIRST | MID | DATE OF BIRTH | O DETAINED O ORDERED TO MCCC O OTHER |

| QUAN | TYPE OF PROPERTY | DESCRIPTION | | SERIAL # | CODE # | VALUE |

individual was waiting for a bus and had a six pack in his arm. He states that he got off the bus and approached him with the same offer as he did the others and this individual agreed to go along with him. He states that they went to his residence where he had oral sex on this individual before killing him. He states he gave him the potion and when the individual went to sleep he strangled him with the strap. He states he subsequently put his head in the freezer and his body in the same blue 57 gallon barrel in his residence. He states that these are the only homicides he has committed and that the only other one was the one that we knew about in 1978 which was the one in Bath, Ohio.

Mr. DAHMER states that he is still willing to cooperate with us and if we have anymore photos or people that are missing and that we may have identification of them he will be glad to view photos to try to make an identification of the other unknown victims. As of this report, we have 10 tentative identifications with some being positive and possibly an 11th that being victim #5 who has the tattoo of Cash D on his chest with pitchforks going up. A check of the Gang Crimes Unit revealed that they had stuck up an individual identified as Mark Lee BROWN-M/B, dob-8/10/63 with an address of 2110 W. State St. or 1025 N. 21st St. and this individual is a BGD. Gang Member from Chicago and that he does have the tattoo Cash D on his right chest area. Detective BARBER will attempt to locate this individual during his tour of duty.

Further investigation pending.

Report per Detective Dennis MURPHY.

DM:jaj 7/25/91

2472 / SEC 5 / PAGE 3?

| REPORTING OFFICER DET. DENNIS MURPHY | PAYROLL # 32893 | LOC CODE 91 | SUPERVISOR SIGNATURE |

PO15-B 5-89 SUPPLEMENT REPORT MILWAUKEE POLICE DEPARTMENT	☑ INCIDENT SUPPLEMENT ☐ ACCIDENT SUPPLEMENT ☐ JUVENILE SUPPLEMENT	PAGE _1_ of _1_	DATE OF REPORT 07-24-91	INCIDENT/ACCIDENT # 91-51767/M2472-M2481

INCIDENT INFORMATION	INCIDENT HOMICIDE (STABBING)		DATE OF INCIDENT/ACCIDENT 07-23-91		REP CON :
	VICTIM LACY, Oliver		LOCATION OF INCIDENT/ACCIDENT (Address) 924 N. 25th Street #213		DIS'

JUVENILE LAST NAME	FIRST	MID	DATE OF BIRTH	☐ DETAINED ☐ ORDERED TO MCCC ☐ OTHER

QUAN	TYPE OF PROPERTY	DESCRIPTION	SERIAL #	CODE #	VALUE

On Wed., 7-24-91, I, Det. KENNEDY on Squad 126, while interviewing the suspect in this offense, that being one Jeffrey L. DAHMER, spoke to him in regards to the fact that he had knowledge to whether or not the acts he was committing were right or wrong. At this time, Mr. DAHMER stated that he was fully aware that the acts he was committing were wrong and that he feels horrified that he was able to carry out such an offense.

He stated that it is obvious that he realized that they were wrong because he went to great time and expense to try to cover up his crimes. He stated that he used quite a bit of caution by setting up alarm systems in his apartment, that being in the outer door, the sliding door leading to his hallway bathroom and bedroom, and his bedroom door. He stated that he set up a fake video camera and told other homosexuals that he had brought to his apartment that it automatically turned on if his door opened up without the alarm being turned off. He stated that this was all done in order to keep people from entering into his apartment and discovering the evidence of his criminal act.

He also stated that he drank excessively to try to forget the nightmare he felt he was living as he remembered the horror of some of the acts that he performed. He stated that he is deeply remorseful now for what he had done and wished that he had never started. He stated that he is not sure why he started committing these offenses and feels that in order to make restitution to the families of those he has killed, that he would like to help the police in any way that he can by trying to identify his victims.

Report dictated by Det. Patrick KENNEDY.

PK/rc 7-24-91

2472 / SEC 5 / PAGE 34

REPORTING OFFICER Det. Patrick KENNEDY	PAYROLL # 48171	LOC CODE 93	SUPERVISOR SIGNATURE

PO15-8 ⊃-89 SUPPLEMENT REPORT MILWAUKEE POLICE DEPARTMENT	☑ INCIDENT SUPPLEMENT O ACCIDENT SUPPLEMENT O JUVENILE SUPPLEMENT	PAGE __1__ of __7__	DATE OF REPORT 07-25-91	INCIDENT/ACCIDENT # 01-51767/M2472 M2481	
INCIDENT INFORMATION	INCIDENT HOMICIDE (STABBING)		DATE OF INCIDENT/ACCIDENT 07-23-91		REP CON #
	VICTIM LACY, Oliver		LOCATION OF INCIDENT/ACCIDENT (Address) 924 N. 25th Street #213		DIST 3
JUVENILE LAST NAME	FIRST	MID	DATE OF BIRTH	O DETAINED O ORDERED TO MCCC O OTHER	
QUAN	TYPE OF PROPERTY	DESCRIPTION	SERIAL #	CODE #	VALUE

On Thursday, 7-25-91, I, Det. KENNEDY, along with Det. Dennis MURPHY, did receive information from LUCAD that the suspect in this offense, that being Jeffrey DAHMER, had requested to speak with us. At this time, I proceeded to LUCAD and retrieved the suspect, Mr. DAHMER, from his cell, and returned with him to the fourth floor, CIB, where he was placed into an interview room, and we again began to talk.

At this time, Jeffrey DAHMER began speaking regarding his early teenage and high school years in Bath, OH. Jeffrey stated that as a teenager of 15 or 16, he realized that he was a homosexual. He stated that he has never been interested in women, and he had no idea why he was a homosexual, but that he distinctly remembers that in high school, and during his teenage years, he became acutely aware of the fact that he was only attracted to men.

He also stated that it was at this time that he began to have fantasies of killing human beings. He stated that at this time, he also began picking up animals which he had found on the road, which had been killed apparently by vehicles, and he would bring them home to his house, and he would use a knife in order to cut them up, and cut them open to see what was on the inside of them and what they looked like. He stated that several of the animals that he cut up, he would completely strip down the flesh and meaty areas, and then use bleach and various other liquids which he found around his household, and experiment to see which ones would clean the bones the best.

He stated that it was also at this time that he actually found a large dog that had been hit by a car and that he brought this dog home, cut it up, looked at its insides, completely cleaned it, and then soaked the bones in a bleach solution, and that he eventually planned to reconstruct the bones and mount the skeleton, much the way a taxidermist would do it. He stated; however, that he never got around to doing this.

He also stated that during this time that he was cutting up animals, he would fantasize what it would be like to cut up a human being. He stated that he realized at this early age that his homosexual fantasies and his fantasies of killing and dismembering human beings were interlocked, and that he received gratification from these fantasies and they occurred many times. He stated that whenever he had fantasies of homosexual activity, he also had fantasies of killing and dismembering. He goes on to state that he felt that

REPORTING OFFICER 24 2 SEC. 5	PAYROLL # 35 PAGE	LOC CODE	SUPERVISOR SIGNATURE

PO15-8 5-89 SUPPLEMENT REPORT MILWAUKEE POLICE DEPARTMENT	☑ INCIDENT SUPPLEMENT O ACCIDENT SUPPLEMENT O JUVENILE SUPPLEMENT	PAGE _2_ of _4_	DATE OF REPORT 7-25-91	INCIDENT/ACCIDENT # 91-51767/M0170 M0101	
INCIDENT INFORMATION	INCIDENT HOMICIDE (STABBING)		DATE OF INCIDENT/ACCIDENT 7-23-91		REP CON #
	VICTIM LACY, Oliver		LOCATION OF INCIDENT/ACCIDENT (Address) 924 N. 25th St. #213		DIST
JUVENILE LAST NAME	FIRST	MID	DATE OF BIRTH	O DETAINED O ORDERED TO MCCC O OTHER	
QUAN	TYPE OF PROPERTY	DESCRIPTION	SERIAL #	CODE #	VALUE

the retrieving of road killed animals and the cutting of them up, satisfied his urges and his fantasies of killing and dismembering human beings.

He goes on to state that after leaving home in Bath, OH to join the Armed Forces, that while in the Army, he was stationed in Germany. When asked why his behavior of cutting up animals and killing and dismembering of human beings did not occur while he was in the Army, he stated that he believes the reason he did not kill or dismember any one while he was serving his tour of duty in Germany, was because he enjoyed the structure of the Army. He stated that during the entire tour of duty, he lived on base and was in a dorm with three other men. Although he did not have any homosexual or heterosexual rela- tionships while he was in Germany, or in the Army, he did satisfy his urge for sexual excitement by masturbation. He stated that he enjoyed the Army and wished that he could have finished his entire tour of duty; however, his abuse of alcohol made that impossible as the Army decided to let him go six months before his tour of duty was up.

When questioned about bodies dismembered and found in Germany during the time he was there, Jeffrey said that he remembers reading in the newspapers in Germany about a black female who was found beheaded and dismembered and left in a field. He related that this was big news at the time, and this is the only reason why it rings a bell with him. He emphatically denied being involved in any of those homicides and indicated that he is not at all interested in females, either sexually or for the purpose of dismembering. He stated that he is only interested in having a relationship with men.

Jeffrey stated that when he was released from the Army, he stated that he was tired of the cold winters that he had endured in Germany and when he was growing up in Ohio, and with the voucher given to him by the Army, he could go anywhere in the United States that he wished, so he stated that he took a voucher for Miami, FL, because he thought it would be nice with the warm weather all the time. He indicated that the entire time that he was in Miami, FL, he did not engage in any homosexual activity, nor did he kill or dismember anyone while he was down there. He stated that he was continually busy trying to make ends meet financially while in Miami, and this is the reason why he had no time to engage in this activity.

Jeffrey stated that he, at one time, was actually living on the beach because of lack of funds, and this was eventually the reason why he moved back to the midwest, so that

family members could help support him until he got reestablished. Jeffrey says that when

60

PO15-8 5-89 SUPPLEMENT REPORT MILWAUKEE POLICE DEPARTMENT	☒ INCIDENT SUPPLEMENT ☐ ACCIDENT SUPPLEMENT ☐ JUVENILE SUPPLEMENT	PAGE _3_ of _4_	DATE OF REPORT 7-25-91	INCIDENT/ACCIDENT # 91-51767/M2472-M2481	
INCIDENT INFORMATION	INCIDENT HOMICIDE (STABBING)		DATE OF INCIDENT/ACCIDENT 7-23-91		REP CON
	VICTIM LACY, Oliver		LOCATION OF INCIDENT/ACCIDENT (Address) 924 N. 25th St., #213		DIS
JUVENILE LAST NAME FIRST MID			DATE OF BIRTH	☐ DETAINED ☐ ORDERED TO MCCC ☐ OTHER	
QUAN TYPE OF PROPERTY DESCRIPTION			SERIAL #	CODE #	VALUE

he first moved in with his grandmother in West Allis, he decided to make a concentrated effort to find some direction in his life. He went on to state that he constantly felt lonely and empty without direction, and that there was no meaning in life for him. His grandmother was a religious women, that being protestant, and a regular church goer and talked to him several times about religion and how it could turn his life around.

He went on to state that when he first moved to West Allis, he had continual fantasies again about homosexuality, and that along with the homosexual fantasies, came the urges to want to dominate, to kill, and to dismember other men. He stated that he constantly fought this urge by attending church with his grandmother, by reading the Bible, and by trying to live his life in an orderly fashion, "to walk the straight and narrow" are the words in which he used. He said he constantly had the interlocked feelings and fantasies of homosexual behavior, killing, and dismembering, and that they finally overcame him as he was finding it more and more impossible to continue with the life style of "church going and right living" as he put it.

At this time, I questioned Jeffrey regarding the skeleton bones which were found in the file cabinet in his bedroom. He stated that this was victim number seven, the black male that he met in Dec. of 1990 by the bookstore on N. 27th St. He said that this is the only victim that he stabbed in the neck in order to kill him. He stated that the reason he did this is because the potion that he had given him of sleeping pills and alchol was beginning to wear off and that the individual was rather strong and muscular, and he did not feel that he would be able to strangle him successfully without putting up a fight; so he took a knife and stabbed him once along the jugular vein in order to kill him. He stated that because this individual was the most attractive that he had met up until that time, he decided to clean and boil the entire skeleton in the solution of water and soilex and to save it. The reason he did this was to keep this individual with him as long as possible.

Regarding victim number ten, tentatively identified as Errol LINDSAY, Jeffrey stated that this is the only one of his victims that he completely took the skin off of. He stated that this was done with a very small, very sharp paring knife and that it took him approximately two hours to completely take all the skin off this victim, while leaving intact the cartiladge, ligament, and fleshy muscular areas.

When talking about his personal relationships, Jeffrey stated that he really has no

INCIDENT INFORMATION	INCIDENT HOMICIDE (STABBING)		DATE OF INCIDENT/ACCIDENT 7-23-91		REP CON #
	VICTIM LACY, Oliver		LOCATION OF INCIDENT/ACCIDENT (Address) 924 N. 25th St., #213		DIST
JUVENILE LAST NAME	FIRST	MID	DATE OF BIRTH	O DETAINED O ORDERED TO MCCC O OTHER	
QUAN	TYPE OF PROPERTY	DESCRIPTION	SERIAL #	CODE #	VALUE

close friends and that he is basically a loner. He stated that he is a loner by choice, and that he has never had any success in continuing any long-range relationships. He stated that he has had friends while he was in high school, but never any best friend that he would continually hang around with. He stated that he likes to be alone, and he expecially likes to be alone when he kills people and cuts them up because it makes him feel more secure and more dominant.

At this time, he went on to say that he realizes what he has done warrants the death penalty; however, he is not sure that he really wants to die as punishment for his offenses. He stated that when he was younger, he started cutting up animals, and he enjoyed the excitement of cutting them up, and that he wished now that he would have just continued to cut up animals and would have stopped with them and not have moved on to human beings. He felt that he originally only started it for the curiosity.

At this time, I questioned Jeffrey regarding the celebrated DRESSLER murder trial which is going on now in Waukesha County regarding the death of an individual by the name of MADDEN. He stated that he is aware of this trial only because he has read it in the paper; but he emphatically denied knowing DRESSLER or MADDEN and stated that he has had no part in that homicide.

Regarding smaller children, Jeffrey stated that although he has been convicted of exposing himself to younger children, and that he has tried to take pictures of minors, that he has no sexual desires to be with a younger child, that he has never attempted to entice a smaller child for sexual purposes, and that he was strictly sexually excited by and attracted to young men of any race or ethnic persuasion from the early teens to the late twenties.

It should also be noted that during this interview and the interview that took place on 7-24-91, several photographs taken from our Identification Division were shown to Jeffrey and he was asked if he has ever met these individuals or if they were in fact any of his victims. These photographs were picked specifically because the individual in the photograph was known to still be alive and it should be noted that each photograph which was shown to him where the individual in the photograph was still alive, Jeffrey stated "I've never seen this man before, and he is definitely not one of my victim's."

It was at this time that the interview was terminated.

Report dictated by Det. Patrick KENNEDY.   PK/rc 7-25-91

REPORTING OFFICER Det. Patrick KENNEDY	PAYROLL # 48171	LOC CODE 93	SUPERVISOR SIGNATURE _Lt. Raymond Smith_

PO15-B 5-89 SUPPLEMENT REPORT MILWAUKEE POLICE DEPARTMENT	0 INCIDENT SUPPLEMENT 0 ACCIDENT SUPPLEMENT 0 JUVENILE SUPPLEMENT	PAGE 1 of	DATE OF REPORT 07-25-91	INCIDENT/ACCIDENT # 91-51767/ M 2472 2481	
INCIDENT INFORMATION	INCIDENT HOMICIDE		DATE OF INCIDENT/ACCIDENT 07-22-91		REP CON #
	VICTIM LACY, OLIVER		LOCATION OF INCIDENT/ACCIDENT (Address) 924 N. 25th St. Apt. 213		DIST
JUVENILE LAST NAME	FIRST	MID	DATE OF BIRTH	0 DETAINED 0 ORDERED TO MCCC 0 OTHER	
QUAN	TYPE OF PROPERTY	DESCRIPTION	SERIAL #	CODE #	VALUE

On Thursday, 7-25-91, I, Det. Patrick KENNEDY, Sq. 126, was notified by LUCAD that the suspect in this offense, Jeffrey DAHMER, had requested to see me.

At this time I proceeded to the fifth floor, LUCAD, where I did meet Jeffrey and he in fact stated he did wish to speak with me. I brought him down with me to the fourth floor CIB interview room, at which time I asked him what it was he wished to speak about.

It was at this time that he requested a cigarette and a cup of coffee, which I gave him. He stated that he just wished to talk about the feelings he had regarding the confession that he had made about all of his victims and his apprehension as to the court appearance he was to make later on in the afternoon. At this time I stated that I would be willing to listen to any comments that he had to make.

He states that the realizes that there is no way he can change anything in regard to what he did to his victims. He also states that he realizes it would be impossible to make amends for the crimes and offenses he has committed towards these people; however, he feels that the only way for him to make a new start in his life is to make a clean breast of things and to be fully honest. He states that he feels this is what he did and he knows it is the only way he can change his life. He states that he knows that this will not change any of the things that he did but that maybe by telling the truth he can start to make things right and put at ease the minds of his victims' relatives. He also stated that he felt that the only way he could start to change his self was to admit exactly what he had done, to state that he is sorry for what he has done and to swear that he will try to change his life in the future.

At this time I was advised by Detective Dennis MURPHY that we were to transport the suspect Jeffrey DAHMER to the Milwaukee County Sheriff's Dept. jail area, and we then walked him to the jail area and turned him over to Deputy SCHUH (phonetic) at the Milwaukee County Sheriff's Dept. for his court appearance.

It should be noted that in previous conversations regarding his court appearance the suspect Jeffrey DAHMER expressed apprehension at appearing in court in the paper jump suit provided him by the City Jail. At this time I advised him that if he wished I could bring some old clothes from my home and give them to him so that he would have some presentable clothes to war for his court appearance. To this Jeffrey DAHMER stated that he

REPORTING OFFICER 2472	5	PAYROLL # 39	LOC CODE	SUPERVISOR SIGNATURE

| INCIDENT INFORMATION | INCIDENT HOMICIDE | | | DATE OF INCIDENT/ACCIDENT 07-22-91 | | REP CON # |
| | VICTIM LACY, OLIVER | | | LOCATION OF INCIDENT/ACCIDENT (Address) 924 N. 25th St., Apt. 213 | | DIST |

| JUVENILE LAST NAME | FIRST | MID | DATE OF BIRTH | O DETAINED O ORDERED TO MCCC O OTHER |

| QUAN | TYPE OF PROPERTY | DESCRIPTION | SERIAL # | CODE # | VALUE |

would be most appreciative if we could bring some clothes in for him, and on the date of his court appearance we did in fact provide him with a button down collared shirt and a pair of pants which fit him, for his court appearance. Upon taking him over to the county jail and turning him over for his court appearance we also requested that they provide him with some county foot apparel, which they did.

Report dictated by Detective PATRICK KENNEDY.

PK:rd 7-26-91

472 SEC 5 PAGE 40

| REPORTING OFFICER DET. P. KENNEDY | PAYROLL # 48171 | LOC CODE 93 | SUPERVISOR SIGNATURE |

	INCIDENT HOMICIDE .		DATE OF INCIDENT/ACCIDENT 07-22-91		REP CON #
INCIDENT INFORMATION	VICTIM LACY, Oliver		LOCATION OF INCIDENT/ACCIDENT (Address) 924 N. 25th St., #213		DIST
JUVENILE LAST NAME	FIRST	MID	DATE OF BIRTH	☐ DETAINED ☐ ORDERED TO MCCC ☐ OTHER	

QUAN	TYPE OF PROPERTY	DESCRIPTION		SERIAL #	CODE #	VALUE

On Friday, 7-26-91, I, Det. Dennis MURPHY, met with Det. John KARABATSOS, who is from the Summit County Sheriff's Department in Akron, Ohio, and with Lt. Richard MUNSEY, who is from the Bath County Police Department in Akron, Ohio. These two individuals flew to Milwaukee to interview the suspect, Jeffrey DAHMER, in regard to the homicide that had occurred in Ohio in 1978, which DAHMER had confessed to.

I informed the detectives that a meeting was set up for 11:00 at the Milwaukee County Jail, in which we were going to meet an associate of Gerald BOYLE; namely, Attorney, Scott HANSON, who would be present for the interview.

At 11:00 A.M., we proceeded to the Milwaukee County Jail where we did meet with Attorney Scott HANSON, and we all proceeded to the County Jail where we met with Jeffrey DAHMER. Attorney Scott HANSON requested that he talk with the defendant prior to our questioning him. Attorney HANSON conversed with Jeffrey for approximately 10-minutes, and then we all sat in the Library Room in the County Jail. I personally informed Jeff that he still could invoke his "Miranda Rights" if he desired, and I again asked him if he wanted to talk with us regarding this homicide investigation. I stated to him that even though his attorney is here, I still had to advise him of his various rights, and he stated that he "understood" his rights. He had been told them numerous times, and he did not wish to invoke his rights, that he would "waive" them, and he would co-operate and talk to us because he wanted to clean up everything.

I then introduced him to Officer's KARABATSOS and MUNSEY, and informed him that they were from the Akron, Ohio Police Department and they were investigating the homicide he had previously confessed to, at which time he stated he would co-operate with them.

We then showed him area photographs of his previous residence at 4480 W. Bath Rd., in Bath, Ohio, and he pointed out the area where he had disposed of the bones in the photographs. This was a heavily wooded area, and he was asked if he could make a diagram indicating same. At which time, Jeffrey drew a diagram of Bath Rd., the driveway, the garage, and the house area, and a small wooded area just to the side of the house. He indicated that this was the area in which he had disposed of the victim's bones. We also asked him if he knew the name, Steven HICKS, and he stated that that was the name of the victim in Ohio, and the reason he remembered it was because it was his first one and he

REPORTING OFFICER SEC. 5 PAGE	PAYROLL # 4 1	LOC CODE	SUPERVISOR SIGNATURE Act. Lt. Raymond ...

INCIDENT INFORMATION	INCIDENT HOMICIDE			DATE OF INCIDENT/ACCIDENT 7/22/91		REP CON #
	VICTIM LACY, Oliver			LOCATION OF INCIDENT/ACCIDENT (Address) 924 N. 25th St., #213		DIST

JUVENILE LAST NAME		FIRST	MID	DATE OF BIRTH	O DETAINED O ORDERED TO MCCC O OTHER

QUAN	TYPE OF PROPERTY	DESCRIPTION		SERIAL #	CODE #	VALUE

stated "you don't forget your first one".

We then showed him a reproduction of the photograph of Steven HICKS, and upon looking at it he stated that this looks like the individual. He was subsequently shown the regular photograph of Steven HICKS which depicts the entire body, and he stated, "I'm almost positive that's him. Yeah, that's him. That's the individual that I killed in Ohio". He was then questioned regarding how this transpired, and he stated that he was driving southbound on Cleveland and Maslin Rd. (phonetic) and he figured it was warm out because the victim did not have a shirt. He stated he thought it was early Fall but he can not be sure. He stated that as he was driving southbound on Cleveland and Maslin Rd., he saw the hitchhiker, and picked him up at Ball and Cleveland and Maslin Rd. He states that he discussed with the individual about buying or smoking "pot" and drinking. They decided to go to his residence, and he stated that this was in the later afternoon or early evening hours. He stated that he made a U-turn and drove back to his residence because no one was home.

He states his father was living in a motel complex about 5-10 miles away, and his mother had already left for Chippewa Falls, WI., and he was living in the residence alone.

He states that when they arrived home, they went into the bedroom and were drinking beer, and after a while the victim wanted to leave. Jeff states that he wanted the victim to stay. The victim was sitting either on the bed or in a chair in a bedroom, and he approached him from behind and hit him with a barbell in the head, and then he used the barbell to strangle him. After this occurred, he states he put him in a crawl space under the house and subsequently dismembered him in the same crawl space. He states that after he dismembered him he put the body in plastic bags and put the bags in the back seat of a blue 4-door auto that was in the garage. He stated that this was about 3:00 A.M., and as he was driving he was stopped by officers who stated he was driving left of center. He stated he was given a drunken driving test which he passed, and then allowed to drive away. He states he thinks he may have gotten a ticket, but he is not sure.

He states he then returned home and put the bags in a drainage pipe behind the house, and let them sit there for a couple of weeks. After this time he took the bags out, broke the bones up in little pieces and proceeded to a rocky cliff area to the back

REPORTING OFFICER	PAYROLL #	LOC CODE	SUPERVISOR SIGNATURE
SEC	PAGE		Det Lt Raymond P. Surik

INCIDENT	INCIDENT HOMICIDE			DATE OF INCIDENT/ACCIDENT 07-22-91		REP COM
INFORMATION	VICTIM LACY, Oliver			LOCATION OF INCIDENT/ACCIDENT (Address) 924 N. 25th St., #213		DIS

JUVENILE LAST NAME	FIRST	MID	DATE OF BIRTH	☐ DETAINED ☐ ORDERED TO MCCC ☐ OTHER

QUAN	TYPE OF PROPERTY	DESCRIPTION	SERIAL #	CODE #	VALUE

side of the house and just to the rear, which about 10ft. above the ground, and he spread the bones around this area. He stated that he then burned the victim's identification and clothes.

Mr. DAHMER states that he believed the victim had been wearing a necklace or something with what appeared to be teeth braces on this necklace. He states that he disposed of this by throwing them in the river by the sewerage plant.

We then questioned Mr. DAHMER as to whether or not he continued his education. He stated that he did start Ohio University in August of 1978, and that he had committed this homicide prior to registering for school. He then thought, well, it was at least 2-weeks prior to going to school in August. He states he can not be sure of the exact time or month that this occurred, but he does readily admit committing the homicide, and upon viewing the photographs and hearing the name states, that that was infact the person he did infact kill.

We then asked Mr. DAHMER if he would draw a diagram depicting where the crawl space was, the drainage pipe, and the cliff area where he disposed of the body. He proceeded to make a drawing on the reverse side of the previous drawing indicating these locations and where he disposed of the bones. This drawing was signed by Jeffrey DAHMER and initialled by myself, Det. KARABATSOS, and Lt. MUNSEY. This will be retained by Lt. MUNSEY for his investigation in Ohio.

I then informed Mr. DAHMER that I had numerous questions from previous statements he had given me, and he stated he would answer anything.

At this time I asked him where he bought the chemicals used; namely the muramic acid. He stated that he bought them at Ace Hardware on 4th St. by Lapham Lighting. He states he bought the 4-boxes a few days before his arrest, just after the last homicide, and he was going to use these chemicals in the 57 gallon barrel. He states he bought the ether, chloroform, and others at Labb's Pharmacy on 27th & Kilbourn. He also stated that the jewelry he had sold at work; namely, a necklace with an Italian horn on, was his personal jewelry and he did not sell or keep anything from any of his victims.

He was also questioned regarding the bones and skeleton that were found in the drawer in his residence, and he stated that these belonged to the same person whose arm was in the freezer, and he stated that this was from the victim by the bookstore who he

REPORTING OFFICER	SEC 5 / PAGE	PAYROLL # 43	LOC CODE	SUPERVISOR SIGNATURE

PO15-B 5-89 SUPPLEMENT REPORT MILWAUKEE POLICE DEPARTMENT	☒ INCIDENT SUPPLEMENT ☐ ACCIDENT SUPPLEMENT ☐ JUVENILE SUPPLEMENT	PAGE 4 of 4	DATE OF REPORT 07-27-91	INCIDENT/ACCIDENT # 91-51767	
INCIDENT INFORMATION	INCIDENT HOMICIDE		DATE OF INCIDENT/ACCIDENT 07-22-91		REP COW
	VICTIM LACY, Oliver		LOCATION OF INCIDENT/ACCIDENT (Address) 924 N. 25th St. #213		DIS
JUVENILE LAST NAME	FIRST	MID	DATE OF BIRTH	☐ DETAINED ☐ ORDERED TO MCCC ☐ OTHER	
QUAN	TYPE OF PROPERTY	DESCRIPTION	SERIAL #	CODE #	VALUE

stated he killed approximately 1-year ago.

I then questioned him where he had worked when he moved to Miami Beach from the service, and he stated that he had worked at Sunshine Subs Shop, which was privately owned and it was on Collins Ave., approximately 1/2 mile from his motel.

Mr. DAHMER was then thanked for his co-operation and subsequently returned to the County Jail.

It should be noted that during the start of our interview Mr. DAHMER had requested to have cigarettes. He was given coffee, but he was unable to smoke in the County Jail, so at approximately 12:15 P.M., I, Det. Dennis MURPHY, proceeded to get an order to produce, which was signed by Judge RANDA, and Jeffrey DAHMER was taken to the CIB Interview Room along with Det. Lt. MUNSEY, Det. KARABATSOS, and Attorney, Scott HANSON. The remaineder of the interview was conducted at that location, and Mr. DAHMER was subsequently returned to the County Jail. Just prior to his return, Attorney HANSON had requested that we not talk to Mr. DAHMER regarding anything unless we contact their agency. I informed Mr. HANSON that Mr. DAHMER has been requesting my presence everyday, and stated he did not wish an attorney present when I arrived to interview him. In the presence of Attorney HANSON, I informed Jeffrey of his attorney's request, and he stated he "understood" it, but stated that he wanted to get everything out in the open. I informed Mr. HANSON that if Jeffrey calls to talk to me and he does not wish the attorney present, I will conduct my interview. Mr. HANSON stated that he understood, and requested again to Mr. DAHMER that he contact him prior to contacting the police. Mr. DAHMER was then returned to the County Jail.

Report per: Det. Dennis MURPHY.

DM/slb 7-27-91

SEC 5 PAGE 44

68

PO15-B 5-89 SUPPLEMENT REPORT MILWAUKEE POLICE DEPARTMENT	☒ INCIDENT SUPPLEMENT ☐ ACCIDENT SUPPLEMENT ☐ JUVENILE SUPPLEMENT	PAGE 1 of 4	DATE OF REPORT 07-27-91	INCIDENT/ACCIDENT # 91-51767 (M2472)	

	INCIDENT HOMICIDE		DATE OF INCIDENT/ACCIDENT 07-22-91		REP CON #
INCIDENT INFORMATION	VICTIM LACY, Oliver		LOCATION OF INCIDENT/ACCIDENT (Address) 924 N. 25th St., #213		DIST
JUVENILE LAST NAME	FIRST	MID	DATE OF BIRTH	☐ DETAINED ☐ ORDERED TO MCCC ☐ OTHER	
QUAN	TYPE OF PROPERTY	DESCRIPTION		SERIAL # CODE #	VALUE

On Friday, 7-26-91, prior to returning the defendant, Jeffrey DAHMER, back to the County Jail and after the interview with Det's Richard MUNSEY and John KARABATSOS, I, Det. Dennis MURPHY and Det. Lt. Ken RISSE and Det. Guy NOVAK, met with DAHMER at the CIB to question him regarding the homicides that he alleged to have committed in West Allis, WI.

Mr. DAHMER stated that he possibly killed his first victim at the Ambassador Hotel because he stated he took him up there gave him a potion and passed out, but he did remember beating him about the chest. He stated that when he woke up the victim was dead, he put the victim in a suitcase that he had picked up at the Grand Avenue Mall, and took a cab to his grandmother's house at 2357 S. 57th St., where he subsequently dismembered the body and disposed of the bones and the tissue in the garbage.

He stated that the 2nd victim, whom he had met at the "219" Club, was conveyed with him in a City Vet Cab, and he readily admitted killing him the same way as the other victims. He stated he believed this individual may have lived on 10th & National, because he thinks that what he told him. He also stated that he offered him money for sex, and that's the reason this individual went with him.

Victim #3, whom he also states he killed in West Allis, he recalls that about 2-weeks after the homicide, he was reading the personal section in the paper and there was a small photo of this victim and it listed him as missing and requested information regarding the individual. He states he can not recall the name, but he does recall seeing this photo in the personal section of the paper.

Mr. DAHMER states that when he returned these victims to his grandmother's house, it was usually in the middle of the night, and usually on a Saturday night. He stated when he brought victim #1 back it was in the middle of the night, and the next day, Sunday, when his grandmother went to church was when he dismembered the body, cut it in little pieces, removed the flesh, muscle, and tissue before breaking up the bones. He stated that he never kept any parts of these.

He states he also did this with victim #2, he brought him over on a Saturday night and dismembered the body on a Sunday morning.

He also states that when he took victim #3 over to the house he had also taken a cab there and was dropped off 2-blocks away, usually up by the Mai-Kai Tavern, and then

REPORTING OFFICER 2372, SF 5	PAYROLL # PAGE 45	LOC CODE	SUPERVISOR SIGNATURE Lt. Lt. Raymond A Such

69

INCIDENT INFORMATION	INCIDENT HOMICIDE		DATE OF INCIDENT/ACCIDENT 07/22/91		REP CON
	VICTIM LACY, Oliver		LOCATION OF INCIDENT/ACCIDENT (Address) 924 N. 25th St., #213		DIS

JUVENILE LAST NAME	FIRST	MID	DATE OF BIRTH	☐ DETAINED ☐ ORDERED TO MCCC ☐ OTHER

QUAN	TYPE OF PROPERTY	DESCRIPTION		SERIAL #	CODE #	VALUE

he would walk to the address. He states that way no one would know where his grandmother lived or where he was staying.

He states that the pills used to put these individuals to sleep were called **#20** and they were prescribed to him by a Dr. OLSON, of West Allis Memorial Hospital.

He also states that there was one more occurrence that happened, but this time the individual woke up prior to him being able to kill him and he was also seen by his grandmother with this individual in the basement and he decided not to kill him. He stated that he did walk this individual to the bus-stop and returned to the residence. It was shortly after this that his grandmother had asked him to leave.

A check with West Allis revealed that there was a "theft" complaint filed on 4-4-88, by Ronald FLOWERS, who was this alleged victim, case #B41212, file #88-07829.

Regarding victim, #4, who was subsequently identified as Anthony SEERS, he stated that he met this victim a few weeks before he went into the Work Release Center, and with him he was dropped off by the Mai-Kai Lounge around Easter of 1989. Infact, he stated it was the night before Easter. He stated that this did happen after his arrest, but he was at his grandmother's house. He states that after brining him to his house on Saturday night, he did have sex with him, cut him up, disposed of the body in the same manner, except for keeping his head, scalp, and genitals. He stated that he did dispose of this body on Easter Sunday.

West Allis officers questioned him regarding any other information he may have in relationship to these alleged homicides in their jurisdiction, and he stated he could not think of anything at this time, but if he does recall he will contact me so that I can inform them of any further information.

Mr. DAHMER was then returned to the County Jail.

I, along with the Ohio Police officers and West Allis Police officers, then subsequently went to the West Allis Police Department where we interviewed the father of Mr. DAHMER; namely, Lionel DAHMER. While we were conducting this interview I received a phone call from Captain Domagalski informing me that the subject, Jeffrey DAHMER, had requested that I come to the jail because he had something important to tell me.

After our interview with his father, I subsequently returned to the County Jail,

REPORTING OFFICER 2472	5	PAYROLL # 46	LOC CODE	SUPERVISOR SIGNATURE

A list of victims of Jeffrey Dahmer

MILWAUKEE (AP) — Here are names, ages and last cities of residence of the 15 people Jeffrey Dahmer pleaded guilty to killing. Also included is the last time they were reported seen or when Dahmer told police he met or killed them.

Ricky Beeks, 33, Rockford, Ill., last seen May 1990.

Joseph Bradehoft, 25, Milwaukee, met Dahmer July 19, 1991.

Jamie Doxtator, 14, of Milwaukee, last seen January 1988.

Richard Guerrero, 25, Milwaukee, disappeared in 1988.

Anthony Hughes, 31, Madison, reported missing May 24, 1991.

Oliver Lacy, 23, Milwaukee, last seen July 12, 1991.

Errol Lindsey, 19, Milwaukee, last seen April 7, 1991.

Ernest Miller, 22, Chicago, last seen Sept. 2, 1990.

Anthony Sears, 26, Milwaukee, last seen March 25, 1989.

Konerak Sinthasomphone, 14, Milwaukee, last seen May 27, 1991.

Edward W. Smith, 28, Milwaukee, reported missing June 1990.

Curtis Straughter, 18, Milwaukee, last seen Feb. 18, 1991.

David C. Thomas, 23, Milwaukee, reported missing Sept. 24, 1990.

Matt Turner, 20, Chicago, met Dahmer in Chicago on June 30, 1991.

Jeremy Weinberger, 23, Chicago, last seen July 6, 1991.

Dahmer was not charged in Milwaukee in connection with the following two deaths, for which he has confessed. He faces trial in Ohio in the Hicks case. Prosecutors said they lacked evidence to charge him in the Tuomi case.

Steven Mark Hicks, 18, Coventry Township, Ohio, killed June 18, 1978.

Steven W. Tuomi, Milwaukee, 24 when last heard from Sept. 15, 1987.

PO15-B 5-89 SUPPLEMENT REPORT
MILWAUKEE POLICE DEPARTMENT

☒ INCIDENT SUPPLEMENT
☐ ACCIDENT SUPPLEMENT
☐ JUVENILE SUPPLEMENT

PAGE 3 of 4
DATE OF REPORT
INCIDENT/ACC #

	INCIDENT	HOMICIDE		DATE OF INCIDENT/ACCIDENT		REP CON
INCIDENT INFORMATION	VICTIM	LACY, Oliver		LOCATION OF INCIDENT/ACCIDENT (Address) 924 N. 25th St., #213		DIS

JUVENILE LAST NAME	FIRST	MID	DATE OF BIRTH	☐ DETAINED ☐ ORDERED TO MCCC ☐ OTHER

QUAN	TYPE OF PROPERTY	DESCRIPTION	SERIAL #	CODE #	VALUE

where Mr. DAHMER informed me that he forgot to tell me about an incident that occurred about 1-year ago where one of them had gotten away. I asked him what he meant, and he stated that he had picked up a Spanish male for the purpose of taking photos and having sex, and he brought him over to his apartment at 924 N. 25th St. He stated that this had occurred prior to victim #7. He states that when he brought this individual over, he did not have anymore sleeping pills left so he attempted to knock him out by hitting him in the back of the neck with his fist or hand. He stated this did not work and the hispanic male fought with him, and after a while they kind of made up and he stayed there the remainder of the night and left in the morning. Mr. DAHMER stated that he had forgotten about this, but he wanted to get it out. I asked him if he recalled any other incidents where this had occurred and he stated he "did not".

I then informed him that we had just spoken with his father, and we had received information that he may have had a sexual experience when he was 14 or 15 yoa., with a person who lived across the street. Mr. DAHMER stated that this did occur, and this person and him had gotten undressed and did some body rubbing and kissing. I asked him if he recalled the name Eric TYSON (phonetic), and he stated this was the individual. He stated he did not consider this a homosexual experience at the time, but stated, "But I guess it is".

I then asked him when he had acquired his fish tank and he stated it was about 6-months ago because he had developed an interest at that time.

I then informed him that there were numerous allegations made against him by people calling and went through a stack of them, at which time he denied all of them. I asked Mr. DAHMER if he had anything more to tell me, and why he did not request to have his attorney prior to talking to me, and he stated that he did not want his attorney there he just wanted to tell me about this other thing that he had forgotten and he didn't need his attorney present for that. I asked if he felt he needed the attorney for any other questioning, and he stated he felt he did not because he has been truthful with me the whole time and he does not feel he needs his attorney present when I'm there. I again informed him of his attorney's request, that he contact the attorney prior to contacting me, and he stated he understands and if he feels he has something important enough to tell me he will call me. I then informed him again that his attorney had requested his co-

REPORTING OFFICER 2472 SEC 5	PAYROLL # 47	LOC CODE	SUPERVISOR SIGNATURE

PO15-8 5-89 SUPPLEMENT REPORT
MILWAUKEE POLICE DEPARTMENT

☒ INCIDENT SUPPLEMENT
☐ ACCIDENT SUPPLEMENT
☐ JUVENILE SUPPLEMENT
PAGE 4 of 4

DATE OF REPORT	INCIDENT/ACCIDENT #
07-27-91	91 51767

INCIDENT	DATE OF INCIDENT/ACCIDENT	REP CON #
HOMICIDE	07-22-91	

VICTIM	LOCATION OF INCIDENT/ACCIDENT (Address)	DIST
LACY, Oliver	924 N. 25th St. #213	

JUVENILE LAST NAME	FIRST	MID	DATE OF BIRTH	☐ DETAINED ☐ ORDERED TO MCCC ☐ OTHER

QUAN	TYPE OF PROPERTY	DESCRIPTION	SERIAL #	CODE #	VALUE

operation, and he stated he would consider it.

Report per: Det. Dennis MURPHY.

DM/slb   7-27-91

2472 SEC 5 PAGE 48

REPORTING OFFICER	PAYROLL #	LOC CODE	SUPERVISOR SIGNATURE
DET. DENNIS MURPHY	32893 91		

PO15-B 5-89 SUPPLEMENT REPORT MILWAUKEE POLICE DEPARTMENT	X INCIDENT SUPPLEMENT O ACCIDENT SUPPLEMENT O JUVENILE SUPPLEMENT	PAGE 1 of 1	DATE OF REPORT 07-29-91	INCIDENT/ACCIDENT # M2472-M2481 91-51767

INCIDENT INFORMATION

INCIDENT HOMICIDE (STABBING)		DATE OF INCIDENT/ACCIDENT 07-23-91	REP COM
VICTIM LACY, Oliver		LOCATION OF INCIDENT/ACCIDENT (Address) 924 N. 25th Street #213	DIS

JUVENILE LAST NAME	FIRST	MID	DATE OF BIRTH	O DETAINED O ORDERED TO NCCC O OTHER TO NCCC

QUAN	TYPE OF PROPERTY	DESCRIPTION	SERIAL #	CODE #	VALUE

On Monday, 07-29-91, we, Detectives Dennis MURPHY and Patrick KENNEDY, received a call from the Milwaukee County Sheriff that the subject, Jeffrey DAHMER, requested to speak to us.

At this time we obtained an order to produce and proceeded to the Sheriff's Department where upon presenting it we were informed that he was presently with the psychiatrist for Attorney BOYLE. An attempt to locate Attorney BOYLE met with negative results and we then informed the Sheriff to contact us when his interview was over.

At approximately 12:05pm we received a call from the County jail indicating that DAHMER was finished with his interview and was available for us. At that time we proceeded to the Milwaukee County Jail where we picked up Jeffrey DAHMER and asked him if he had contacted his attorney regarding his request to see us. He stated he did and that his attorney would meet us at the CIB.

We proceeded to the CIB where Jeffrey stated he would talk to us and wanted to talk to us even though his attorney wasn't present because he stated that he told us everything already. He stated that he's not involved in any other crimes and he will talk to us regarding anything or answer any questions we may have relative to this investigation. We asked him if he wanted to again call his attorney and he again stated "no," that he would wait until she arrives.

I then asked him several questions regarding a statement he had made regarding the homicide in Bath, Ohio in regards to a call I received from Lieutenant Richard MUNSEY relative to the investigation. I asked him what he had done with the knife he had used to cut up the vitim, namely Steven HICKS, and he stated that he believes he threw it in the river. I questioned him as to whose car he used when he stated that he was driving down the road when he picked up the hitchhiker and subsequently in a car later on in the evening after the death and he stated he used his father's blue 4 door which his father had let him use to go to a movie. He indicated that his mother had already left for Chippewa Falls and his father was still living in the motel at this time. He stated that when he killed Steve his mother was gone. I also questioned him regarding how much time he had spent with the victim prior to killing him and he stated that they were

2472   5 - 49
___/ SEC_____/ PAGE

REPORTING OFFICER	PAYROLL #	LOC CODE	SUPERVISOR SIGNATURE
			Det Lt Raymond Such

PO15-B 5-89 SUPPLEMENT REPORT MILWAUKEE POLICE DEPARTMENT	O INCIDENT SUPPLEMENT O ACCIDENT SUPPLEMENT O JUVENILE SUPPLEMENT	PAGE____of____	DATE OF REPORT 7-30-91	INCIDENT/ACCIDENT # 91-51767/ M-2472-2481		
INCIDENT INFORMATION	INCIDENT HOMICIDE		DATE OF INCIDENT/ACCIDENT 7-23-91			REP CON #
	VICTIM LACY, Oliver		LOCATION OF INCIDENT/ACCIDENT (Address) 924 North 25th St.			DIST
JUVENILE LAST NAME	FIRST	MID	DATE OF BIRTH	O DETAINED O ORDERED TO MCCC O OTHER		
QUAN	TYPE OF PROPERTY	DESCRIPTION		SERIAL #	CODE #	VALUE

together for a couple of hours and they were just drinking beer.

I also went back to his earlier childhood when he had been cutting the dogs and I asked him if he did, in fact, ever cut up a dog and hang it up in the tree in Ohio and he stated that he only hung one dog in the tree and doesn't know why he did this. He also stated that he does not, nor did he have, any girlfriends in Milwaukee or in Ohio. He did admit going to the prom but stated that he only went to see what it was like because he was junior and the girl he went with was a senior and they just went more or less to accompany each other to the prom.

He stated that he does not recall any other thing regarding the Bath, Ohio homicide and if we have any further questions regarding it he would be glad to answer them for us.

Report dictated by: Det. Dennis MURPHY

DM:dls 07-29-91

2472   5   50
SEC   PAGE

REPORTING OFFICER DEt. D. MURPHY	PAYROLL # 32893 91	LOC CODE	SUPERVISOR SIGNATURE Det Lt Raymond R Such

75

| PO15-B 5-89 SUPPLEMENT REPORT MILWAUKEE POLICE DEPARTMENT | □ INCIDENT SUPPLEMENT □ ACCIDENT SUPPLEMENT □ JUVENILE SUPPLEMENT | PAGE _1_ of _1_ | DATE OF REPORT 07-29-91 | INCIDENT/ACCIDENT #/ M2472-M2481 91-51767 |

| INCIDENT INFORMATION | INCIDENT HOMICIDE (STABBING) | | DATE OF INCIDENT/ACCIDENT 07-23-91 | | REP CON # |
| | VICTIM LACY, Oliver | | LOCATION OF INCIDENT/ACCIDENT (Address) 924 N. 25th Street #213 | | DIST 3 |

JUVENILE LAST NAME	FIRST	MID	DATE OF BIRTH	□ DETAINED □ ORDERED TO MCCC □ OTHER

QUAN	TYPE OF PROPERTY	DESCRIPTION		SERIAL #	CODE #	VALUE

On Monday, 07-29-91, we, Detectives Dennis MURPHY and Patrick KENNEDY, after walking Mr. DAHMER over to the CIB from the Milwaukee County Sheriff's lock up and informing that he had the right to have his attorney present during questioning he stated that he did not need to have his attorney present and, in fact, he had called her and she was on her way but he would talk to us until she does arrive.

I informed him that we had a call from Carlos CRUZ who stated that he had been in the service with Mr. DAHMER while in Germany. Mr. DAHMER stated that he does remember him and, in fact, he has nothing to hide regarding Germany. He stated that he does remember spending Thanksgiving at Mr. CRUZ'S residence and he stated also present was an individual with the last name of DAVIS, another girl who was with DAVIS and also Mr. CRUZ'S wife. He indicated that he did have Thanksgiving dinner at that location and he did become involved in an argument with Mr. DAVIS regarding where they were going to spend the evening because there were not that many bedrooms. He stated that he was drunk because he had drank heavily and it was snowing hard, similar to a blizzard, but he stated that he did not leave the house. He related that he remembers staying there and leaving in the morning but he doesn't remember leaving at night nor does he remember being covered with blood or having blood on any type of clothing. He stated that Mr. CRUZ'S wife should be able to verify his statement that he did not leave that night or at any time once he arrived.

He again denies being involved in any homicides in Germany and stated that he could not recall any other occurances where he may have been away from the post other than when he went to Octoberfest for three days in Munich which he believes was in August of 1980. Again Mr. DAHMER denies being involved in any homicides in Germany or in any other place other than the ones he has already confessed to.

Report dictated by: Det. Dennis MURPHY

DM:dls 07-29-91

24472   5   51

SEC_____ / PAGE_____

REPORTING OFFICER Det. D. MURPHY	32893 PAYROLL # 91	LOC CODE	SUPERVISOR SIGNATURE

INCIDENT	HOMICIDE	DATE OF INCIDENT/ACCIDENT 07-23-91		REP CON
VICTIM	LACY, Oliver	LOCATION OF INCIDENT/ACCIDENT (Address) 924 N. 25th St., Apt. #213		DI #3

JUVENILE LAST NAME	FIRST	MID	DATE OF BIRTH	☐ DETAINED ☐ ORDERED TO HCCC ☐ OTHER

QUAN	TYPE OF PROPERTY	DESCRIPTION	SERIAL #	CODE #	VALUE

NARRATIVE:

On Monday, 07-29-91, we Detectives Dennis MURPHY and Patrick KENNEDY while inter-viewing the subject, Jeffrey DAHMER at the CIB in the presence of his attorney, Wendy PATRICKUS, we showed him numerous photographs of missing black males, one white male and one hispanic male. Upon viewing B of I #242222 (Aaron VICKER), he stated this is defini-tely not one of the subjects. He then viewed B of I #243552 (Terrence MOORE) and he stated this is definitely not one of the subjects. He viewed B of I #211904 (Michael SAVAGE) and he also stated this was not one of the subjects. He then viewed B of I numbers: #244202, #157760, #233740,..... and he stated none of these are any of the indi-viduals that were his victims. He also viewed B of I #109328 (Gary GAYBORNE, W/M) and he stated this was definitely not one of the victims.

I then proceeded to show him another B of I photograph #200484 (David C. THOMAS) and he stated, "This looks like the victim who I possibly killed after the man in bookstore", (who was subsequently the 8th Victim --- if you go in order). This follow up was given to Detective O'KEEFE to take this photograph, along with photograph that had been taken by the suspect of his homicide victim to the family in order to make identification.

The next B of I photograph shown to him was #190872 (Richard GUERRERO), and he stated that he could not be sure, but the victim (who was Victim #3 in Milwaukee) was a hispanic male and had had his photograph in the personals in the Milwaukee Journal. A copy of this paper was obtained from 01-07-89 and upon viewing this photograph in the personals he stated, "Yes", this is the hispanic male I killed at my grandmother's house (2357 S. 57th St.)". He further stated this occurred sometime in March of 1988. IN WEST ALLIS

Both the identifications of THOMAS and GUERRERO were subsequently made as positive identifications and were listed as homicide victims.

On Tuesday, 07-30-91, again while questioning DAHMER at the CIB in the presence of his attorney (PATRICKUS), we showed him a photo array consisting of four hispanic males, B of I numbers: #209415, #234074, #234356 and #227440. Upon viewing these four photographs, DAHMER picked out B of I #234356 and stated this photograph looks like the first hispanic male he met on 2nd St., (Victim #2) which occurred approximately in January

2472 SEC 5 PAGE 52

REPORTING OFFICER	PAYROLL #	LOC CODE	SUPERVISOR SIGNATURE

| INCIDENT HOMICIDE | | | DATE OF INCIDENT/ACCIDENT 07-23-91 | | REP CON |
| INFORMATION VICTIM LACY, Oliver | | | LOCATION OF INCIDENT/ACCIDENT (Address) 924 N. 25th St., Apt. #213 | | DIS #3 |

| JUVENILE LAST NAME | FIRST | MID | DATE OF BIRTH | ☐ DETAINED ☐ ORDERED TO MCCC ☐ OTHER |
| | | | | |

QUAN	TYPE OF PROPERTY	DESCRIPTION	SERIAL #	CODE #	VALUE

of 1988. This is a photograph of Jay E. DOXTATOR, I/M, DOB 03/01/73 of 1010 W. Pierce St., and reported missing on 01-18-88. Further investigation was passed on to Detective MCHENRY and they will attempt to make positive identification on this individual.

Further investigation is pending.

Report per Detective Dennis MURPHY.

DM/htf   07-31-91

↑72   SEC   5   PAGE   53

| REPORTING OFFICER DET. DENNIS MURPHY | PAYROLL # 32893 | LOC CODE 91 | SUPERVISOR SIGNATURE |

PO15-6 5-89 SUPPLEMENT REPORT	X INCIDENT SUPPLEMENT		DATE OF REPORT	INCIDENT/ACCIDENT #
MILWAUKEE POLICE DEPARTMENT	O ACCIDENT SUPPLEMENT	PAGE 1 of 4	07-29-91	91-51767/M2472-M2481
	O JUVENILE SUPPLEMENT			

| INCIDENT INFORMATION | INCIDENT HOMICIDE (STABBING) | | DATE OF INCIDENT/ACCIDENT 07-23-91 | | REP CON # |
| | VICTIM LACY, Oliver | | LOCATION OF INCIDENT/ACCIDENT (Address) 924 N. 25th Street #213 | | DIST 3 |

JUVENILE LAST NAME	FIRST	MID	DATE OF BIRTH	O DETAINED O ORDERED TO MCCC O OTHER

QUAN	TYPE OF PROPERTY	DESCRIPTION		SERIAL #	CODE #	VALUE

On Monday, 07-29-91, I, Detective KENNEDY, along with Det. Dennis MURPHY, were contacted by Deputy MALLICK (phonectic), of the Milwaukee County Sheriff's Jail. He stated at this time, which was approximately 9:45am, that the suspect, Jeffrey DAHMER, had requested to speak with us.

We proceeded to the jail after obtaining an order to produce and returned with the suspect to the 4th floor CIB and placed Mr. DAHMER in an interview room. At this time Mr. DAHMER stated that he did, in fact, wish to speak with us regarding the offense.

I advised Mr. DAHMER that I had some further questions regarding the Asian male whom he had met at the Grand Avenue mall. Regarding the Asian male he stated that he met him while he was walking around the Grand Avenue mall. He indicated that after introducing himself to the victim, he offered him $50.00 to accompany him back to his apartment to pose and have some drinks and watch videos. He stated that he advised the Asian male that the posing would be in nude or semi-nude states. The Asian male agreed to accompany him back to his apartment and they returned to his 25th Street address by bus. He feels that they returned home at approximately 5:00pm and once in the apartment he had the victim disrobe down to his black bikini panties and that he posed for several photographs which he took with his Polaroid camera. These photos can be found on Milwaukee Police inventory. He stated that during the time of the posing he also mixed his drink of rum, coffee and sleeping pills and offered it to the victim who drank it. He went on to state that during this entire time the victim spoke in perfect English and was completely able to understand English and spoke it fluently. He indicated that at about this time the rum/coffee concoction with the sleeping pills in it begun to take effect and as the victim became drowsey he walked him into the bedroom area. During the time that he walked him into the bedroom area and sat on the bed DAHMER stated that the victim, Tony HUGHES, whom he had killed several days earlier, was lying naked on the floor of his bedroom. He stated that he believes that the victim saw Tony HUGHES' body, however, did not react to it. He feels that this was because the rum/coffee/sleeping pill mixture was beginning to affect him. He went on to state that he put a video on and they watched it until the victim fell asleep. He related that during this time he began kissing and body rubbing the victim and he feels that he may have had oral sex, mouth to penis, on the victim, however, he denies at this time that he had penis to anus

REPORTING OFFICER 2472 SEC	5 PAGE	PAYROLL # 5 4	LOC CODE	SUPERVISOR SIGNATURE Det./Lt. Raymond Kwich

PO15-B 5-89 SUPPLEMENT REPORT MILWAUKEE POLICE DEPARTMENT	X INCIDENT SUPPLEMENT O ACCIDENT SUPPLEMENT O JUVENILE SUPPLEMENT	PAGE 2 of 2	DATE OF REPORT 07-29-91	INCIDENT/ACCIDENT # 91-51767/M2472-M2481
INCIDENT INFORMATION	INCIDENT HOMICIDE (STABBING)		DATE OF INCIDENT/ACCIDENT 07-23-91	REP CON #
	VICTIM LACY, Oliver		LOCATION OF INCIDENT/ACCIDENT (Address) 924 N. 25th Street #213	DIST
JUVENILE LAST NAME	FIRST	MID	DATE OF BIRTH	O DETAINED O ORDERED TO MCCC O OTHER
QUAN	TYPE OF PROPERTY	DESCRIPTION	SERIAL #	CODE #	VALUE

sex with the victim. He stated that after he realized the he was unable to arouse the victim by mouth to penis sex and by body rubbing and kissing he continued to watch the video and to drink beer until he himself fell asleep. He indicated that after a few hours of sleep he woke up and it was quite late out, approximately 11:00 or 12:00, maybe later. He looked about and realized that the victim was still sleeping from the effects of his drink and he decided to go to the tavern located on 27th Street known as the Gare Bear Bar to continue drinking.

He stated that he left the apartment, went to the Gare Bear Bar and drank beer until closing time. At closing time, after leaving the tavern, he stated that he began to walk eastbound on West State Street and observed the victim sitting completely naked on the southeast corner of 25th and State. He stated that the victim was sitting on the curb. He related that there were two black females standing by him and they appeared to be hysterical. He walked up to the victim, whom he realized was speaking to the black females in Asian. The victim was disoriented and appeared to be intoxicated by alcohol, however, he realized that he must still be under the influence of the drink containing the sleeping pills he had given him. At this time he advised the ladies that the victim was, in fact, a friend on his and that he attempted to pull the victim in the direction of his apartment. He stated that the women continued screaming at him, "we don't know if you really know this guy and we've called the Police, why don't you wait until the Police get here." He stated that he continued pulling the victim towards his apartment and that the victim did offer some slight resistance to this. When he got to the alley behind the Hong Fat Company he noticed that the Fire Department had approached from the east end of the alley and the Milwaukee Police Department was coming from the west end of the alley. He indicated that at this time he noticed that the victim had a slight laceration above his left eye and was bleeding from this. He stated that at this time there was no other signs of blood on either the anal or genital area of victim. As the Police and Fire Department arrived he stopped with the boy and he noticed that the Fire Department personnel simply stood by and did not make any efforts to attend to the victim. He stated that the he feels that the Police Officer took a yellow plastic type blanket and wrapped it around the boy and he noticed that the black females who he had seen with the boy on 25th and State appeared to still be hysterical and were screaming

REPORTING OFFICER 2472	SEC 5	PAGE	PAYROLL 55	LOC CODE	SUPERVISOR SIGNATURE Alt.Lt. Raymond Such

INCIDENT INFORMATION	INCIDENT HOMICIDE (STABBING)		DATE OF INCIDENT/ACCIDENT 07-23-91		REP COM
	VICTIM LACY, Oliver		LOCATION OF INCIDENT/ACCIDENT (Address) 924 N. 25th Street #213		DIS

JUVENILE LAST NAME	FIRST	MID	DATE OF BIRTH	O DETAINED O ORDERED TO MCCC O OTHER

QUAN	TYPE OF PROPERTY	DESCRIPTION	SERIAL #	CODE #	VALUE

at the Police Officers. At this time he stated that a Police Officer approached him and asked him what was going on. He stated that he handed the Police Officer his Ambrosia Chocolate Company personnel ID and stated who he was and gave a fake name for the victim. He stated that he believes he told the Police that the victim was 19 years old and he thought this was appropriate, as although the victim was young, he believed him to be approximately that age. He stated that he told the Police that the victim was, in fact, a close friend of his and gave him a fake name. He indicated that the victim had stayed with him several times in the past and that whenever he drinks he gets crazy and has been known to walk out of the apartment in the nude. He stated that the Officers attempted to speak with the victim, however, he stood there speaking only in an Asian dialect and appeared to be intoxicated and smelled of alcohol. He stated at this time he feels he convinced the Police that this was some type of homosexual relationship that had some alcohol problems and that he would take care of the victim if he was allowed to return with him to his apartment. He stated at this time two Officers escorted both he and the victim back to his apartment building.

He went on to state that during the time that the Officers were speaking with him regarding the Asian boy the black females who had been screaming hysterically in the beginning of this, left the scene, however, he is unsure were they went to.

He related that the victim was in no way an acquaintance of his before this evening, that he had never seen him before and had absolutely no idea that he was, in fact, the brother of the minor that he had taken pictures of on an earlier offense. He indicated that it was a chance meeting at the Grand Avenue mall and that to his knowledge besides this offense and the offense where he took pictures of an Asian boy that there have been no other encounters, either personally, casually or sexual, with any other oriental males.

At this time I again questioned Jeffrey DAHMER as to the bleeding from the anus of the victim and whether or not the bleeding would be visable to Police Officers. He stated emphatically that there was no blood coming from the anus or genital area of the victim as he had not had any anal intercouse or injured the victim in any way prior to this meeting with the Police. He stated that the night was pitch black and the alley was also dark. He feels the Police attempted to interview and investigate the incident

REPORTING OFFICER 2472	SEC 5	PAGE 56	PAYROLL #	LOC CODE	SUPERVISOR SIGNATURE Det Lt Raymond Such

INCIDENT INFORMATION	INCIDENT HOMICIDE (STABBING)			DATE OF INCIDENT/ACCIDENT 07-23-91		REP CON #
	VICTIM LACY, Oliver			LOCATION OF INCIDENT/ACCIDENT (Address) 924 N. 25th Street #213		DIST
JUVENILE LAST NAME	FIRST	MID		DATE OF BIRTH	O DETAINED O ORDERED TO MCCC O OTHER	
QUAN	TYPE OF PROPERTY	DESCRIPTION		SERIAL #	CODE #	VALUE

to the best of their ability at the time, however, he feels he was able to convince Police of the homosexual nature of the incident and that, in fact, all would be well if he was allowed to assist in taking care of the victim.

    Report dictated by: Det. Patrick KENNEDY

PK:dls 07-29-91

M 2472 SEC 5 / PAGE 57

REPORTING OFFICER Det. Patrick KENNEDY	PAYROLL # 48171	LOC CODE 93	SUPERVISOR SIGNATURE

INCIDENT INFORMATION	INCIDENT HOMICIDE (STABBING)			DATE OF INCIDENT/ACCIDENT 07-23-91		REP COM
	VICTIM LACY, Oliver			LOCATION OF INCIDENT/ACCIDENT (Address) 924 N. 25th Street #213		DIS 3
JUVENILE LAST NAME	FIRST	MID	DATE OF BIRTH		☐ DETAINED ☐ ORDERED TO HCCC ☐ OTHER	
QUAN	TYPE OF PROPERTY	DESCRIPTION		SERIAL #	CODE #	VALUE

On Monday, 07-29-91, we, Detectives Dennis MURPHY and Patrick KENNEDY, received a call from the Milwaukee County Sheriff that the subject, Jeffrey DAHMER, requested to speak to us.

At this time we obtained an order to produce and proceeded to the Sheriff's Department where upon presenting it we were informed that he was presently with the psychiatrist for Attorney BOYLE. An attempt to locate Attorney BOYLE met with negative results and we then informed the Sheriff to contact us when his interview was over.

At approximately 12:05pm we received a call from the County jail indicating that DAHMER was finished with his interview and was available for us. At that time we proceeded to the Milwaukee County Jail where we picked up Jeffrey DAHMER and asked him if he had contacted his attorney regarding his request to see us. He stated he did and that his attorney would meet us at the CIB.

We proceeded to the CIB where Jeffrey stated he would talk to us and wanted to talk to us even though his attorney wasn't present because he stated that he told us everything already. He stated that he's not involved in any other crimes and he will talk to us regarding anything or answer any questions we may have relative to this investigation. We asked him if he wanted to again call his attorney and he again stated "no," that he would wait until she arrives.

I then asked him several questions regarding a statement he had made regarding the homicide in Bath, Ohio in regards to a call I received from Lieutenant Richard MUNSEY relative to the investigation. I asked him what he had done with the knife he had used to cut up the vitim, namely Steven HICKS, and he stated that he believes he threw it in the river. I questioned him as to whose car he used when he stated that he was driving down the road when he picked up the hitchhiker and subsequently in a car later on in the evening after the death and he stated he used his father's blue 4 door which his father had let him use to go to a movie. He indicated that his mother had already left for Chippewa Falls and his father was still living in the motel at this time. He stated that when he killed Steve his mother was gone. I also questioned him regarding how much time he had spent with the victim prior to killing him and he stated that they were together for a couple of hours and they were just drinking beer.

I also went back to his earlier childhood when he had been cutting the dogs and I

REPORTING OFFICER		PAYROLL #	LOC CODE	SUPERVISOR SIGNATURE
M 2472	SEC 5 / PAGE 58	58		

83

INCIDENT INFORMATION	INCIDENT HOMICIDE (STABBING)		DATE OF INCIDENT/ACCIDENT 07-23-91	REP CON #
	VICTIM LACY, Oliver		LOCATION OF INCIDENT/ACCIDENT (Address) 924 N. 25th Street #213	DIST

JUVENILE LAST NAME	FIRST	MID	DATE OF BIRTH	☐ DETAINED ☐ ORDERED TO MCCC ☐ OTHER

QUAN	TYPE OF PROPERTY	DESCRIPTION		SERIAL #	CODE #	VALUE

asked him if he did, in fact, ever cut up a dog and hang it up in the tree in Ohio and he stated that he only hung one dog in the tree and doesn't know why he did this. He also stated that he does not, nor did he have, any girlfriends in Milwaukee or in Ohio. He did admit going to the prom but stated that he only went to see what it was like because he was junior and the girl he went with was a senior and they just went more or less to accompany each other to the prom.

He stated that he does not recall any other thing regarding the Bath, Ohio homicide and if we have any further questions regarding it he would be glad to answer them for us.

Report dictated by: Det. Dennis MURPHY

DM:dls 07-29-91

2472 M_____/ SEC_____ 5 / PAGE_____ 59

REPORTING OFFICER Det. Dennis MURPHY	PAYROLL # 32893	LOC CODE 91	SUPERVISOR SIGNATURE

PO15-B 5-89 SUPPLEMENT REPORT
MILWAUKEE POLICE DEPARTMENT
O INCIDENT SUPPLEMENT
O ACCIDENT SUPPLEMENT
O JUVENILE SUPPLEMENT
PAGE 1 of 7
DATE OF REPORT 7-29-91
INCIDENT/ACCIDENT # 91-51767 7 M-2472-M-2481

	INCIDENT	HOMICIDE	DATE OF INCIDENT/ACCIDENT 7-23-91		REP CON
INCIDENT INFORMATION	VICTIM	LACY, Oliver	LOCATION OF INCIDENT/ACCIDENT (Address) 924 North 25th St., #213		DIS

JUVENILE LAST NAME	FIRST	MID	DATE OF BIRTH	O DETAINED O ORDERED TO MCCC O OTHER

QUAN	TYPE OF PROPERTY	DESCRIPTION	SERIAL #	CODE #	VALUE

On Mon., 7-29-91, I, Det. KENNEDY, on Squad 126, along with Det. Dennis MURPHY, were in an interview room located in the CIB on the fourth floor. At this time we had the suspect in this offense, Jeffrey DAHMER, who had previously requested to speak with us regarding this offense. I advised Mr. DAHMER that I had a series of questions I would like to ask him regarding the offense, to which he stated he was willing to answer them.

At this time I asked him regarding the patties of meat which we found in the lower freezer in his apartment. To this he stated they were not exactly patties, however they were strips of muscle and flesh which he had taken from his thirteenth victim. He stated he met this victim in front of the bus station and the reason these were not thrown out, along with other parts found with the so called "patties" was because he had placed them on the bottom of his standing freezer and that they had become frozen to the bottom and he was unable to get them out. He stated his usual routine after cutting up his victims, was to only throw out two and possibly three bags of human flesh and bones at a time and at this time he would hide the bags underneath other bags of garbage which were located behind his apartment building on 25th St. He stated the remainer of flesh, chunks and strips of body parts which he had cut off the victims, he would place in plastic bags and freeze until a more approriate time to throw them out. He stated this was done in order to help stop detection of his crime. He felt that if he would throw out entire cut up body parts at one time, it would be easier for people to detect his activities, so therefore he would freeze, or keep refrigerated, body parts until he was able to more discreetly dispose of them through the trash.

Regarding the computer which was found in his apartment, Jeffrey stated he became interested in computers while he was doing his tour in the House of Correction. He stated he thought it would be fun and interesting and that he would use it for personal finance, daily planning, games, and personal business. He stated there will be several discs found in his apartment, however, that he never recorded or put anything into his discs regarding the offenses that he has been questioned about. He stated the computer did not turn out to be as interesting to him as he felt it would and that he barely used it and that slightly before his arrest he was attempting to sell the computer and had an offer

V ± 5 % SE 5 PAGE 60

REPORTING OFFICER	PAYROLL #	LOC CODE	SUPERVISOR SIGNATURE
			Det Lt Raymond R Smith

INCIDENT INFORMATION	INCIDENT HOMICIDE		DATE OF INCIDENT/ACCIDENT 7-23-91		REP CON #
	VICTIM LACY, Oliver		LOCATION OF INCIDENT/ACCIDENT (Address) 924 North 25th St.		DIST
JUVENILE LAST NAME	FIRST	MID	DATE OF BIRTH	O DETAINED O ORDERED TO MCCC O OTHER	

| QUAN | TYPE OF PROPERTY | DESCRIPTION | | SERIAL # | CODE # | VALUE |

regading so.

Regarding whether or not he had ever been in Columbus, Georgia, or Fort Bennings, Jeffrey stated that while he was taking his military police training at Fort McClellan, Alabama, he kept getting drunk on base and ended up getting beat up by several other members of his unit. He stated they did this because he had caused the entire platoon to suffer extra physical training and punishment because of his abusive drinking pattern. He stated that one day after the entire unit was disciplined because one of his infractions, a large black private and a large white private took him into the men's room and pysically beat him bloody. He stated that during this beating he received a concussion and the ear drum of his left ear was fractured. He stated that from this injury he was transferred to Fort Bennings in Georgia, for treatment. He stated he was there for only two days and then returned to his barracks at Fort McClellan. He stated that after washing out of the MP training school, he was transferred to Fort Sam Houston, Texas where he was trained as a medic. He stated this training agreed with him more and he felt he did well while there.

Regarding questions as to whether or not he belonged to a health club, he stated he was a lifetime "President's Member" of the Vic Tanny Health Club and he was eligible to attend any Vic Tanny Health Club throughout the nation. He stated he frequently visited the Vic Tanny Health Club on North Hawley Road and that he went regularly for about a year, however, after that time constraints and his job, along with his drinking problem prevented him from going any longer.

Regarding having a locker at the Ambrosia Chocolate Company, he stated that while he was employed at Ambrosia Chocolate Company, he did have a yellow painted locker, he believes the number was "214." He stated that to the best of his knowledge, there was nothing of value or of personal belongings in that locker at the time of his termination, however he is not sure.

Regarding how long ago he bought the standing freezer found in his apartment, he stated that he bought the standing freezer several months after he had killed the victim known as "Cash D." He stated the reason he bought the freezer was because he was having difficulty storing the cut off flesh and bones which he had cut from his victims. He

| REPORTING OFFICER | SES 5 PAGE | PAYROLL # 6 | LOC CODE | SUPERVISOR SIGNATURE |

INCIDENT INFORMATION	INCIDENT HOMICIDE		DATE OF INCIDENT/ACCIDENT	REP CON
	VICTIM LACY, Oliver		LOCATION OF INCIDENT/ACCIDENT (Address) 924 NORTH 25TH ST.	DIS

JUVENILE LAST NAME	FIRST	MID	DATE OF BIRTH	O DETAINED O ORDERED TO MCCC O OTHER

QUAN	TYPE OF PROPERTY	DESCRIPTION		SERIAL #	CODE #	VALUE

stated he felt that by buying the freezer, it would be easier for him to store the cut up flesh and bones until he was able to dispose of them discreetly through the garbage to the rear of his apartment.

Regarding the penis from the black male which he kept and which he painted white, he stated he bought a skin color paint and painted the penis simply because it seemed like a fasinating idea and he wanted the penis to look more natural. He was unable to give any further reason as to why he painted this penis.

Regarding the head of the victim, BRADEHOFT and why it was partially decomposed when found in the freezer, Jeffrey stated that after he killed the victim, BRADEHOFT, he placed him on the bed in his bedroom and covered him with a blanket and left him there for approximately two days. He stated he remembers it was hot during those two days and that the air conditioning in his apartment does not really cool off the bedroom that well. He stated it had been at least a day and a half before he checked on his victim and that when he pulled the blankets back after approximately two days, he noticed that decomposition had already begun and that the head had acquired some maggots. He stated he quickly cut up the victim and disposed of him in the usual way, except for keeping the head and placing it in the freezer.

Regarding the black nylon strap which he stated he used to strangle several of his victims and which was photographed by himself, hanging one of his victims from his shower in his bathroom, I questioned Jeffrey as to the whereabouts of the strap and he stated he was unsure which victim he got rid of the strap with, however he stated it became soaked with blood and he decided to throw it out and that he disposed of it through his garbage located in the alley at his building.

Regarding the knives which he used, he stated that the large knife with the six inch blade and the black plastic handle, he bought at the knife shop in the mall and he had returned to the mall at least two or three times in order to get it sharpened, as the store would sharpen the knife for free. He stated this is the knife he used most often when cutting up his victims, however the two small three inch bladed parry knives with the black plastic handles, he stated he bought at Lechtner's Kitchen Mart in the Grand Avenue Mall. He stated he did use these knives, however they were not very strong. The smaller

REPORTING OFFICER	PAYROLL #	LOC CODE	SUPERVISOR SIGNATURE
2 5	62		

INCIDENT	HOMICIDE		DATE OF INCIDENT/ACCIDENT 7-23-91		REP CON #
VICTIM	LACY, Oliver		LOCATION OF INCIDENT/ACCIDENT (Address) 924 North 25th St.		DIST

JUVENILE LAST NAME	FIRST	MID	DATE OF BIRTH	O DETAINED O ORDERED TO MCCC O OTHER

QUAN	TYPE OF PROPERTY	DESCRIPTION	SERIAL #	CODE #	VALUE

of the two parry knives, one of which is photographed and a copy of which can be found on MPD inventory is the knife which he used to crave the skin off of the one victim that he totally skinned.

Regarding the battery complaint which he filed with the Milwaukee Police Department in November of 1988, he stated he met an individual and asked him if he would come back to his apartment for pictures. He stated that although he was no longer living in the apartment on North 24th St., he had just moved out in October and felt it would still be vacant. He stated he still had the key for that apartment and that he and the suspect went back to that apartment. However upon attempting to enter, he realized it had been rented out and a female was living there. He stated that upon realizing this, he and the suspect walked down the stairwell of the apartment building at 808 North 24th St. and continued to drink beer. He went on to indicate that after all the beer was gone, he bent over and received a hard blow from behind. He is unsure what he was struck with, however because of his intoxication and the fact the blow was so hard, he knows he passed out. He stated when he came to, he was at the police station and that officers, after taking his complaint, took him to West Allis Memorial Hospital, where he was stitched up. He believes the suspect, who was a black male, also stole about $350 from his pockets and he does remember comimg to the third floor of the Police Administration Building and viewing photos regarding this offense, however he was unable to pick anyone out of the line up.

Regarding whether or not he knew a white male, approximately 54 years old, by the name of Tom MODEE, who apparently was a sexual acquaintance of one of his victims, Ernest MILLER, he stated he never met any of his victim's friends and has no idea who Thomas MODEE is.

At this time I questioned Jeffrey regarding the fact that he apparently left the victims, who were already killed, lying about his apartment. He stated he never left anyone for more then two days, however he did leave several of his victims uncut up and naked, lying about his apartment, either in his bed or on his bedroom floor. He stated there wre several reasons why he did this. The first reason was because on several of the victims he intended and did return at a later date and had oral and anal sex, and kissing and touching of the body, after they were dead. He also stated that sometimes because of time

REPORTING OFFICER	5	PAYROLL # 63	LOC CODE	SUPERVISOR SIGNATURE

INCIDENT INFORMATION	INCIDENT HOMICIDE		DATE OF INCIDENT/ACCIDENT 7-23-91		REP COM
	VICTIM LACY, Oliver		LOCATION OF INCIDENT/ACCIDENT (Address) 924 North 25th St.		DIS

JUVENILE LAST NAME	FIRST	MID	DATE OF BIRTH	⊙ DETAINED ⊙ ORDERED TO MCCC ⊙ OTHER

QUAN	TYPE OF PROPERTY	DESCRIPTION	SERIAL #	CODE #	VALUE

constraints and work, he was unable to proceed with cutting up and disposing of the bodies at the time, so he simply left them. He stated also that there were other times, because of his drinking and the late hours he was keeping, that he was just too exhausted to try to cut up the body and dispose of it, so he left them there.

Regarding the letter which was written to Judge GARDNER while he was in the House of Correction, he stated that he remembers talking to a white male inmate in the House of Correction regarding his predicament and wanting to get out. He stated that this inmate put the idea in his head to write a letter to the judge regarding a change in his sentence. He stated the inmate appeared to be knowledgeable in such matters and actually wrote out a letter which he copied in his own handwriting. He stated the words and the ideas in the letters which he wrote to Judge GARDNER were not even his, however, he thought that they sounded all right and decided to use them to see if they would work. He stated that although he did write the letter, the ideas, words, and composition were the work of another inmate.

At this time I questioned Jeffrey regarding the long period of time which lapsed between his first homicide which he committed in Bath, Ohio, and the first homicide which he committed here in Milwaukee. At this time we established that the first homicide which he committed here in Milwaukee occurred probably in November of 1987. This was the victim that he took to the Ambassador Hotel.

Jeffrey stated he feels that the first homicide that happened in Bath, Ohio, was unplanned and somewhat of an accident. He stated this haunted him terribly for many years and that he had nightmares and was troubled by it during the entire time he was in the service. He emphatically denied committing any crimes while he was in the United States Armed Forces and stated he feels that one of the reasons that he did not get involved in criminal activity was because of the structure of the military and the fact that he never had a residence or an apartment of his own. He feels he was continually surrounded by other soldiers and did not have an opportunity to commit any offenses. He stated that after leaving the military and moving to Miami, Florida, that he was short of funds and was living on the beach after he ran out of cash. He stated he lived on the beach for approximately two months in between hotels and that there, too, he did not have an oppor-

REPORTING OFFICER	PAYROLL # 64	LOC CODE	SUPERVISOR SIGNATURE

	INCIDENT		DATE OF INCIDENT/ACCIDENT /67 / M-2472	REP
INCIDENT INFORMATION	VICTIM	HOMICIDE	LOCATION OF INCIDENT/ACCIDENT (Address)	DIS
JUVENILE LAST NAME:	LACY, OTTWURST	MID	DATE OF	○ DETAINED ○ ORDERED TO MCCC ○ OTHER
QUAN	TYPE OF PROPERTY	DESCRIPTION	SERIAL #	CODE #	VALUE

tunity to commit an offense. He stated he was busy working in the sub shop trying to make money or trying to find a place to stay and that Miami did not turn out to be the opportunity that he felt it would be when he left the service. He stated after calling his father and advising him of the financial trouble he was having in Miami, he was given a plane ticket to return to Ohio, and eventually moved to his grandmother's house in West Allis.

He stated when he first moved to West Allis with his grandmother, it was at this time that he decided to try to put behind him the nightmare he had constantly re-lived regarding his first homicide. He stated his grandmother was a religious woman and at this time he began attending church with her and apparently was looking into religious ideals in an attempt to change his life. He stated he recalls reading the Bible and attempting to look for a job and to live the so called "straight and narrow life." He stated that although he constantly tried to delve into the religious aspects of life, he constantly had fantasies of homosexual activity and mutilation of human beings. He stated that eventaully during this period of time the fantasies and the urges for, as he called them, "the darker side," bothered him and that he decided to quit attending church and looking into religion, and for awhile he delved in the occult. He stated he felt he did this because he felt that since religion wasn't working, maybe he should just delve into the occult and to satanism. However, after reading several books and dabbling in it, he realized this was not for him and then he again gave in to his homosexual tendencies. He stated he began by going to the bookstores where he obtained information regarding gay areas in Milwaukee. He stated he also started reading gay and homosexual pornography and eventually became acquainted with the bars in the homosexual areas of town. From there he began to frequent the gay baths and was a regular member of the gay baths and spent the night several times. He in fact stated that several times he used a liqueur which had been tampered with by his sleeping pills in the gay baths, however he did not commit any violent acts while there. He only druged some of his gay friends who he had met and spent the night with in the gay baths. He stated he believes this is the reason why there was such long span between homicides, as he was going through all of these mental changes, trying to leave the old life behind and that once he finally again gave in to his homo-

REPORTING OFFICER		PAYROLL	LOC CODE	SUPERVISOR SIGNATURE
2472	5	PAGE 65		

	INCIDENT			DATE OF INCIDENT/ACCIDENT		REP CON #
INCIDENT INFORMATION	HOMICIDE			7-23-91		
	VICTIM			LOCATION OF INCIDENT/ACCIDENT (Address)		DIST
	LACY Oliver			924 North 25th St.		

JUVENILE LAST NAME	FIRST	MID	DATE OF BIRTH	O DETAINED O ORDERED TO MCCC O OTHER

QUAN	TYPE OF PROPERTY	DESCRIPTION	SERIAL #	CODE #	VALUE

sexual desires, that it slowly began to escalate over years until he finally gave in to his fantasies of killing and dismembering men after homosexual acts and culminated in his first homicide here in Milwaukee at the Ambassador Hotel.

At this time he was given several other questions regarding his tour of duty in Germany and a chronological explanation of the events of his life and Det. Dennis MURPHY will file a detailed supplementary regarding this part of the interview.

It should also be noted that during this interview, I asked Jeffrey if in fact all the information he has been giving us regarding this offense is true and correct. At this point Jeffrey was very adamant, stating, What would be the point of lying now? You realize that the whole purpose for me cooperating with you and giving you this information is for me to clear my conscious so that I can go on with my life. What I've told you is the truth. Why should I lie now?" At this time the interview was terminated.

Report per Det. Patrick KENNEDY.

PK/lh   7-29-91

84 2 SEC 5 PAGE 66

REPORTING OFFICER	PAYROLL #	LOC CODE	SUPERVISOR SIGNATURE
Det. P. KENNEDY	48171 93		

INCIDENT INFORMATION	INCIDENT HOMICIDE		DATE OF INCIDENT/ACCIDENT 7-23-91		REP COM #
	VICTIM LACY, Oliver		LOCATION OF INCIDENT/ACCIDENT (Address) 924 North 25th St., #213		DIST
JUVENILE LAST NAME	FIRST	MID	DATE OF BIRTH	O DETAINED O ORDERED TO MCCC O OTHER	
QUAN	TYPE OF PROPERTY	DESCRIPTION		SERIAL #	CODE #	VALUE

On Tue., 7-30-91, I, Det. KENNEDY, along with Det. Dennis MURPHY, were called by Deputy COOPER of the Milwaukee County Sheriff's jail and he informed us at this time that the suspect, Jeffrey DAHMER, had requested to speak with us. At this time we proceeded to the 5th Floor Lock Up of the Milwaukee County Jail and returned to the 4th Floor of the C.I.B., with the suspect, Jeffrey DAHMER, and placed him into an interview room.

At this time I was informed by Jeffrey DAHMER that he would like to speak with me some more regarding the above offense.

At this time Jeffrey DAHMER stated that during the time that he was committing these offenses, he had been incarcerated in House of Correction for the offense of taking photographs of a minor. He stated that during his incarceration he was given a "day pass" on Thanksgiving Day. He stated that during his day pass he was ashamed to face his family who were gathered at his grandmother's house in West Allis for Thanksgiving dinner and that after dinner he left the residence and went to a local West Allis tavern where he began to drink heavily. He stated after he became intoxicated, he ended up down in the homosexual gay area of Milwaukee, that being 200 South 2nd St. and he bar hopped from bar to bar. He stated he is unsure, but he feels that this time he entered the 219 Club, where he ended up sitting next to an older white male, approximately 35 - 40 years old, who had dark curlish shoulder length hair and a beard. He stated the two talked and drank heavily, and that he (DAHMER) apparently blacked out because of over indulgence in alcohol.

He stated he recalls waking up the next morning and he was in a strange apartment. He stated that at this time he was hogtied. He described this as being tied behind his back and then suspended by hooks and ropes from the ceiling and that both his legs were separated and tied and also elevated and that the suspect described earlier that he had met in the 219 Club, was using a white striped candle and placing it in his anal area. He stated that when he realized what was happening, he began screaming and swearing at the suspect, demanding that he be cut down and let go. He stated the suspect did cut him down and he quickly grabbed his clothing and attempted to leave the apartment, when the suspect attempted to stop him and stated, "What's your hurry? Let's stop and talk about this."

67

REPORTING OFFICER	PAYROLL #	LOC CODE	SUPERVISOR SIGNATURE
5			

	INCIDENT	HOMICIDE		DATE OF INCIDENT/ACCIDENT 7-23-91		REP COM #
INCIDENT INFORMATION	VICTIM	LACY, Oliver		LOCATION OF INCIDENT/ACCIDENT (Address) 924 North 25th St.		DIST

JUVENILE LAST NAME	FIRST	MID	DATE OF BIRTH	O DETAINED O ORDERED TO MCCC O OTHER

QUAN	TYPE OF PROPERTY	DESCRIPTION		SERIAL #	CODE #	VALUE

He stated at this time he was in no mood to speak with the suspect and quickly left the residence and made his way back to the House of Correction.

He stated that approximately a day or two after this encounter, he had a bowel movement and that a six inch portion of candle was ejected from his anal area at this time. He stated he was highly intoxicated at the time of this encounter and that he is unsure whether or not he would be able to identify this suspect through photographs. He stated he chalked this up to being an experience that he had to endure because his high risk life style and the homosexual area of town. He stated that at this time he was actually the victim.

At this time I questioned Jeffrey DAHMER regarding the blood which we found splattered around the walls surrounding his bed in the bedroom of his apartment on 25th St. and regarding the blood which was found dried and soaked into the mattress of his bedding. He stated this blood was the result of the seventh victim, who has been identified as Ernest MILLER. He stated he met Ernest MILLER in front of the bookstore on 27th St. and that after taking him home to his apartment and drugging him with his sleeping pill rum concoction, that the victim apparently began to wake up from the potion as he was lying on his bed. He stated the victim had a muscular build and he felt he would be unable to strangle him as he was coming out of his daze, so he used his knife to cut him in the carotid artery. He stated that by cutting the carotid artery of the victim, the blood began to splatter all about the bed and the walls. He stated he did not do a very good job on cleaning up the blood afterward and this is the remaining blood which is located on the wall and the bedding in his apartment.

At this time I questioned him regarding the apparel, that being clothing, that he would wear during the time he was dismembering his victims. He stated that whenever he dismembered his victims, he was always completely naked, that he wore no shoes, socks, or any clothing of any type. He stated this was not in fact done because of sexual gratification, but simply for necessity because the job of cutting and dismembering his victims was quite messy and he did not wish to get blood and body fluids about his clothing.

At this time I was informed by Lt. Kenneth MEULER that detectives from the Chicago Police Department wished to speak with the suspect, DAHMER, regarding possible connections

REPORTING OFFICER	-5	PAYROLL #	LOC CODE	SUPERVISOR SIGNATURE
	PAGE 68			

INCIDENT INFORMATION	INCIDENT HOMICIDE		DATE OF INCIDENT/ACCIDENT 7-23-91		REP CON #
	VICTIM LACY, Oliver		LOCATION OF INCIDENT/ACCIDENT (Address) 924 North 25th St.		DIST

JUVENILE LAST NAME	FIRST	MID	DATE OF BIRTH	O DETAINED O ORDERED TO MCCC O OTHER

QUAN	TYPE OF PROPERTY	DESCRIPTION		SERIAL #	CODE #	VALUE

in offenses they were investigating in their jurisdiction. It should also be noted that Attorney Wendy PATRICKUS, from Gerald BOYLE's office, appeared and sat in on this interview.

At this time Det. CARROLL and Det. KEENAN, from the Chicago Police Department entered the interview room and questioned the suspect, Jeffrey DAHMER, regarding his frequent excursions by bus to the Chicago area. At this time Jeffrey DAHMER stated that he had visited the Chicago gay area on approximately ten or eleven different occasions and that while he was there, he usually frequented the gay taverns located on Clark St. or Halsted St. He specifically mentioned men's bathhouses, one by the name of Man's Country Bath Club located on Clark St. in Chicago, the Unicorn Club, which is also a gay bath house located on Halsted. At this time the detectives from Chicago also asked Jeffrey DAHMER if he had made any personal acquaintances while he was in Chicago, to which the suspect answered that all the male homosexuals he met in Chicago were strictly one night stands and he did not become personally involved with any of them. He also stated he never left the gay area or the gay bath houses with any of his acquaintances and accompanied them to their personal homes or apartments. He stated that the males he met in Chicago were of all different racial and ethnical backgrounds including both black and white males. He also stated that on several occasions while he was visiting bath houses in Chicago, he brought his sleeping pills and used them in a rum concoction to drug several of his "gay pick ups" (as he called them) during the one night stands. He stated that only one of them realized he had been drugged and the following morning accused him of putting something in his drink and struck him about the face before leaving. He stated he was never reported to any of the owners of the bath house or to the Chicago Police regarding his activities.

Upon being questioned further regarding his gay activities in the Chicago area, he stated to the detectives that he received his information regarding gay bars, gay bath houses, and gay functions in the Chicago area by reading gay publications which can be picked up readily in various locations both here in Milwaukee and in Chicago. At this time Jeffrey DAHMER denied being involved in any violent or homicidal acts while he was in the Chicago area and stated that the only two males which he had met in Chicago and

REPORTING OFFICER	PAYROLL #	LOC CODE	SUPERVISOR SIGNATURE
2	5	B9	

	INCIDENT				

INCIDENT INFORMATION

INCIDENT	HOMICIDE		DATE OF INCIDENT/ACCIDENT 7-23-91		REP CON
VICTIM	LACY, Oliver		LOCATION OF INCIDENT/ACCIDENT (Address) 924 North 25th St.		DIS

JUVENILE LAST NAME	FIRST	MID	DATE OF BIRTH	O DETAINED O ORDERED TO MCCC O OTHER

QUAN	TYPE OF PROPERTY	DESCRIPTION	SERIAL #	CODE #	VALUE

brought back to Milwaukee and subsequently murdered are the individuals whom he has already discussed with the Milwaukee Police and those incidents have been documented thoroughly. At this time the detectives concluded their interview.

At this time myself, Det. KENNDY, along with Attorney Wendy PATRICKUS, were informed that detectives from the West Allis Police Department also would like to speak with Jeffrey DAHMER and they were admitted into the interview room. At this time Det. NOVAK and Det. RISSE, entered the interview room and questioned the suspect Jeffrey DAHMER regarding the possibility of any bones or materials left over from the victims which he had murdered at his grandmother's house located in West Allis. The purpose of this was to determine whether or not a search warrant would be needed in order to dig up areas around his grandmother's house. At this time Jeffrey DAHMER stated that there would be no need to get a search warrant because all of the bones were disposed of in the trash and carried from the home. He denied burying any of the bones or personal affects of his victims which he killed in the West Allis home, anywhere on the property in West Allis and he denies spreading the bones around any other area in West Allis. He stated that all of his victims were disposed of through the trash and taken away by West Allis public trash collection. At this time they also questioned Jeffrey DAHMER regarding the instruments he used to cut up his victims in West Allis, to which he stated he is unsure what type of knife he used, however he is positive it was not a kitchen utensil from his grandmother's kitchen, that he bought the knife and disposed of the knife the same way he did the body, that being through the trash.

Regarding the GUERRERO identification, the West Allis detectives were interested in how he was positive that the victim that he had killed was in fact GUERRERO and he stated that after viewing the ID photo provided by the Milwaukee Police, he was also given newspaper pictures dated during the time element in which GUERRERO was missing and stated that he distinctly remembered reading the newspaper article and seeing the picture of his victim in the newspaper and realizing that was in fact the victim he had brought back to his grandmother's house and this is why he is sure that GUERRERO is in fact one of his victims.

Lastly the detectives inquired regarding his victim, SEARS. He stated he met the

REPORTING OFFICER	5	PAYROLL # 70	LOC CODE	SUPERVISOR SIGNATURE

INCIDENT INFORMATION	INCIDENT HOMICIDE		DATE OF INCIDENT/ACCIDENT	REP, CON #
	VICTIM LACY, Oliver		LOCATION OF INCIDENT/ACCIDENT (Address) 924 North 25th St.	DIST

JUVENILE LAST NAME	FIRST	MID	DATE OF BIRTH	O DETAINED O ORDERED TO MCCC O OTHER

QUAN	TYPE OF PROPERTY	DESCRIPTION	SERIAL #	CODE #	VALUE

victim, SEARS, at the door at closing time at LeCage, which is a tavern located on 2nd and National. He stated he had been drinking and the victim, SEARS, was standing with a white male. He stated he was actually approached by SEARS and that the conversation that followed, he asked if SEARS would be interested in accompanying him back to his grandmother's house for some homosexual activity and drinks. He stated SEARS was more then eager to accompany him and was actually more the aggressor in this encounter. He stated that the friend of SEARS, the white male who drove them back to his grandmother's location in his vehicle and that he and SEARS sat in the back on the way to his grandmother's house and on the way the victim, SEARS, performed an act of oral sex on him (DAHMER). At this time the detectives from West Allis concluded their interview.

Report per Det. Patrick KENNEDY.

PK/lh   7-30-91

2472   5   71

REPORTING OFFICER Det. P. KENNEDY	48171	PAYROLL # 93	LOC CODE	SUPERVISOR SIGNATURE

INCIDENT INCIDENT INFORMATION	INCIDENT HOMICIDE		DATE OF INCIDENT/ACCIDENT 07-23-91		REP COM
	VICTIM LACY, Oliver		LOCATION OF INCIDENT/ACCIDENT (Address) 924 N. 25th St., Apt. #213		DIS #3
JUVENILE LAST NAME	FIRST	MID	DATE OF BIRTH	O DETAINED O ORDERED TO MCCC O OTHER	
QUAN	TYPE OF PROPERTY	DESCRIPTION	SERIAL #	CODE #	VALUE

NARRATIVE:

On Tuesday, 07-30-91, we Detectives Dennis MURPHY and Patrick KENNEDY while inter-viewing the subject, Jeffrey DAHMER in the presence of his attorney, Wendy PATRICKUS, aske him numerous questions regarding the Bath County Ohio Homicide which occurred in 1978.

I asked Mr. DAHMER where was the trash barrel he used to burn the victim's clothes by his house, and he stated behind the cliff where he threw the bones near the property line; the trash container was on his property, but the cliff was mostly on the next property just to the west of his residence. He stated he burned all of the victim's clothes, plus his i.d. in this trash container.

We also questioned him regarding the location of the tree where he hung the dog, and he stated it was in the lot next to his residence, namely the woods after the lot. He stated this would probably be east of his house in the wooded area past the next lot. He further stated it was the same wooded area, where a girl had committed suicide in 1977. Regarding the dog, he stated it was a road kill and he cut it open and removed the insides and hung it in the tree.

I then questioned him further regarding where he had disposed of the knife in the river which was used in the homicide, and he stated the river ran along the treatment plant and the bridge ran across the river. He stated it was the closest bridge to the treatment plant, near the landfill site. He then drew a map for me indicating this loca-tion. He then stated that he parked the car on this bridge, got out and threw the knife and the victim's necklace about 10 ft out into the river which was approximately 50 ft wide. He stated the name of this town may be Cuyahoga Falls in Ohio; he stated that sounds like the town.

We also questioned him regarding the time he was stopped by the police in June of 1978, and he stated the police stopped him around 3:00 AM (in the morning), because he was driving left of center. He stated when he was stopped he was detained for approximately 1/2 hour and was given a drunk test. He stated he was made to walk the line and do the finger to nose test; he passed both test and was eventually given a ticket. He further stated when the police stopped him there was one car and one officer, but this officer

REPORTING OFFICER 5	PAYROLL # 72	LOC CODE	SUPERVISOR SIGNATURE

INCIDENT INFORMATION	INCIDENT HOMICIDE		DATE OF INCIDENT/ACCIDENT 07-23-91		REP CON
	VICTIM LACY, Oliver		LOCATION OF INCIDENT/ACCIDENT (Address) 924 N. 25th St., Apt. #213		DIS #3

JUVENILE LAST NAME	FIRST	MID	DATE OF BIRTH	☐ DETAINED ☐ ORDERED TO HCCC ☐ OTHER

QUAN	TYPE OF PROPERTY	DESCRIPTION	SERIAL #	CODE #	VALUE

called for back up and another car and officer arrived. I asked him if he had been drinking and he stated he was not. I asked him how did he act when the police stopped him and he stated he was very nervous, but he tried to act calm. I then asked did the police look in the car and he stated, yes with their flashlights and they then asked what were in the bags that were on the rear seat. He stated there were three bags on the back seat and he informed the police that it was garbage and that he had not had the chance to take them to the landfill and he was going to do that tommorrow. I then asked him if there was an odor coming from these bags which he stated had contained the body parts of the victim. DAHMER stated there may have been a slight odor he is not sure; the windows of the car were rolled up to the best of his recollection. I asked him what was the reason he told the officers that he was out driving around, and he stated he told the officers that his parents were recently divorced and he couldn't sleep, so he just went out for a drive to get this off of his mind. I then asked him if he was arrested previously and he stated to the best of his knowledge he had not been arrested prior to this stop and he subsequently received a ticket for driving left of center.

I asked him what was his intentions with the three bags containing the body parts and he stated he was going to take them and throw them down the gulley in the road, but before he got to that location he was stopped by the police. He stated once he was issued his ticket, he then made a u-turn and then proceeded back to the residence and placed these bags in the drainage pipe behind the house. I then asked him how long it had been since the murder and he stated it was possibly the next day or so after the murder that he did this with the intentions of disposing the body in this manner, but being that he was stopped he left the bags in the drainage pipes for a week or two, removed them and subsequently broke them up with either a large rock or a sledge hammer and then spread them around the first cliff in his yard.

DAHMER stated at the time the police were talking to him he was near the side of the car and they made him walk to the rear of the car to take the drunken driving road field sobriety test.

DAHMER further stated he could not recall the type of knife he used to cut up and dismember the body, only that it was possibly one from his house and he threw it in the river with the victim's necklace.

REPORTING OFFICER SEC. 5 PAGE 73	PAYROLL #	LOC CODE	SUPERVISOR SIGNATURE Det. H. Raymond R. Smith

INCIDENT INFORMATION	INCIDENT HOMICIDE			DATE OF INCIDENT/ACCIDENT 07-23-91		REP CON
	VICTIM LACY, Oliver			LOCATION OF INCIDENT/ACCIDENT (Address) 924 N. 25th St., Apt. #213		DIS #3

JUVENILE LAST NAME	FIRST	MID	DATE OF BIRTH	O DETAINED O ORDERED TO MCCC O OTHER

QUAN	TYPE OF PROPERTY	DESCRIPTION	SERIAL #	CODE #	VALUE

I contacted Lieutenant Richard MUNSY (phonetic) regarding these statements and informed him that I would fax a copy of the diagram DAHMER made for me indicating where the treatment plant, river and bridge were located, along with a revised copy of the diagram he had made for us on a previous interview indicating where the second cliff area was and where the trash barrel was.

Report per Detective Dennis MURPHY.

DM/htf 07-31-91

2472 SEC 5 PAGE 74

REPORTING OFFICER DET. DENNIS MURPHY	PAYROLL # 32893	LOC CODE 91	SUPERVISOR SIGNATURE Det. Lt. Raymond A. Smith

INCIDENT INFORMATION	INCIDENT HOMICIDE		DATE OF INCIDENT/ACCIDENT 07/23/91		REP COM #
	VICTIM LACY, Oliver		LOCATION OF INCIDENT/ACCIDENT (Address) 924 N. 25th St., Apt. #213		DIST 3

JUVENILE LAST NAME	FIRST	MID	DATE OF BIRTH	O DETAINED O ORDERED TO MCCC O OTHER

QUAN	TYPE OF PROPERTY	DESCRIPTION	SERIAL #	CODE #	VALUE

NARRATIVE:

On Tuesday, July 30, 1991, I, Detective KENNEDY along with Detective Dennis MURPHY, while interviewing the suspect Jeffrey DAHMER in an interview room of the CIB, were accompanied by Attorney Wendy PATRIKAS when the following questions regarding possible inquiries into other connections of the above offense were given to Mr. DAHMER. At this time, I questioned him regarding the fact that information was received from out of state jurisdictions that in 1981 we received information that a man fitting his description was in the Hollywood Mall which is located in Hollywood, Florida and that this white male fitting his description apparently attempted to pick up an individual and that this individual making this report states that this was the same day that the victim, Adam WALSH, was last seen and then later found decapitated with body parts missing. Regarding this inquiry, the subject Jeffrey DAHMER states he admits that he was in Florida during the time that Adam WALSH offense occurred. He states he realized this because of the news media at the time; however, he denies any part in the offense regarding Adam WALSH and states that he was never at any time in Hollywood, Florida or the Hollywood Mall.

Regarding a report from the Gay and Lesbian Community Center at UWM which states that in June or early July of 1991, they received a phone call at approximately 8:45 P.M. which stated "I just killed a sick fucking fag last night and I feel real good about it" and went on to state other spurters regarding homosexual orientation and the fact of killing them and that this tape was reported to the Milwaukee Police and felt that it was regarding Jeffrey DAHMER. Jeffrey DAHMER at this time denies ever making any phone calls to the Gay and Lesbian Community at UWM. As a matter of fact, he states that at no time did he make any phone calls to anyone including the victims of his offenses regarding his offenses. He states that he never called the family of the victims of his offenses and he never called any Gay or Lesbian hot-lines to admit to his offenses. He also states that he has absolutely no hatred for homosexuals and that he, in fact, prefers homosexuals and to use his words in a twisted or preverted way he actually loves them.

Regarding a report that an individual from Talmadge, Ohio reports that on July 6, 1981 he was hitchhiking when he was picked up by a white male who resembles Jeffrey DAHMER and that this individual had a portion of a human leg in the front seat of his auto. Jeffrey DAHMER at this time states that he never owned a vehicle in Ohio at the time this report was supposedly made and that he was in Miami, Florida during this time and denies

REPORTING OFFICER	PAYROLL # 75	LOC CODE	SUPERVISOR SIGNATURE

PO15-B 5-89 SUPPLEMENT REPORT MILWAUKEE POLICE DEPARTMENT	O INCIDENT SUPPLEMENT O ACCIDENT SUPPLEMENT O JUVENILE SUPPLEMENT	PAGE 2 of 2	DATE OF REPORT 07/30/91	INCIDENT/ACCIDENT # 91-51767/M2472 M2481		
INCIDENT INFORMATION	INCIDENT HOMICIDE		DATE OF INCIDENT/ACCIDENT 07/23/91			REP CON #
	VICTIM LACY, Oliver		LOCATION OF INCIDENT/ACCIDENT (Address) 924 N. 25th St., Apt. #213			DIST
JUVENILE LAST NAME	FIRST	MID	DATE OF BIRTH	O DETAINED O ORDERED TO NCCC O OTHER		
QUAN	TYPE OF PROPERTY	DESCRIPTION		SERIAL #	CODE #	VALUE

being involved in this.

Regarding a report taken from the Fresno Police Department that a foot was found in Fresno County on March 30, 1991 in a vacant field, Jeffrey DAHMER states that he has never been in California and specifically has never been in Fresno, California in his entire life and he denies any involvement in this offense.

Regarding the We-Tip information that we received stating that the suspect Jeffrey DAHMER recently worked in the Moreno View Manor Nursing Home under the alias of Mike NASERS, Jeffrey DAHMER states that he has never in his life used an alias and he has never worked in a nursing home here in Milwaukee or anywhere else in the world.

Regarding an inquiry sent to the Milwaukee Police by the Woodstock Police Department regarding a suspect wanted for a double murder in their jurisdiction, that suspect being a Richard J. CHURCH-M/W, dob-3/24/69. At this time, I showed Mr. DAHMER a photograph of Richard J. CHURCH and he stated that he believes that he has seen this picture before on some crime show, possibly America's Most Wanted; however, he denies ever meeting or knowing the suspect, Mr. CHURCH, and also denies he is a victim in any of his offenses.

Regarding a We-Tip we received stating that the suspect, Jeffrey DAHMER, had hidden body parts from some of his victims in the walls of his apartment and plastered them over, Jeffrey DAHMER states that he emphatically denies hiding any body parts of any of his victims in the walls of his apartment and states that all body parts which he kept from his victims have been taken into the custody of the Milwaukee Police Department.

Regarding information given by United States Armed Forces regarding Jeffrey DAHMER'S stay in Germany, he denies this entire report and a detail supplemental by Detective Dennis MURPHY has been filed regarding this information.

At this time, the interview with Jeffrey DAHMER was terminated and he was taken back to the Milwaukee County Sheriff's Department and turned over at approximately 4:45 P.M. on July 30, 1991.

Report per Detective Patrick KENNEDY.

PK:jaj 7/31/91

2 5 PAGE 7

REPORTING OFFICER DET. PATRICK KENNEDY	PAYROLL # 48171	LOC CODE 93	SUPERVISOR SIGNATURE

THE CANNIBAL

Face of madman who killed 17 and ate them

From STEWART DICKSON in New York

THIS is the face of real-life Silence Of The Lambs killer Jeffrey Dahmer who has confessed to butchering 17 men.

Police believe the crazed madman ate many of his victims while the rest were killed, his friends say.

Yesterday, the 31-year-old factory worker appeared in a Wisconsin court accused of four murders - with more fresh charges expected to be laid soon.

As the unshaven killer was making his brief appearance before the US judge, more grisly details of his horrific life were revealed by his stepmother Shari.

She told how her husband once found bones in a massive vat at a flat where their son often stays.

Small

"We smelled a harsh odour coming from the basement flat," she said.

His father Lionel investigated and found bones and residue in a huge vat.

"We couldn't tell if they were human or animal."

Jeffrey said it was an animal he had found.

"Even when he was quite young he liked to use acid to scrape the meat off dead animals."

And Shari told how Dahmer often took men to the flat in his gran's house.

Torture

"One time he was down there with a man when his mother opened the door.

"She could see only his bare chest. He warned her, 'You don't want to come down here.'

"She thought they were naked so she didn't go down."

Police found severed heads, torsos, boxes of body parts and photos and videos of tortured victims in Dahmer's apartment.

The sick killer was arrested after an intended victim escaped and was found by police running down a street - his hands still handcuffed.

'Butcher' link on air base

CANNIBAL Jeffrey Dahmer is suspected of killing five women in Germany while serving with US forces.

The women were all murdered and their bodies mutilated near an air base where he was stationed as a medical orderly more than ten years ago.

A copy of a narrative in each copy of Bild Kreuznach told a German newspaper yesterday: "We have a burning interest in Dahmer. We are checking to see if he could be the killer."

He said there were similarities between the murders even though all the German victims were women and only men were murdered in Milwaukee.

102

Body parts litter apartment

Milwaukee man arrested at scene; up to 12 bodies might be involved

By ANNE E. SCHWARTZ
of The Journal staff

Milwaukee police are calling the discovery of numerous body parts, possibly from as many as a dozen bodies, the most gruesome slaying case in the city's history.

Among the body parts found overnight were three human heads in a refrigerator, police said.

"There's bones in the chocolate!"

Art courtesy of Susan Eve Padron.

103

	INCIDENT	HOMICIDE		DATE OF INCIDENT/ACCIDENT 7-23-91		REP CON
INCIDENT INFORMATION	VICTIM	LACY, Oliver		LOCATION OF INCIDENT/ACCIDENT (Address) 924 North 25th St., #213		DIS

JUVENILE LAST NAME	FIRST	MID	DATE OF BIRTH	O DETAINED O ORDERED TO MCCC O OTHER

QUAN	TYPE OF PROPERTY	DESCRIPTION	SERIAL #	CODE #	VALUE

On Tue., 7-30-91, we, Det. Dennis MURPHY and Patrick KENNEDY, reinterviewed the defendant, Jeffrey DAHMER, at the CIB in the presence of his attorney, Wendy PATRICKUS. At this interview which began at approximately 11:30AM, we asked him several questions regarding some of the victims and regarding various calls that had come in to our department.

We questioned him regarding victim #1, whom he stated died at the Ambassador Hotel and he related that he met this individual about one week before Thanksgiving in 1987. He stated he had rented a room at the Ambassador Hotel and had previously prepared sleeping pills in a glass by breaking the pills down to a powdery form and leaving this form in the glass. He stated that when he and the victim returned to the hotel, he made a rum and coke in the glass with the pills. He stated he gave this drink to the individual and the individual subsequently passed out. Mr. DAHMER stated he had also drank a lot and was lying in bed with this individual and he passed out. When he awoke, he discovered the victim dead and blood coming from the side of his mouth. He stated that he also noticed on the victim, severe bruising on his chest and that he (DAHMER) had bruising on his forearms, so he surmised that he had beaten the victim about the chest, possibly killing him. After this occurred, Mr. DAHMER took the room for another night, proceeded to the Grand Avenue Mall, where he purchased a large suitcase from Woolworth's. He stated the suitcase had a zipper with a leather buckle going around the suitcase. He stated he placed the victim in the suitcase and conveyed him to his grandmother's residence via a cab.

Once at his grandmother's residence, he used a knife to dismember the body and he disposed of the body parts in the trash. He stated he did not use his grandmother's knife, but used one of his knives that he possibly bought at the mall, but he is not sure. He also stated that he did dispose of the suitcse.

We questioned him further regarding his use of the sleeping pills and he stated that in all of the cases, he would have the sleeping pill broken down into a powder form in the bottom of either a glass or a cup and when he would prepare the drink for the individual, using either coffee or rum and coke, he would use the glass or cup that contained the

REPORTING OFFICER	PAYROLL #	LOC CODE	SUPERVISOR SIGNATURE

| INCIDENT INFORMATION | INCIDENT HOMICIDE | | DATE OF INCIDENT/ACCIDENT 7-23-91 | REP CON |
| VICTIM LACY, Oliver | | | LOCATION OF INCIDENT/ACCIDENT (Address) 924 North 25th St. | DIS |

| JUVENILE LAST NAME | FIRST | MID | DATE OF BIRTH | O DETAINED O ORDERED TO MCCC O OTHER |

| QUAN | TYPE OF PROPERTY | DESCRIPTION | | SERIAL # | CODE # | VALUE |

powdered sleeping pill substance. He stated this would dissolve readily and the victim was unable to determine that anything was in his drink.

We also questioned him regarding any other murders he may be involved in, namely a homicide where two murders occurred in Corpus Christi, Texas, between 1981 and 1983, and he denied any knowledge of this offense. He stated he was not in Corpus Christi, Texas and that he did not know of the murders there. I informed him that the clues had led to Decatur, Illinois, and asked him if he had ever been in Decatur, Illinois, and he stated he had never been to Decatur, Illinois. Mr. DAHMER denied any involvement in any other homicides outside the ones he has already admitted to and stated that he is not invovled in any others.

Additional questions were asked and presented to Mr. DAHMER and his responses will be reflected on separate supplementary reports.

Report per Det. Dennis MURPHY.

DM/lh   7-31-91

5 - 78

PAGE

| REPORTING OFFICER Det. D. MURPHY | PAYROLL # 32893   91 | LOC CODE | SUPERVISOR SIGNATURE |

| | INCIDENT | HOMICIDE | | DATE OF INCIDENT/ACCIDENT 7-23-91 | | REP CON # |
| INCIDENT INFORMATION | VICTIM | LACY, Oliver | | LOCATION OF INCIDENT/ACCIDENT (Address) 924 North 25th St., #213 | | DIST |

| JUVENILE LAST NAME | FIRST | MID | DATE OF BIRTH | O DETAINED O ORDERED TO MCCC O OTHER |

| QUAN | TYPE OF PROPERTY | DESCRIPTION | SERIAL # | CODE # | VALUE |

On Wed., 7-31-91, I, Det. KENNEDY, along with Det. Dennis MURPHY, were contacted by the Milwaukee County Sheriff's jail, that the suspect, Jeffrey DAHMER, wished to speak with us. At this time, after obtaining an order to produce, we arrived at the fifth floor of the Milwaukee County Jail, where we met the suspect, Jeffrey DAHMER, and returned with him to the fourth floor of the CIB and placed him into an interview room. While in the interview room, we were accompanied by his defense attorney, Wendy PATRICKUS, and at this time we conducted the following interview.

I asked Jeffrey DAHMER if he would answer some questions regarding inquiries made from other jurisdictions. He stated to the affirmative to this. I asked him regarding Kingsford, Michigan, who are investigating a white male by the name of Michael SMITH, who has been missing since 5-27-91. At this time I showed him a picture regarding Michael SMITH, asking if this could possibly be the first victim he had met in Wisconsin and murdered in the Ambassador Hotel. After viewing the photos he stated that he had never seen this individual before and denied that he is involved in the missing of Michael SMITH.

At this time, I asked Jeffrey DAHMER regarding information received that an individual by the name of Terry MINUS was involved with him in occult study while in Germany, and the fact that this individual stated that Jeffrey DAHMER leased a farm in Sandusky, Ohio, where he has buried remains of several of his victims. Mr. DAHMER stated that this is untrue, he knows no one by the name of Terry MINUS and that he was never into the occult while he was in Germany. He also stated he was never in the Marine Corp., which this individual alludes to.

Regarding information from Dr. James CERVENANSKY, who is a physician at West Allis Memorial Hospital, Dr. CERVENANSKY reported that on 1-7-91, he received a phone call from an individual who identified himself as SHRIEBER and stated he was a doctor. He went on to state that this doctor stated he was performing an autopsy on an individual who had been dead for approximately six days, and while cutting around the leg area, all the toes began to move. Dr. CERVENANSKY stated this individual stated he was wondering if this was proper for this to happen and was wondering if this was possibly Jeffrey DAHMER calling to get information regarding his victims. To this Mr. DAHMER stated he has never used any

| REPORTING OFFICER | PAYROLL # | LOC CODE | SUPERVISOR SIGNATURE |

INCIDENT INFORMATION	INCIDENT	HOMICIDE		DATE OF INCIDENT/ACCIDENT 7-23-91		REP CON #
	VICTIM	LACY, Oliver		LOCATION OF INCIDENT/ACCIDENT (Address) 924 North 25th St.		DIST

JUVENILE LAST NAME	FIRST	MID	DATE OF BIRTH	O DETAINED O ORDERED TO MCCC O OTHER

QUAN	TYPE OF PROPERTY	DESCRIPTION		SERIAL #	CODE #	VALUE

alias, in particular the alias of Dr. SHRIEBER and that he never called West Allis Memorial Hospital in regards to moving toes on one of his autopsies.

Regarding information received from the Brookfield Police Department that an individual by the name of Jeffrey DAHMER pawned a ring on 8-8-88, at a gold and silver office located in their city, to which Mr. DAHMER stated he in fact did buy a blue topaz ring with a gold setting from Bailey, Banks, and Biddle, located at Northridge Mall in Milwaukee for approximately $1500, sometime in the summer months of 1987. He stated he bought this ring because he has always had an interest in jewelry and especially rings and that at the time he felt the large topaz was attractive to him. He stated that approximately a year later, because of his drinking habits, he was running low on cash and took that ring to a gold and silver establishment on Bluemound Road, where after bargaining with the individual working behind the desk, he obtained $189 for his topaz ring. He stated the ring did not belong to any of his victims and he again denied selling any of the jewelry which he obtained from any of his victims and that if there was any jewelry on any of his victims, he simply it them out in the trash, along with body parts.

Regarding an inquiry made from the Joliet Illinois Police Department regarding a missing by the name of Terry ROUSE, W/M, approximately 24 years old, who has apparently been missing since 5-10-91, inquiries were made as to whether he was a possible victim of Mr. DAHMER's. After viewing the photos and newpaper article sent along with the inquiry, Mr. DAHMER denied ever seeing this individual or that he was one of his victims.

Regarding an inquiry sent by the Police Department in Fresno, California, who sent along a picture of a white male by the name of PURTELL, whose leg part they found in Nortern California, Mr. DAHMER viewed the photo and stated he has never seen this indiviudal before. He again reiterated the fact that he has never been in California at any time in his life. He denied any part in this offense.

Again Mr. DAHMER was asked regarding if he had ever been in Hollywood, Florida, and any connection he may possibly have with Adam WALSH. Mr. DAHMER again, adamantly stated he has never been in Hollywood, Florida. He has never been in the Hollywood, Florida mall, and he in fact had nothing to do with the abduction and subsequent dismemberment of the young boy by the name of Adam WALSH. He denied committing any murders while living in

REPORTING OFFICER		PAYROLL #	LOC CODE	SUPERVISOR SIGNATURE
2	5	80		S/t Lt Raymond

| INCIDENT | HOMICIDE | | DATE OF INCIDENT/ACCIDENT | 7-23-91 | REP CON # |
| INFORMATION | VICTIM | LACY, Oliver | LOCATION OF INCIDENT/ACCIDENT (Address) 924 North 25th St. | | DIST |

| JUVENILE LAST NAME | FIRST | MID | DATE OF BIRTH | ☐ DETAINED ☐ ORDERED TO MCCC ☐ OTHER |

| QUAN | TYPE OF PROPERTY | DESCRIPTION | | SERIAL # | CODE # | VALUE |

Florida.

At this time Mr. DAHMER was questioned regarding recent newspaper stories that stated that as an eight year old boy in Ohio, he was sexually assaulted by a neighbor. To this Mr. DAHMER stated this is untrue, that the first time he experienced any sexual behavior was when he was approximately 14 year old and that was with the young man who lived across the street by the name of Eric TYSON (phonetic). He stated that Eric was one or two years younger then him and that they mutually consented and got together on several occasions in a tree house where they simply kissed and touched each other's body.

I then questioned Mr. DAHMER regarding a possible victim of his, that being Luis PINET, Puerto Rican male, DOB: 10-25-74. At this time I showed Mr. PINET's photo, which was a family photo, to Mr. DAHMER and after viewing it, he stated that this in fact is the individual whom he fought with in his apartment on approximately 7-8-90. Regarding the incident with Mr. PINET, he stated the day previous to the fighting with Mr. PINET, he had met Luis PINET at the Phoenix tavern and had asked him to accompany him home to his apartment for some homosexual activity and offered him money to pose for nude photos. He stated that on this occasion Mr. PINET readily accompanied him home to his apartment and they had "normal homosexual sex." He stated at this time they spoke of meeting again the following night at the Phoenix. He stated that Mr. PINET left on his own accord that night.

Mr. DAHMER stated that the following nigh the went to the Phoenix tavern located on South 2nd St., where he again saw Mr. PINET. He stated at this time Mr. PINET again voluntarily decided to return with him to his apartment and at this time they took a taxi from the Phoenix tavern to 23rd and Wells, where they got out and walked. At 23rd and Wells, Mr. DAHMER stated he stopped and bought himself some cigarettes and from there they walked to his apartment building. He stated the reason why he would have the taxi drop him off several blocks from his apartment was in order to keep the taxi driver from knowing exaxtly where he lived at and to see if anyone had been following him, as he did not want anyone to detect his activities. He stated that after buying the cigarettes, they walked to his apartment and once inside, they had conversation, however he can not recall the words. He stated that at this time he asked Luis if he would get undressed and

| REPORTING OFFICER | PAYROLL # | LOC CODE | SUPERVISOR SIGNATURE |

108

INCIDENT INFORMATION	INCIDENT		DATE OF INCIDENT/ACCIDENT		REP COM #
	HOMICIDE		7-23-91		
	VICTIM		LOCATION OF INCIDENT/ACCIDENT (Address)		DIST
	LACY, Oliver		924 North 25th St.		

JUVENILE LAST NAME	FIRST	MID	DATE OF BIRTH	☐ DETAINED ☐ ORDERED TO MCCC ☐ OTHER

QUAN	TYPE OF PROPERTY	DESCRIPTION	SERIAL #	CODE #	VALUE

allow him to take several photos of him in the nude, which Luis complied with. He stated Luis lay on the bed and he took several photos, however they did not come out, so he asked Luis to turn on to his stomach so he could take some back shots of Luis with is Polaroid camera. Mr. DAHMER stated at this time he was starting to become intoxicated and had run out of sleeping pills to put into his rum coffee potion in order to give to the victim. He stated that in preparation for this evening and knowing he was out of sleeping pills, he had gone to the hardware store and purchased himself a rubber mallet hammer. He stated he did this because it was cheaper then filling his prescription which cost approximately $30. He stated his intention was to strike the victim on the head with his hammer and knock him out so that he would be able to strangle the victim while he was unconscious. He stated at this time as Mr. PINET was lying on his stomach, he retrieved his hammer and struck the victim on the back part of his neck. He felt that by striking him on the back of his neck, he would cut off blood going to his brain and cause the victim to pass out, however this only made Luis PINET angry and at this time they got into a physical fight. He stated that during the fight, he tried to explain to Luis PINET he only struck him because he thought he was going to take the money, rob him and run out without giving him photos. After fighting for awhile on the front room floor, the victim promised he would not call the police and was allowed to leave the apartment.

He stated the victim left the apartment and apparently went to the corner phone booth in order to call for a ride home and after discovering he had no cash, returned to the apartment and knocked on the door. Mr. DAHMER stated he opened the door and admitted Mr. PINET back into his room and that they sat on the bed in his bedroom and spoke about the incident all night. Mr. DAHMER stated there was no homosexual sex between them for the rest of the evening and they simply sat up all night talking about the fact that Mr. DAHMER had struck him with a hammer and whether or not Mr. PINET was going to report him to the police. Mr. DAHMER stated he felt comfortable that the talk he had with Mr. PINET regarding the entire incident, had calmed down to the point where Mr. PINET was not going to complain to the police about him and that early the next morning he allowed Mr. PINET to leave the apartment. He stated he does not recall seeing Mr. PINET again, after this incident and this was all the information he was able to give me regarding this offense.

REPORTING OFFICER	PAYROLL #	LOC CODE	SUPERVISOR SIGNATURE
5	82		

INCIDENT INFORMATION	INCIDENT	HOMICIDE		DATE OF INCIDENT/ACCIDENT 7-23-91		REP CON
	VICTIM	LACY, Oliver		LOCATION OF INCIDENT/ACCIDENT (Address) 924 North 25th St.		DI

JUVENILE LAST NAME	FIRST	MID	DATE OF BIRTH	O DETAINED O ORDERED TO MCCC O OTHER

QUAN	TYPE OF PROPERTY	DESCRIPTION	SERIAL #	CODE #	VALUE

At this time Mr. DAHMER was asked several questions, again pertaining to his tour of duty while in the Armed Forces and stationed in Germany, and Det. MURPHY will file a detailed supplementary report regarding the interview given on these questions.

Report per Det. Patrick KENNEDY.

PK/lh   7-31-91

2 SF 5 - 83
PAGE

REPORTING OFFICER Det. P. KENNEDY	PAYROLL # 48171 · 93	LOC CODE	SUPERVISOR SIGNATURE

INCIDENT INFORMATION	INCIDENT HOMICIDE (STABBING)		DATE OF INCIDENT/ACCIDENT 07-23-91		REP COM #
	VICTIM LACY, Oliver		LOCATION OF INCIDENT/ACCIDENT (Address) 924 N. 25th Street #213		DIST 3

JUVENILE LAST NAME	FIRST	MID	DATE OF BIRTH	O DETAINED O ORDERED TO MCCC O OTHER

QUAN	TYPE OF PROPERTY	DESCRIPTION	SERIAL #	CODE #	VALUE

Refer to Lacy Follow Up Number:

On Wed., 7-31-91, we, Det. Dennis MURPHY and Patrick KENNEDY, along with Defense Attorney Wendy PATRICKUS, were present at the Criminal Investigation Bureau in an interview with the defendant, Jeffrey DAHMER, who had requested our presence to attempt to identify other victims, and to answer any questions we may have relevant to this investigation.

Mr. DAHMER was shown a couple of photographs of individuals regarding this investigation and a supplementry report will be called in by Det. KENNEDY regarding these photographs. We then asked Mr. DAHMER numerous questions regarding our investigation and he answered them freely.

We questioned him when he left Miami Beach, and he stated that it was about Sept. of 1981 and that he possibly flew by Pan Am Airlines to Cleveland Airport in Ohio. He stated that when he left Florida, he left on a ticket supplied by his grandmother. We also questioned him regarding his activities in Miami Beach when he moved there, and he stated that he moved there right from the service, and that when he left the service, he left all of his Army uniforms and clothing in Germany. He stated that he did not want to wear anything green once he was out of the military, and he never had an Army fatigue jacket. He also stated that he never wore any type of baseball cap or other cap.

We then asked him numerous questions about his apartment and articles used during the commission of the offenses and he stated that he used drill bits to drill holes in the heads to flush them out and these drill bits should be in a box or they were in the box in his apartment or they were on the floor. He stated that the Police should have recovered this.

He also stated that the spray paint that he used, which was a fake granite type, blueish color, should have a pamphlet in one of his drawers in the residence. He stated that he does not recall the brand name, but the can was light complected. He stated that he bought this at Pallet's Art Store on Water St. This will be checked out by Det. Randy BAIER.

Regarding the makeup he used to color the genitals that he kept of one of his victims, he stated that he bought a skin tone type make up at Sears at South Ridge and this was a specialized makeup that used for hiding marks or discolored skin. He stated that

REPORTING OFFICER	PAYROLL # 84	LOC CODE	SUPERVISOR SIGNATURE
5			Act Lt. Raymond Smith

INCIDENT INFORMATION	INCIDENT HOMICIDE (STABBING)			DATE OF INCIDENT/ACCIDENT		REP COM #
	VICTIM LACY, Oliver			LOCATION OF INCIDENT/ACCIDENT (Address) 924 N. 25th St., #213		DIST

JUVENILE LAST NAME	FIRST	MID	DATE OF BIRTH	☐ DETAINED ☐ ORDERED TO MCCC ☐ OTHER

QUAN	TYPE OF PROPERTY	DESCRIPTION	SERIAL #	CODE #	VALUE

the reason that he colored this is because he wanted it more of a flesh color.

We then asked him questions regarding where he may have gone on vacation out of the states and he stated that in 1976, he went with the family to Puerto Rico on a two week vacation, and that's the first time that he had ever drank rum. He stated that he was with his parents and that nothing happened while he was in Puerto Rico.

He also stated that during all the initial meetings with his victims, he always offered money for sex or taking photos or watching videos, or a combination of these; but stated that it was not for heavy sex, he just hoped it would lead to that.

We questioned Jeff regarding some of the victims, and he stated that one of the victims, namely Ed SMITH, who was the bald headed guy, victim number six, and we asked him if he knew this individual by the nick name of "Sheik". He stated that he did not know his real name nor his nick name, but this individual did wear a headband like an Arib type headband. He stated that he did take photographs, but he tore them up and threw them out.

He stated that most of the homicides took place either on weekends or when he had time off from work. He also stated that he does not drive a car, never owned a car in Wisconsin, and that he did accept rides home from the Ambrosia Chocolate factory a couple of times from his supervisors, but he never used his car, nor anyone elses while in Wisconsin.

DAHMER at this time again stated that he was not involved in any other homicides and that if he can recall any information that would help us for our investigation, he will contact either myself--Det. MURPHY, or Det. KENNEDY with this information.

Mr. DAHMER did bring along with him a book that he had received by mail from the Vanity Fair Magazine, and this book's title was "Killing for Company", written by Brian MASTERS. This book depicted a case of a suspect, Dennis NILSEN, who would kill people, dismember them, and throw them in plastic bags and dispose of them. This case is possibly similar to Mr. DAHMER'S, and Vanity Fair requested an interview from him. This information was given to his attorney in our presence, and she kept the copy of the book.

An appointment was set up that we obtain an order to produce on Thursday, 8-1-91 and have a meeting at the Criminal Investigation Bureau at 1:30 with Mr. DAHMER, his attorney, and Wendy PATRICKUS to show him additional photos we expect to arrive today of possible victims. Also to ask any additional questions that may arise through the evening.

Report dictated by Det. Dennis MURPHY.

DM/rc 7-31-91

REPORTING OFFICER	PAYROLL #	LOC CODE	SUPERVISOR SIGNATURE
Det. Dennis MURPHY	32893	91	

PO15-B 5-89 SUPPLEMENT REPORT MILWAUKEE POLICE DEPARTMENT	☐ INCIDENT SUPPLEMENT ☐ ACCIDENT SUPPLEMENT ☐ JUVENILE SUPPLEMENT	PAGE _1_ of _4_	DATE OF REPORT 7-31-91	INCIDENT/ACCIDENT # 91-51767 / M-2472-M-2481	
INCIDENT INFORMATION	INCIDENT HOMICIDE		DATE OF INCIDENT/ACCIDENT 7-23-91		REP CON #
	VICTIM LACY, Oliver		LOCATION OF INCIDENT/ACCIDENT (Address) 924 North 25th St., #213		DIST
JUVENILE LAST NAME	FIRST	MID	DATE OF BIRTH	☐ DETAINED ☐ ORDERED TO MCCC ☐ OTHER	
QUAN	TYPE OF PROPERTY	DESCRIPTION		SERIAL #	CODE #	VALUE

On Wed., 7-31-91, we, Det. Dennis MURPHY and Patrick KENNEDY, in the presence of Attorney Wendy PATRICKUS, who is the attorney for Jeffrey DAHMER, interviewed Jeffrey at the CIB, Room 421. Mr. DAHMER was interviewed regarding a teletype we had received from the German Federal Criminal Police, requesting we ask certain investigative questions which may help them determine if Mr. DAHMER was in their country at the time some homicides had occurred or whether he was station in the Army at this time. This teletype was sent to our department by a Legat BONN. This teletype requested we ask approximately eleven questions relative to our investigation, which were as follows.

Which police agency was leading the investigation in the United States, and that is the Milwaukee Police Department located at 749 West State St., Milwaukee, Wisconsin, 53233.

Next I requested the background of Mr. DAHMER, including his blood type and whether or not he has any knowledge of German. At the present time in this investigation, we do not know his blood type and he stated he does not speak any German. Mr. DAHMER was born on 5-21-60, in Milwaukee, Wisconsin at Deaconess Hospital. He attended and graduated from the Revere High School in Akron, Ohio. He attended from September of 1975 until June, of 1978, and he received his high school diploma. He then went on to Ohio State University in Columbus, Ohio, where he attended from September of 1978 until December of 1978, but he did not graduate. He then immediately enlisted in the Army on December 29, 1978. He was rated as Private E1 and enlisted in Cleveland, Ohio. Following his enlistment, he was sent to Military Police School in Ft. McClellan, Alabama, for an eight week course, which he did not complete. On May 11, 1979, he was sent to the Army Hospital School at Fort Sam Houston, Texas, in San Antonio, where he attended a six week course to become a Medical Specialist. Upon completion of this course, he was assigned to Headquarter Company, 286 Armor Division, 2nd Battalion, 68th Armor in Baumholder, Germany. He was stationed at that post from June of 1979, until March 24, 1981.

Upon his discharge, he was sent to Fort Jackson, in South Carolina, where he was discharged on March 26, 1981, from the United Stated Army, at which time he took a plane to Miami Beach, Florida, where he remained until approximately September of 1981. He then

5   86

REPORTING OFFICER	PAYROLL #	LOC CODE	SUPERVISOR SIGNATURE

113

PO15-B 5 89 SUPPLEMENT REPORT   O INCIDENT SUPPLEMENT   PAGE 2 of 4   DATE OF REPORT | INCIDENT/ACCIDENT #
MILWAUKEE POLICE DEPARTMENT   O ACCIDENT SUPPLEMENT   7-31-91   91-51767/ M-2472-2481
                     O JUVENILE SUPPLEMENT

INCIDENT		DATE OF INCIDENT/ACCIDENT	REP CON #
INCIDENT INFORMATION	INCIDENT HOMICIDE	7-23-91	
	VICTIM LACY, Oliver	LOCATION OF INCIDENT/ACCIDENT (Address) 924 North 25th St.	DIST

JUVENILE LAST NAME	FIRST	MID	DATE OF BIRTH	O DETAINED O ORDERED TO MCCC O OTHER

QUAN	TYPE OF PROPERTY	DESCRIPTION	SERIAL #	CODE #	VALUE

returned to his Bath, Ohio, where he had been living prior to joining the service. He remained in Bath, Ohio, until approximately December of 1981, when he moved to Milwaukee, Wisconsin, and lived at 2357 South 57th St., in West Allis, Wisconsin. He remained there with his grandmother until approximately 1988, when he moved about May of 1988, or in that vicinity, to 808 North 24th St. He then was arrested for taking pictures of a minor, charged with Second Degree Sexual Assault, and subsequently sentenced to a year under the "work release program" and five years probation. Approximately June of 1989, he began serving his term and was released in March of 1990. He moved back in with his grandmother at 2357 South 57th St., until May of 1990, when he then moved in to the apartment at 924 North 25th St. It was at this location where he remained until his arrest.

He stated that while he was stationed in Germany, he went to Munich for October Fest of 1980, and went to the Lansthole (phonetic) for about two months of training. He also stated he would go to Ideroberstein, Germany, for dinner, but never would remain overnight. He stated these were the only places he would travel to in Germany.

We did question Mr. DAHMER about any crimes he may have committed in Germany and he denied being involved in any offenses. We questioned him regarding any sexual abuse crimes against children or other sexual crimes and he again denied being involved in any of these offenses. He stated he did not deal with any homosexuals while he was in Germany, and he would satisfy himself by looking at magazines and masturbation.

Mr. DAHMER did leave Germany as soon as his military duties ended. He stated he has not visited Germany since he left the Army, nor did he have a passport. He also stated he does not have any relatives living in Germany and that he has been a homosexual all his life. He stated he is not interested in women or not intentionally in juveniles, and he stated the age group he participated with the homosexuals ranged from the late teens, 18 - 19, to the middle to early 20's. He stated if the individual is younger but looks older, he will attempt to have a relationship with him.

In regards to the number of victims in the United States, Mr. DAHMER admits to killing seventeen people. Of these, one is from out of Wisconsin, that was his first victim in June of 1978, and that was a white male who he killed in Bath, Ohio. The next victim was in November of 1987, and that was a white male, 25 years of age, whom he killed in

REPORTING OFFICER	PAYROLL #	LOC CODE	SUPERVISOR SIGNATURE
5	87		Alt Lt. Raymond C Such

PO15-B 5-89 SUPPLEMENT REPORT
MILWAUKEE POLICE DEPARTMENT

O INCIDENT SUPPLEMENT
O ACCIDENT SUPPLEMENT
O JUVENILE SUPPLEMENT

PAGE 3 of 4

DATE OF REPORT - O INCIDENT/ACCIDENT # M-2472-2481

	INCIDENT	HOMICIDE		DATE OF INCIDENT/ACCIDENT 1991		REP CON #
INCIDENT INFORMATION	VICTIM	LACY, Oliver		LOCATION OF INCIDENT/ACCIDENT (Address) 924 North 25th St.		DIST

JUVENILE LAST NAME	FIRST	MID	DATE OF BIRTH	O DETAINED O ORDERED TO MCCC O OTHER

QUAN	TYPE OF PROPERTY	DESCRIPTION	SERIAL #	CODE #	VALUE

Milwaukee. The next victim was a Hispanic male, about 16 or 18, whom he killed in January of 1988. The next victim was a Hispanic male, about 25 years of age, whom he killed in approximately March of 1988. The next victim was a black male, about 25 years of age, whom he killed in March of 1989. The next victim was a black male about 33 years of age, whom he killed in May of 1990, after he was released from serving his time for the sexual assault complaint. The next victim was a black male about 28 years of age, whom he killed in July of 1990. The next victim was a black male about 23 years of age, whom he killed in September of 1990. The next victim was a black male about 23 years of age, whom he killed in October or November of 1990. The next victim was a black male about 17 years of age, whom he killed in February of 1991. The next victim was a black male, 18 years of age, whom he killed in March of 1991. The next victim was a black male, 31 years of age, whom he killed in May of 1991. The next victim was a black male, 14 years of age, who was also killed in May of 1991. The next victim was a black male, 20, whom he killed in June of 1991. The next victim was a Puerto Rican male, 23, who he killed in July of 1991. The next victim was a black male, 23, whom he killed in July of 1991. The last victim was a white male, 25, who he killed in July of 1991. The exact dates of these homicides can not be determined at this time.

As far as the sexual preference and/or race, religion, or education of the individuals that the suspect perferred, the suspect stated it was not a matter of race, religion, or education, it was just a matter of opportunity. He stated that he offered each one of these individuals money to be photographed, to view videos, or to have sex, and after he persuaded them to come into his apartment, he would give them a sleeping potion, #10 and once they went to sleep, he would strangle them either manually or with a strap, photograph most of them after death, sometimes have sex with them after death, and then subsequently dismember them and on approximately eleven of the victims, kept the skulls and approximately four torsos, the hands, a couple hearts, and other inner organs.

We again asked Mr. DAHMER numerous times, whether or not he was involved in any homosexual relationships or any commissions of any crimes or offenses while he was stationed in Germany and he denied being involved in any.

REPORTING OFFICER	PAYROLL #	LOC CODE	SUPERVISOR SIGNATURE
5	88		

115

Witness: Dahmer said he'd 'eat my heart'

Man who brought police to apartment takes stand at trial

PO15-8 5-89 SUPPLEMENT REPORT
MILWAUKEE POLICE DEPARTMENT
O INCIDENT SUPPLEMENT
O ACCIDENT SUPPLEMENT
O JUVENILE SUPPLEMENT
PAGE 4 of 4
DATE OF REPORT 7-31-91 INCIDENT/ACCIDENT # 91-51787 M-2472-2481

	INCIDENT	HOMICIDE		DATE OF INCIDENT/ACCIDENT 7-23-91		REP COM #
INCIDENT INFORMATION	VICTIM	LACY, Oliver		LOCATION OF INCIDENT/ACCIDENT (Address) 924 North 25th St.		DIST

JUVENILE LAST NAME	FIRST	MID	DATE OF BIRTH	O DETAINED O ORDERED TO MCCC O OTHER

QUAN	TYPE OF PROPERTY	DESCRIPTION	SERIAL #	CODE #	VALUE

A copy of the fingerprints and the photos will be included in this report. It is also requested that we sent a 1980 photograph of the subject, Jeffrey DAHMER, along with this report, but we do not have one. We suggest that you contact the Military Service for his 1979 Military photo.

Report per Det. Dennis MURPHY and Det. Patrick KENNEDY.

DM/lh   7-31-91

2472 SEC. 5 PAGE 89

REPORTING OFFICER Det. D. MURPHY	PAYROLL # 32893 91	LOC CODE	SUPERVISOR SIGNATURE

INCIDENT		DATE OF INCIDENT/ACCIDENT		REP COM #
INCIDENT	HOMICIDE (STABBING)	07-23-91		

INFORMATION	VICTIM	LOCATION OF INCIDENT/ACCIDENT (Address)	DIST
	LACY, Oliver	924 N. 25th Street #213	3

JUVENILE LAST NAME	FIRST	MID	DATE OF BIRTH	O DETAINED
				O ORDERED TO MCCC
				O OTHER

COAN	TYPE OF PROPERTY	DESCRIPTION	SERIAL #	CODE #	VALUE

On Wednesday, 07-31-91, we, Detectives Dennis MURPHY and Patrick KENNEDY, reinterviewed the defendant, Jeffrey DAHMER, at the Detective Bureau. This interview was conducted with his attorney, Wendy PATRICKUS, present. After his attorney had left and we were just about to convey Mr. DAHMER back to the county jail he requested another cup of coffee and a cigarette. We provided him with this and upon sitting with him we asked him whether or not he would be willing to answer some questions regarding the last offense, namely the attempt homicide, file #91-51770, which had lead to his arrest. Mr. DAHMER stated that he did not need his attorney present, that he has cooperated with us fully and he will continue to cooperate with us. He wished to tell us what he recalls of the incident.

Mr. DAHMER stated that about a week prior to this offense which had occurred on 07-22-91, he met the subject, Tracy EDWARDS, at the bus stop infront of the Eagles Club at 24th and Wisconsin. Mr. DAHMER stated that he was just sitting there drinking a beer and thinking when the victim asked DAHMER for a cigarette. There was small talk and then the victim got on the bus.

Mr. DAHMER stated that about a week later, 07-22-91, he was having pizza and some beers at the Grand Avenue mall. After he finished this he walked down to the 3rd Street front entrance of the mall and he saw the victim with two other of his friends. He stated that he approached them and they had small talk, this was at about 5:00 or 6:00pm. He stated that he then asked the victim if he wanted to make approximately $50.00 to $75.00 to go home with him so that he can take some pictures of him and watch some videos. He indicated that the victim then went over and talked to his friends and they agreed to go to his apartment. He stated that they all walked over to the liquor store, the victim and both of his friends, which is located at 6th and Wisconsin. He stated that he went into the liquor store, bought a bottle of rum and coke and, he believes a 6 pack. He related that as he walked out his two friends were gone so he and the victim proceeded to the Greyhound bus station where they took a taxi. He stated that he got out of the taxi infront of the Eagles Club so that nobody would know where he lived and they walked to his residence.

He indicated that they walked through the back door because that's the way he always goes, it's the door closest to his apartment. He stated that once he got into

REPORTING OFFICER	PAYROLL #	LOC CODE	SUPERVISOR SIGNATURE
2179 SEC 5 / PAGE 90			

118

	INCIDENT HOMICIDE (STABBING)		DATE OF INCIDENT/ACCIDENT 07-23-91		REP CON #
INCIDENT INFORMATION	VICTIM LACY, Oliver		LOCATION OF INCIDENT/ACCIDENT (Address) 924 N. 25th Street #213		DIST
JUVENILE LAST NAME	FIRST	MID	DATE OF BIRTH	☐ DETAINED ☐ ORDERED TO MCCC ☐ OTHER	
QUAN	TYPE OF PROPERTY	DESCRIPTION		SERIAL #	CODE #	VALUE

the apartment he made a drink of rum and coke and he did not have any sleeping pills left so it was just rum and coke. He stated that they were sitting there talking about going to the gay bars in Chicago and they started watching videos, namely Exorcist II. He then started talking about taking some pictures, namely bondage pictures, and he told the victim that he wanted to handcuff him. He stated that he got the first cuff on him as they were sitting on the edge of the bed in the bedroom.

Mr. DAHMER stated that then things begin to get fuzzy and he does not remember having a knife or putting a knife up to the victim. He stated that he must have blacked out. He also stated that he does not remember telling the victim anything about showing him things that he would not believe. Mr. DAHMER stated that he then recalled hearing a knock at the door, which he answered, and he observed two Police Officers along with the victim standing in the hallway. He related that he invited them in and the victim still had the handcuff on his wrist. The next thing he can recall is that one of the Police Officers went into the bedroom and then he heard him say, "cuff him," at which time the other Officer placed handcuffs on him. He indicated that when he placed the handcuffs on him he began to struggle. He stated that he continued to struggle even when the Officers opened the refrigerator door. I asked Mr. DAHMER whether or not he told the Officers where the handcuff key was because the Officers could not remove the cuffs and stated that he might have said they were in the bedroom but he doesn't remember. He also related that he didn't remember showing any photos to the victim nor does he remember threatening the victim with a knife. He did state that the reason he uses handcuffs is so that he can keep control of his victims. He stated that he keeps the knife in the bedroom. I asked Mr. DAHMER if he remembered stating anything to the victim about threatening him or about cutting his heart out and he stated that he does not recall doing this. I asked Mr. DAHMER why he fought with the Police and he stated it was probably because he did not want to be arrested, and that he did not want them to see what was in the refrigerator. Mr. DAHMER stated that he cannot recall everything regarding this due to the fact that he had been drinking and thought he was intoxicated. Mr. DAHMER does recall when the Police arrived but stated he does not recall the victim leaving nor does he know when the victim left his apartment.

DM:dls 08-01-91

| REPORTING OFFICER
Det. Dennis MURPHY | PAYROLL #
9472 SEC | LOC CODE | PAGE | SUPERVISOR SIGNATURE |

| | INCIDENT HOMICIDE (STABBING) | | DATE OF INCIDENT/ACCIDENT 07-23-91 | REP CON |
| INCIDENT INFORMATION | VICTIM LACY, Oliver | | LOCATION OF INCIDENT/ACCIDENT (Address) 924 N. 25th St. #213 | DIS |

| JUVENILE LAST NAME | FIRST | MID | DATE OF BIRTH | O DETAINED O ORDERED TO MCCC O OTHER |

| QUAN | TYPE OF PROPERTY | DESCRIPTION | | SERIAL # | CODE # | VALUE |

I asked him where the handcuff key was, and he stated that he threw the handcuffs and the key in the garbage earlier and retrieved the handcuffs and not the key. He states that he would have been unable to remove the cuffs if he had placed them on the victim unless he removed the hands from the victim.

Report per: Det. Dennis MURPHY.

DM/dls   8-1-91

2472 — 5 PAGE 92

| REPORTING OFFICER DET. DENNIS MURPHY | PAYROLL # 32893 | LOC CODE 91 | SUPERVISOR SIGNATURE |

PO15-B 5-89 SUPPLEMENT REPORT MILWAUKEE POLICE DEPARTMENT	☒ INCIDENT SUPPLEMENT ☐ ACCIDENT SUPPLEMENT ☐ JUVENILE SUPPLEMENT	PAGE 1 of 1	DATE OF REPORT 08-01-91	INCIDENT/ACCIDENT # 91-51767/M2472-M2481	
INCIDENT INFORMATION	INCIDENT HOMICIDE (STABBING)		DATE OF INCIDENT/ACCIDENT 07-23-91		REP CON #
	VICTIM LACY, Oliver		LOCATION OF INCIDENT/ACCIDENT (Address) 924 N. 25th Street #213		DIST 3
JUVENILE LAST NAME	FIRST	MID	DATE OF BIRTH	O DETAINED O ORDERED TO HCCC O OTHER	
QUAN	TYPE OF PROPERTY	DESCRIPTION		SERIAL #	CODE #	VALUE

On Thursday, 08-01-91, we, Detectives Dennis MURPHY and Patrick KENNEDY, proceeded to the Milwaukee County Jail after receiving a call at 1:00pm from Deputy MALEK indicating that Jeffrey DAHMER was requesting to talk to us. Upon obtaining an order to produce we escorted Mr. DAHMER to the CIB, along with his attorney, Wendy PATRICKUS. At the Detective Bureau, in an interview room, we interviewed Mr. DAHMER in regards to his activities in Bath, Ohio in June 1978 as to the location where he had disposed of the knife. Lieutenant MUNCEY of the Bath, Ohio Police Department had faxed me a map of the area by the Sewage Treatment plant locating where the bridges were and requested that I show this to the defendant and have him point out where he disposed of the knife.

At this time Mr. DAHMER drew an "X" in the middle of the Cuyahoga River, approximatley in the middle of the Bath Road bridge and stated that he threw the knife about 10 feet out into the water. I then faxed this map back to Lieutenant MUNCEY.

I also asked him several questions regarding the homicide scene as to whether or not he had broken the knife he used and dropped it where the bones where recovered. He stated that he did not recall doing that. I asked him if his parents knew anything about this homicide or any of the other homicides and he stated that they did not know anything regarding this. I also informed him that a pruning shears were found at the location where the bones were being recovered and he stated that he did not use a pruning shears nor does he know anything about it. I was also informed that there was a tool box in the crawl space under the house. I asked him if he knew anything regarding this tool box and he stated that the time he was living there and the time he dismembered the body under the crawl space there was no tool box there. This information was passed on to Lt. MUNCEY.

Report dictated by: Det. Dennis MURPHY
DM:dls 08-01-91

2472 SEC 5 PAGE 93

INCIDENT INFORMATION	INCIDENT HOMICIDE (STABBING)		DATE OF INCIDENT/ACCIDENT 07-23-91		REP CON
	VICTIM LACY, Oliver		LOCATION OF INCIDENT/ACCIDENT (Address) 924 N. 25th Street #213		DIS 3
JUVENILE LAST NAME	FIRST	MID	DATE OF BIRTH	O DETAINED O ORDERED TO MCCC O OTHER	
QUAN	TYPE OF PROPERTY	DESCRIPTION		SERIAL #	CODE #	VALUE

On Thursday, 8-01-91, we, Detectives Dennis MURPHY and Patrick KENNEDY, were advised by Milwaukee County Sheriff's Jail that the suspect, Jeffrey DAHMER, wished to speak with us regarding the above offense. At this time we proceeded to the fifth floor lock up at the Milwaukee County Sheriff's Jail where we met the suspect, Jeffrey DAHMER, and his attorney, Wendy PATRICKUS. At this time they accompanied us to the fourth floor of the CIB where they were placed in an interview room. We questioned Jeffrey DAHMER regarding the follow matters.

Regarding information received from Charleston, South Carolina and a picture showing James BIEDERMAN, W/M, who has been missing from that state, DAHMER looked at the picture and stated that he has never seen this individual before and has never, in fact, been in South Carolina.

Regarding information received from Portage County, Ohio and specifically Ravenna, Ohio, regarding a missing white male by the name of Charles KOCH, who has been missing since 07-14-83, Mr. DAHMER stated that on that date he was in Milwaukee and did not have access to a car during his entire stay in Milwaukee. During the year of 1983 he did not make any return trips to visit family or friends in Ohio. He denied being involved in the missing of this individual.

Regarding information received from the county of Allegheny Police Department that being in Pittsburg, PA., with a picture sent of Anthony MICHAELOWSKI, who is a white gay male street hustler who has been missing. He was found dismembered in December of 1988. The Police in that jurisdiction requested that Jeffrey DAHMER look at the picture and decide whether or not he has ever been in Pittsburg or been involved in this offense. After viewing the photos, Jeffrey DAHMER stated that he had never seen this individual before and denies being involved in this offense.

Regarding Adam WALSH, the Hollywood, Florida Police Department sent along photos of the victim, Adam WALSH, who's head was found in that county approximately 10 years ago during the time when Mr. DAHMER was living in Miami Florida. Again, Mr. DAHMER stated, after viewing the photo, that he is in no way connected with the death of Adam WALSH and he has never seen this individual before except on t.v. and through flyers.

Regarding information received from Suffolk, Virginia regarding a missing person by the name of Walter HOBBS. Mr. DAHMER viewed the photo of Walter HOBBS and stated that

| REPORTING OFFICER 2472 sec 5 | PAYROLL # | LOC CODE | SUPERVISOR SIGNATURE Det. Lt. Raymond Suit |

INCIDENT INFORMATION	INCIDENT HOMICIDE (STABBING)		DATE OF INCIDENT/ACCIDENT 07-23-91		REP CON #
	VICTIM LACY, Oliver		LOCATION OF INCIDENT/ACCIDENT (Address) 924 N. 25th Street #213		DIST

JUVENILE LAST NAME	FIRST	MID	DATE OF BIRTH	O DETAINED O ORDERED TO MCCC O OTHER

QUAN	TYPE OF PROPERTY	DESCRIPTION	SERIAL #	CODE #	VALUE

he has never seen this individual before and stated that he has never been to Virginia and denies being involved in the missing of this person.

Regarding a photograph sent of a black male by the name of Prince BUSH, who has been missing since May 1987, Mr. DAHMER viewed this photo and stated that he has never seen this individual before and that he, in fact, has nothing to do with his missing.

At this time Mr. DAHMER stated that he wished to speak again regarding his relationship with the individual known to this department as Luis PINET. He stated that there were a few facts he forgot to mention regarding his relationship with Mr. PINET and he wished to reiterate them.

Mr. DAHMER stated that he had seen Mr. PINET working at the 219 Club as a clean up helper for some time before he actually got to know him. He stated that he observed Mr. PINET cleaning up glasses and sweeping up floors in that tavern several times late in the evening. He stated that the first time he met Mr. PINET was in the Phoenix tavern and that he found him attractive so he approached him and offered him $200.00 to return with him to his apartment to pose nude for some pictures and to have some homosexual sex. He stated that they took a cab to his apartment on North 25th Street where they mutually consented to engaging in sexual activity which involved kissing, masturbation and oral sex. He stated that he also took several pictures of Mr. PINET, however, he did not like the way they turned out so he tore them up and threw them out. He indicated that Mr. PINET willingly spent the night with him on that evening and before leaving in the morning he advised Mr. PINET that if he met him at 12:00 the next day he would, in fact, give him money for the previous night's activity. Mr. DAHMER stated that they agreed to meet at 12:00. Mr. DAHMER took this to mean 12 noon and decided that he would, in fact, make Mr. PINET one of his victims. He stated that at this time he was out of his sleeping pills which he had used in previous potions to knock out his victims and did not have the $30.00 in order to refill his prescription. So early in the morning he went to the Army/Navy Surplus store on West Wisconsin Avenue where he bought a plastic hammer. He stated that he bought this hammer and planned to use it to strike Mr. PINET on the head in order to render him unconscious so that he could strangle him and make him one of his victims.

He related that he returned to the Phoenix bar at 12 noon, however, Mr. PINET was

REPORTING OFFICER 9479 SEC.	PAYROLL # 95 PAGE	LOC CODE	SUPERVISOR SIGNATURE Sgt. Raymond Buell

| INCIDENT INFORMATION | INCIDENT HOMICIDE (STABBING) | | | DATE OF INCIDENT/ACCIDENT 07-23-91 | REP COM # |
| | VICTIM LACY, Oliver | | | LOCATION OF INCIDENT/ACCIDENT (Address) 924 N. 25th Street #213. | DIST |

JUVENILE LAST NAME	FIRST	MID	DATE OF BIRTH	☐ DETAINED ☐ ORDERED TO MCCC ☐ OTHER

QUAN	TYPE OF PROPERTY	DESCRIPTION	SERIAL #	CODE #	VALUE

not there so he went about his business for the day. He stated that later on that evening he again returned to the gay area of town, that being 200 S. 2nd Street, where upon bar time, that being approximately 2:30am, he again saw Mr. PINET standing inside the Phoenix tavern. At this time Mr. PINET again agreed to accompany him back to his apartment and they took a cab. He stated that once at the apartment they again engaged in sex which involved kissing, masturbation and oral sex. Then Mr. DAHMER stated that he wished to take a few more pictures of him in the bedroom. He stated that it was during this picture taking session when Mr. PINET was lying on his face with his back and head exposed, while lying on the bed, that Mr. DAHMER took out his plastic hammer and struck Mr. PINET in the back of the neck in an attempt to render him unconscious. Mr. DAHMER stated that upon striking Mr. PINET he became angry and he got up at which time a small argument ensued. Mr. DAHMER then stated that the only reason he struck him was because he felt Mr. PINET was going to take the $200.00 and leave without spending the night. He stated that Mr. PINET did not buy that explaination and he left stating that he was going to call the Police. Mr. DAHMER stated that Mr. PINET, in fact, left the apartment and the apartment building, however, approximately 10 minutes later he heard pounding on the outer apartment lobby door and when he went to investigate Mr. PINET was standing there requesting to get back in and asking for money. Mr. DAHMER stated that at this time Mr. PINET followed him back to his apartment and once inside Mr. DAHMER grabbed him by the neck and attempted to strangle him and a fight ensued. He related that they fought for a couple of minutes when Mr. DAHMER simply stopped fighting and decided to calm the situation down by stating, "lets talk." He stated that Mr. PINET agreed although he was highly agitated and they went into the bedroom where they sat down. Mr. DAHMER stated after calming him down he asked Mr. PINET if he would, in fact, allow him to tie his hands behind his back and Mr. PINET agreed. Mr. DAHMER stated that he tied Mr. PINET'S hands behind his back, however, not very tight and they continued to talk. He indicated that during the next $\frac{1}{2}$ hour or so Mr. PINET wiggled free from the extension cord he had tied on his hands and attempted to leave the apartment when Mr. DAHMER, in fact, grabbed his six inch bladed, black plastic handled, knife. He stated that he believes that PINET thought this was a gun and decided to sit down again. He related that they again began to talk and talked approximately until 7:00am. Mr. DAHMER stated

REPORTING OFFICER 2472 SEC 5	PAYROLL #	LOC CODE	SUPERVISOR SIGNATURE

INCIDENT INFORMATION	INCIDENT HOMICIDE (STÅBBING)		DATE OF INCIDENT/ACCIDENT 07-23-91		REP CON #
	VICTIM LACY, Oliver		LOCATION OF INCIDENT/ACCIDENT (Address) 924 N. 25th Street #213		DIST

JUVENILE LAST NAME	FIRST	MID	DATE OF BIRTH	○ DETAINED ○ ORDERED TO MCCC ○ OTHER

QUAN	TYPE OF PROPERTY	DESCRIPTION		SERIAL #	CODE #	VALUE

that during the talk he was trying to convince PINET not to tell the Police about the night's activities and he continued to apologize for striking him with the hammer. Mr. DAHMER stated that although he did intend to kill PINET and make him one of his victims, that because of the previous nights sexual activities and that fact that they had spent hours talking, he began to sober up and know Mr. PINET on a more personal level and had decided that he would not kill him. He indicated that at approximately 7:00am in the morning he walked Mr. PINET to the bus stop on 24th and Wisconsin and gave him money for cab fare. He indicated that was the last he saw of Mr. PINET until about 5 or 6 months later as he was walking in the Grand Avenue mall he observed Mr. PINET walking in the mall as well. He stated that Mr. PINET approached him and said "hi." He related that there was no further conversation but approximatley March of 1991 as Mr. DAHMER was sitting in the mall eating ice cream PINET observed him, walked up to him and initiated a conversation. He stated that they had small talk for a while and then both went their separate ways.

This is all the information that Mr. DAHMER stated he had regarding the incident with Mr. PINET and this part of the interview was terminated.

Other questions were asked of Mr. DAHMER regarding the night that he was arrested and a detailed supplemental regarding this portion of the interview will be filed by Detective Dennis MURPHY.

Report dictated by: Det. Patrick KENNEDY

PK:dls 08-01-91

2472 SEC. 5 PAGE 97

REPORTING OFFICER Det. Patrick KENNEDY	PAYROLL # 48171	LOC CODE 93	SUPERVISOR SIGNATURE

STATE OF WISCONSIN   CRIMINAL DIVISION   MILWAUKEE COUNTY

STATE OF WISCONSIN, Plaintiff   **CRIMINAL COMPLAINT**

vs.

Jeffrey L. Dahmer   05/21/60
924 N. 25th St.
Milwaukee, WI

       Defendant.

CRIME(S):
See Charging Section Below
STATUTE(S) VIOLATED
See Charging Section Below
COMPLAINING WITNESS:
Kenneth Meuler
CASE NUMBER:

THE ABOVE NAMED COMPLAINING WITNESS BEING DULY SWORN SAYS THAT THE ABOVE
NAMED DEFENDANT IN THE COUNTY OF MILWAUKEE, STATE OF WISCONSIN

COUNT 01:   FIRST DEGREE INTENTIONAL HOMICIDE

on or about June 30, 1991, at 924 North 25th Street, City and County of
Milwaukee, did cause the death of another human being, Matt Turner a/k/a
Donald Montrell, with intent to kill that person contrary to Wisconsin
Statutes section 940.01(1).

COUNT 02:   FIRST DEGREE INTENTIONAL HOMICIDE

on or about July 7, 1991, at 924 North 25th Street, City and County of
Milwaukee, did cause the death of another human being, Jeremiah Weinberger,
with intent to kill that person contrary to Wisconsin Statutes section
940.01(1).

COUNT 03:   FIRST DEGREE INTENTIONAL HOMICIDE

on or about July 15, 1991 at 924 North 25th Street, City and County of
Milwaukee, did cause the death of another human being, Oliver Lacy, with
intent to kill that person contrary to Wisconsin Statutes section
940.01(1).

COUNT 04:   FIRST DEGREE INTENTIONAL HOMICIDE

on or about July 19, 1991 at 924 North 25th Street, City and County of
Milwaukee, did cause the death of another human being, Joseph Bradehoft,
with intent to kill that person contrary to Wisconsin Statutes section
940.01(1).

COUNT 05:   HABITUAL CRIMINALITY

on January 30, 1989 Jeffrey L. Dahmer was convicted in the Circuit Court of
Milwaukee County in Circuit Court Case Number F-882515 of the felony
offenses of Second Degree Sexual Assault and Enticing a Child for Immoral
Purposes in violation of 940.225(2)(e) and 944.12 of the Wisconsin Statutes
and that said convictions remain of record and unreversed and therefore

2472 SEC. 5   98

defendant is a repeater pursuant to Wisconsin Statutes 939.62, and is subject to a total sentence of not more than ten (10) years on each count recited in addition to the mandatory life sentence for each count of First Degree Intentional Homicide.

Upon conviction of Counts One, Two, Three and Four, Class A Felonies, the penalty is life imprisonment as to each count.

Complainant states that he is a Detective Lieutenant with the City of Milwaukee Police Department and bases this complaint upon the following:

(1)   Upon the statement of the defendant, which statement is against his (the defendant's) penal interest that:

(a)   On June 30th, 1991 after the Gay Pride Parade in Chicago, he met a black male at the Chicago Bus Station and offered him money to pose nude and also view videos he (the defendant) had at his apartment back in Milwaukee; he (the defendant) with this black male returned to Milwaukee on a Greyhound Bus and then took a City Vet cab to his (the defendant's) residence in Apartment 213 at 924 North 25th Street, in the City and County of Milwaukee, State of Wisconsin; he (the defendant) gave the black male something to drink which had been drugged and that the man passed out and he (the defendant) used a strap to strangle the man and then dismembered him and kept his head and put it in the freezer in his apartment and placed his body in a 57 gallon barrel that he had in his residence; further that he (the defendant) looked at a photograph supplied by the Chicago Police Department of <u>Matt Turner</u> a/k/a <u>Donald Montrell</u> and indicated that he thought this was the person that he had killed in this incident.

(b)   The defendant further stated that on or about July 5th, 1991 he met a Puerto Rican male at Carol's Gay Bar on Wells Street in Chicago and that he offered the man money to come with him to Milwaukee to pose for him and to view videos; they took a Greyhound Bus from Chicago to Milwaukee and then took a cab to his apartment at 924 North 25th Street in the City and County of Milwaukee, State of Wisconsin; this man stayed with him for two days and on the first day they had oral sex and on the second day the man indicated that he wanted to leave and he (the defendant) didn't want the man to leave so he gave him a drink with a sleeping potion in it and strangled him manually and then took photos of him and dismembered him and then took more photos and kept the man's head in the freezer and body in the 57 gallon drum; he (the defendant) looked at a photo supplied by the Chicago Police Department of <u>Jeremiah Weinberger</u> and indicated that this was the man that he had killed in this incident.

(c)   The defendant further stated that on or about July 15th, 1991 he met a black male on 27th Street between State and Kilbourn in Milwaukee and that the man stated he was going to his cousin's house; he invited the man to his residence to pose for photos and the man agreed to come and model; when they got to the residence, they removed their clothes and did body rubs and he gave the man a drink which had sleeping potion in it and when the man fell asleep, he strangled him and then had anal sex with him after death; he dismembered him and placed the man's head in the bottom of the

(2)

2472 / SEC 5 . 99

127

refrigerator in a box and kept the man's heart in the freezer to eat later; he also kept the man's body in the freezer that he kept the man's identification which identified the man as <u>Oliver Lacy</u>, date of birth 6/23/67.

(d) The defendant further stated that on or about July 19th, 1991 he met a white male on Wisconsin Avenue near Marquette University and the man was waiting for a bus and had a six pack under his arm; he (the defendant) got off a bus at that location and approached the man and offered him money to pose and view videos and the man agreed and they returned to the defendant's residence at 924 North 25th Street in the City and County of Milwaukee, State of Wisconsin; they had oral sex and then he gave the man a drink with a sleeping potion in it and then strangled him with a strap while he slept; he dismembered this man and put his head in the freezer and his body in the same blue 57 gallon barrel where he had placed the bodies of the black male and the Puerto Rican male; he kept this man's identification card which identified him as <u>Joseph Bradehoft</u>, date of birth 1/24/66.

(2) Upon the statement of <u>Dr. Jeffrey Jentzen</u>, Medical Examiner for Milwaukee County, that on July 23rd, 1991 he was called by the Milwaukee Police Department to Apartment 213 at 924 North 25th Street in the City and County of Milwaukee, State of Wisconsin and inside the apartment at that location, among other evidence, he observed a refrigerator with a freezer section and that the refrigerator contained a head and the freezer section contained human body parts; also there was a floor standing freezer which was found to contain three human heads and other body parts and there was a 57 gallon drum which contained human body parts. Jentzen further stated that at the Milwaukee County Medical Examiner's Office these human body parts were examined and that fingerprints were lifted from hands that had been found at the scene and also attempts at dental identification was made; that <u>Dr. L.T. Johnson</u> whom he (Jentzen) knows to be a forensic odontologist did the dental examination and that fingerprint lifts were submitted to the Milwaukee Police Department Bureau of Identification for analysis.

(3) Upon the statement of <u>Dr. L.T. Johnson</u>, a forensic odontologist, that he (Johnson) at the Milwaukee County Medical Examiner's Office examined one of the human heads recovered from the freezer at 924 North 25th Street with known dental records of <u>Jeramiah Weinberger</u> and determined that the severed human head that he examined in comparison with those records was the head of Jeramiah Weinberger.

(4) Upon the statement of <u>Wayne Peterson</u>, that he (Peterson) is a Bureau of Identification technician and supervisor employed by the City of Milwaukee Police Department and that he (Peterson) made comparisons of fingerprints lifted by the Milwaukee County Medical Examiner's Office from body parts recovered at 924 North 25th Street on July 23rd, 1991 with known prints of various persons and was able to identify the prints of <u>Oliver Lacy</u>, <u>Joseph Bradehoft</u>, and <u>Matt Turner</u> a/k/a <u>Donald Montrell</u> as having been lifted from human body parts discovered in that apartment.

(3)

472   5   PAGE 1 0 0
SEC.

(5) Complainant further states that he has viewed a certified copy of
Judgment of Conviction in Milwaukee County Circuit Court Case No. F-882515
and a copy of that Judgment of Conviction is attached hereto and
incorporated herein and the aforementioned Judgment of Conviction indicates
that the defendant was convicted of felony offenses in Milwaukee County
within five years of the offenses listed in this complaint and that he (the
defendant) is therefore a Habitual Criminal.

**** END OF COMPLAINT ****

SUBSCRIBED AND SWORN TO BEFORE ME
AND APPROVED FOR FILING JULY 25, 1991

E Michael McCann
Deputy Asst. District Attorney

Kenneth Meuler
Complaining Witness

(4)

2472   5   101
M_____, SEC_____, PAGE_____

CIRCUIT COURT
STATE OF WISCONSIN   CRIMINAL DIVISION   MILWAUKEE COUNTY

- -

STATE OF WISCONSIN, Plaintiff   **AMENDED CRIMINAL COMPLAINT**

vs.

Jeffrey L. Dahmer   05/21/60
924 N. 25th St.
Milwaukee, WI

Defendant.

CRIME(S):
See Charging Section Below
STATUTE(S) VIOLATED
See Charging Section Below
COMPLAINING WITNESS:
Donald Domagalski
CASE NUMBER:
F-912542

- -

THE ABOVE NAMED COMPLAINING WITNESS BEING DULY SWORN SAYS THAT THE ABOVE
NAMED DEFENDANT IN THE COUNTY OF MILWAUKEE, STATE OF WISCONSIN

COUNT 01: FIRST DEGREE INTENTIONAL HOMICIDE

on or about March 26, 1989, at 2357 South 57th Street, City of West Allis,
County of Milwaukee, did cause the death of another human being, Anthony
Sears, with intent to kill that person contrary to Wisconsin Statutes
section 940.01(1).

COUNT 02: FIRST DEGREE INTENTIONAL HOMICIDE

during the Spring or early Summer of 1990, at 924 North 25th Street, City
and County of Milwaukee, did cause the death of another human being,
Raymond Smith a/k/a Ricky Beeks, with intent to kill that person contrary
to Wisconsin Statutes section 940.01(1).

COUNT 03: FIRST DEGREE INTENTIONAL HOMICIDE

on or about September 3, 1990, at 924 North 25th Street, City and County of
Milwaukee, did cause the death of another human being, Ernest Miller, with
intent to kill that person contrary to Wisconsin Statutes section
940.01(1).

COUNT 04: FIRST DEGREE INTENTIONAL HOMICIDE

on or about September 24, 1990, at 924 North 25th Street, City and County
of Milwaukee, did cause the death of another human being, David Thomas,
with intent to kill that person contrary to Wisconsin Statutes section
940.01(1).

COUNT 05: FIRST DEGREE INTENTIONAL HOMICIDE

on or about February 18, 1991, at 924 North 25th Street, City and County of
Milwaukee, did cause the death of another human being, Curtis Straughter,
with intent to kill that person contrary to Wisconsin Statutes section
940.01(1).

2472   5   102
SEC   PAGE

130

COUNT 06: FIRST DEGREE INTENTIONAL HOMICIDE

on or about April 7, 1991, at 924 North 25th Street, City and County of Milwaukee, did cause the death of another human being, Errol Lindsey, with intent to kill that person contrary to Wisconsin Statutes section 940.01(1).

COUNT 07: FIRST DEGREE INTENTIONAL HOMICIDE

on or about May 24, 1991, at 924 North 25th Street, City and County of Milwaukee, did cause the death of another human being, Tony Anthony Hughes, with intent to kill that person contrary to Wisconsin Statutes section 940.01(1).

COUNT 08: FIRST DEGREE INTENTIONAL HOMICIDE

on or about May 27, 1991, at 924 North 25th Street, City and County of Milwaukee, did cause the death of another human being, Konerak Sinthasomphone, with intent to kill that person contrary to Wisconsin Statutes section 940.01(1).

COUNT 09: FIRST DEGREE INTENTIONAL HOMICIDE

on or about June 30, 1991, at 924 North 25th Street, City and County of Milwaukee, did cause the death of another human being, Matt Turner a/k/a Donald Montrell, with intent to kill that person contrary to Wisconsin Statutes section 940.01(1).

COUNT 10: FIRST DEGREE INTENTIONAL HOMICIDE

on or about July 7, 1991, at 924 North 25th Street, City and County of Milwaukee, did cause the death of another human being, Jeremiah Weinberger, with intent to kill that person contrary to Wisconsin Statutes section 940.01(1).

COUNT 11: FIRST DEGREE INTENTIONAL HOMICIDE

on or about July 15, 1991 at 924 North 25th Street, City and County of Milwaukee, did cause the death of another human being, Oliver Lacy, with intent to kill that person contrary to Wisconsin Statutes section 940.01(1).

COUNT 12: FIRST DEGREE INTENTIONAL HOMICIDE

on or about July 19, 1991 at 924 North 25th Street, City and County of Milwaukee, did cause the death of another human being, Joseph Bradehoft, with intent to kill that person contrary to Wisconsin Statutes section 940.01(1).

(2)

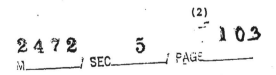

2472   5   103
M_____/ SEC_____/ PAGE

131

HABITUAL CRIMINALITY

on January 30, 1989, Jeffrey L. Dahmer was convicted in the Circuit Court of Milwaukee County in Circuit Court Case Number F-882515 of the felony offenses of Second Degree Sexual Assault and Enticing a Child for Immoral Purposes in violation of 940.225(2)(e) and 944.12 of the Wisconsin Statutes and that said convictions remain of record and unreversed and therefore defendant is a repeater pursuant to Wisconsin Statutes 939.62, and is subject to a total sentence of not more than ten (10) years on each count recited in addition to the mandatory life sentence for each count of First Degree Intentional Homicide.

Upon conviction of each count of First Degree Intentional Homicide, a Class A Felony, the penalty is life imprisonment.

Complainant states that he is a Captain of Police with the City of Milwaukee Police Department and bases this complaint upon the following:

VICTIM ANTHONY SEARS, D.O.B. 1/28/65

1) Upon the statement of the defendant, which statement is against his (the defendant's) penal interest, that he met Anthony Sears (whom he identified in a photograph) at a club called LaCage; that a friend of Anthony Sears drove him (the defendant) and Anthony Sears to the area of his (the defendant's) grandmother's house in the City of West Allis, County of Milwaukee, State of Wisconsin; that his grandmother's house is 2357 South 57th Street; that after they arrived at that residence, they had sex and he gave Anthony Sears a drink with sleeping pills in it; that he strangled him and dismembered the body; that he kept Anthony Sears' head and boiled it to remove the skin; further, that he kept the skull and painted it.

2) Upon the statement of Jeffrey Connor, an adult citizen, that he (Connor) was with Anthony Sears on the evening of March 25th, 1989 and on that evening they were at a bar on 6th and National; they closed the bar and that Anthony Sears had met a white male named Jeff who said that he was here from Chicago and was visiting his grandmother who lived at 56th and Lincoln; that he (Connor) then gave Jeff and Anthony Sears a ride to the vicinity of 56th and Lincoln where they (Jeff and Sears) got out of the car and walked southbound.

3) Upon complainant's personal knowledge of addresses in Milwaukee County and that the intersection of 56th and Lincoln is north of and in close proximity to the address 2357 South 57th Street in the City of West Allis.

4) Upon the statement of Dr. Jeffrey Jentzen, Milwaukee County Medical Examiner, that during the early morning hours of July 23rd, 1991 he (Jentzen) with Milwaukee police officers and other members of the County of Milwaukee Medical Examiner's Office was present at 924 North 25th Street in the City and County of Milwaukee, State of Wisconsin in Apartment 213; that he was present at that location when seven human skulls (three of which were painted) four human heads, and numerous other body parts were recovered; that all the human remains recovered were transported to the Milwaukee County Medical Examiner's Office.

(3)

132

5)   Upon the statement of Dr. L.T. Johnson, a Forensic Odontologist, that he (Johnson) made a comparison of the painted human skulls recovered from 924 North 25th Street in the City and County of Milwaukee, State of Wisconsin during the early morning hours of July 23rd, 1991 with known dental records of Anthony Sears and determined that one of the painted skulls is that of Anthony Sears.

VICTIM RAYMOND SMITH A/K/A RICKY BEEKS D.O.B. 8/10/57

1)   Upon the further statement of the defendant that approximately two months after he (the defendant) moved into Apartment 213 at 924 North 25th Street in the City and County of Milwaukee, State of Wisconsin he met a black male at the 219 Club and offered him money to be photographed and have a drink and watch videos; that the man agreed and came with him (the defendant) to 924 North 25th Street, Apartment 213; that at that location he (the defendant) gave the man a drink which was drugged and the man fell asleep; that he (the defendant) then strangled the man and removed the man's clothing and had oral sex with him; further, that he dismembered the body but kept the skull and later painted it; further, that he (the defendant) identified photographs of Raymond Lamont Smith as being photographs of the man to whom he had done this.
2)   Upon the further statement of Dr. L.T. Johnson that he (Johnson) examined the painted skulls recovered at 924 North 25th Street in the City and County of Milwaukee, State of Wisconsin during the early morning hours of July 23rd, 1991 with known dental records of Raymond Lamont Smith and determined that one of the aforementioned skulls is that of Raymond Smith.
3)   Upon your complainant's personal observation of a copy of the defendant's rental application for the living premises at 924 North 25th Street, Apartment 213; that the aforementioned rental agreement has an initial lease date of May 13th, 1990.

VICTIM ERNEST MILLER, D.O.B. 5/5/67

1)   Upon the statement of Vivian Miller, an adult citizen, that she (Miller) is the aunt of Ernest Miller and that on September 1st, 1990 Ernest Miller came from his home in Chicago to Milwaukee to visit for the Labor Day weekend and that he left her home during the early morning hours of September 3rd, 1990 and she has not seen him or heard from him since.
2)   Upon the further statement of the defendant that during the summer of 1990 he met a black male (whom he identified through a photograph of Ernest Miller as being Ernest Miller) in front of a book store in the 800 block of North 27th Street in the City and County of Milwaukee, State of Wisconsin and that he offered the man money to return to his (the defendant's) apartment at 924 North 25th Street in the City and County of Milwaukee, State of Wisconsin; that when they returned to his apartment they had sex and then he (the defendant) drugged Ernest Miller and killed him by cutting his throat; further, that after taking photos of him, he dismembered the body and disposed of the flesh except for the biceps which he kept in the freezer; he also kept the skull which he painted after the skin was removed, and he kept the skeleton which he bleached.
3)   Upon the further statement of Dr. L.T. Johnson that he (Johnson) has compared the painted skulls recovered on July 23rd, 1991 from the

(4)

defendant's apartment at 924 North 25th Street in the City and County of
Milwaukee, State of Wisconsin with known dental records of Ernest Miller
and determined that one of the aforementioned painted skulls is that of
Ernest Miller.

VICTIM DAVID C. THOMAS D.O.B. 12/21/67

1) Upon the further statement of the defendant that he in the Autumn
of 1990 met a black male in the vicinity of 2nd and Wisconsin in the City
and County of Milwaukee, State of Wisconsin and offered the man money to
come to his apartment at 924 North 25th Street; when they got to his
apartment they drank and talked but he had no sex with this man because the
man wasn't his type; that he gave the man a drink with a sleeping potion in
it and killed him even though he did not want to have sex with him because
he thought the man would wake up and be angry; that he dismembered the body
but did not keep any of the body parts because the man wasn't his type;
further, that he photographed the man while he was in the process of
dismembering him.

2) Upon the statement of Chandra Beanland, an adult citizen, that she
(Beanland) is the girlfriend of David C. Thomas and that she reported him
missing on September 24th, 1990 to the Milwaukee Police Department.

3) Upon the statement of Brian O'Keefe, a City of Milwaukee Police
Detective, that he (O'Keefe) contacted the family of David C. Thomas in the
course of this investigation and specifically spoke with Leslie Thomas who
identified herself as David C. Thomas' sister and that he (O'Keefe) showed
Leslie Thomas the facial portion of the photograph which the defendant
identified as having been taken during the course of dismembering David
Thomas; further, that the facial portion showed no injuries at the time it
was shown to Leslie Thomas and that Leslie Thomas identified the person in
the photograph as being her brother, David Thomas; that the Thomas family
supplied a photograph of David Thomas sleeping which they had; further that
the face in this family photograph appeared to him (O'Keefe) to depict the
same individual as in the photograph the defendant had taken while
dismembering this victim.

VICTIM CURTIS STRAUGHTER D.O.B. 4/16/73

1) Upon the statement of Katherine Straughter, an adult citizen, that
she (Straughter) is the grandmother of Curtis Straughter and that she last
saw her grandson on February 18th, 1991.

2) Upon the further statement of the defendant that in February of
1991 he observed Curtis Straughter (whom he identified through a
photograph) waiting for a bus by Marquette University and offered him money
to come back to his apartment at 924 North 25th Street in the City and
County of Milwaukee, State of Wisconsin; that Straughter did accompany him
back and at the apartment he (the defendant) gave Curtis Straughter a
drugged drink and had oral sex with him; the defendant then strangled him
with a strap and dismembered the body; he also took photos and kept the
man's skull.

3) Upon the further statement of Dr. L.T. Johnson that he (Johnson)
compared the unpainted skulls recovered from the defendant's apartment with
known dental records of Curtis Straughter and determined that one of the
unpainted skulls was that of Curtis Straughter.

(5)

134

VICTIM ERROL LINDSEY D.O.B. 3/3/72

1) Upon the statement of Yahuna Barkley, an adult citizen, that she (Barkley) is the sister of Errol Lindsey and that she last saw him on April 7th, 1991 when he went to the store and that she has not seen him since that time.

2) Upon the further statement of the defendant that in the Spring of 1991 he met Errol Lindsey (whom he identified by photograph) on the corner of 27th and Kilbourn in the City and County of Milwaukee, State of Wisconsin and that he offered Errol Lindsey money to return with him (the defendant) to his apartment at 924 North 25th Street in the City and County of Milwaukee, State of Wisconsin; that after they returned to his apartment he gave Lindsey a drugged drink and after he fell asleep he strangled Lindsey and then had oral sex with him; he then dismembered the body and saved the skull.

3) Upon the further statement of Dr. L.T. Johnson that he (Johnson) compared the unpainted skulls recovered from the defendant's apartment on July 23rd, 1991 with known dental records of Errol Lindsey and determined that one of the unpainted skulls is that of Errol Lindsey.

VICTIM TONY ANTHONY HUGHES, D.O.B. 8/26/59

1) Upon the further statement of the defendant that in May of 1991 he met Tony Anthony Hughes (whom he identified through a photograph) who was deaf and mute in front of the 219 Bar on Second Street in the City and County of Milwaukee, State of Wisconsin; that he communicated with Hughes by writing and it appeared that Hughes could read lips; that he offered Hughes $50 to come to his (the defendant's) apartment at 924 North 25th Street in the City and County and Milwaukee, State of Wisconsin to take photos and view videos; further, that he gave Hughes a drink with a sleeping potion and then killed him and dismembered his body and kept his skull.

2) Upon the further statement of Dr. L.T. Johnson that he (Johnson) has compared the unpainted skulls found in the apartment of the defendant with known dental records of Tony Hughes and determined that one of the unpainted skulls is that of Tony Hughes.

3) Upon the statement of Shirley Hughes, an adult citizen, that she (Hughes) is the mother of Tony Hughes and that Tony Hughes came to Milwaukee from Madison during the late afternoon or evening of May 24th, 1991 and that she has not seen him since and further that her son, Tony Hughes, is deaf and mute.

VICTIM KONERAK SINTHASOMPHONE D.O.B. 12/2/76

1) Upon the statement of Sounthone Sinthasomphone, an adult resident, that he is the father of Konerak Sinthasomphone who was 14 years of age and that during the afternoon of May 26th, 1991 his son left home and did not return and he has not seen him since.

2) Upon the further statement of the defendant that he (the defendant) in late May of 1991 met a young Oriental male (whom he identified by photograph as Konerak Sinthasomphone) in front of Grand Avenue Mall in Milwaukee and that they went back to his (the defendant's) apartment at 924

(6)

2472

5   107

135

North 25th Street in the City and County of Milwaukee, State of Wisconsin; that Sinthasomphone posed for two photographs while he was alive and that he (the defendant) gave Sinthasomphone a drink laced with a sleeping potion and that they then watched videos and while they were watching videos, Sinthasomphone passed out; that he (the defendant) then had oral sex with Sinthasomphone and then he (the defendant) went to a bar to get some beer because he had run out; that while he was walking back from the bar located on 27th just North of Kilbourn, he saw Sinthasomphone staggering down the street and he (the defendant) went up to Sinthasomphone and then the police stopped him; that he told the police that he was a friend of this individual and that the individual had gotten drunk and done this before; that the police escorted them back to his (the defendant's) apartment and he told the police he would take care of Sinthasomphone because he was his friend; that they went into the apartment and after the police left, he killed Sinthasomphone by strangling him and then had oral sex with him and then he took more photographs and dismembered the body and kept the skull.

3) Upon the further statement of Dr. L.T. Johnson that he (Johnson) compared the unpainted skulls recovered from the apartment at 924 North 25th Street with known dental records of Konerak Sinthasomphone and determined that one of the skulls which was recovered from that location is that of Konerak Sinthasomphone.

VICTIM MATT TURNER A/K/A DONALD MONTRELL D.O.B. 7/3/70

1) Upon the further statement of the defendant that on June 30th, 1991 after the Gay Pride Parade in Chicago, he met a black male at the Chicago Bus Station and offered him money to pose nude and also view videos at his apartment back in Milwaukee; he (the defendant), with this black male, returned to Milwaukee on a Greyhound Bus and then took a City Vet cab to his (the defendant's) residence in Apartment 213 at 924 North 25th Street, in the City and County of Milwaukee, State of Wisconsin; he (the defendant) gave the black male something to drink which had been drugged and the man passed out and he (the defendant) used a strap to strangle the man and then dismembered him and kept his head and put it in the freezer in his apartment and placed his body in a 57 gallon barrel that he had in his residence; further that he (the defendant) looked at a photograph supplied by the Chicago Police Department of Matt Turner a/k/a Donald Montrell and indicated that he thought this was the person that he had killed in this incident.

VICTIM JEREMIAH WEINBERGER D.O.B. 9/29/67

1) Upon the further statement of the defendant that on or about July 5th, 1991 he met a Puerto Rican male at Carol's Gay Bar on Wells Street in Chicago and that he offered the man money to come with him to Milwaukee to pose for him and to view videos; they took a Greyhound Bus from Chicago to Milwaukee and then took a cab to the defendant's apartment at 924 North 25th Street in the City and County of Milwaukee, State of Wisconsin; this man stayed with him for two days and on the first day they had oral sex and on the second day the man indicated that he wanted to leave and he (the defendant) didn't want the man to leave so he gave him a drink with a sleeping potion in it and strangled him manually and then took photos of

(7)

him and dismembered the body; he then took more photos and kept the man's head in the freezer and body in the 57 gallon drum; he (the defendant) looked at a photo supplied by the Chicago Police Department of Jeremiah Weinberger and indicated that this was the man that he had killed in this incident.

2) Upon the statement of Dr. L.T. Johnson that he (Johnson) at the Milwaukee County Medical Examiner's Office compared one of the human heads recovered from the freezer at 924 North 25th Street with known dental records of Jeremiah Weinberger and determined that the severed human head that he examined in comparison with those records was the head of Jeremiah Weinberger.

VICTIM OLIVER LACY D.O.B. 6/23/67

1) Upon the further statement of the defendant that on or about July 15th, 1991 he met a black male on 27th Street between State and Kilbourn in Milwaukee and that the man stated he was going to his cousin's house; he invited the man to his residence to pose for photos and the man agreed to come and model; when they got to the residence at 924 North 25th Street in the City and County of Milwaukee, State of Wisconsin, they removed their clothes and did body rubs and he gave the man a drink which had sleeping potion in it; when the man fell asleep, he strangled him and then had anal sex with him after death; he dismembered the body and placed the man's head in the bottom of the refrigerator in a box and kept the man's heart in the freezer to eat later; he also kept the man's body in the freezer; he kept the man's identification which identified the man as Oliver Lacy, date of birth 6/23/67.

VICTIM JOSEPH BRADEHOFT D.O.B.1/24/66

1) Upon the further statement of the defendant that on or about July 19th, 1991 he met a white male on Wisconsin Avenue near Marquette University; the man was waiting for a bus and had a six pack under his arm; he (the defendant) got off a bus at that location and approached the man and offered him money to pose and view videos and the man agreed; they returned to the defendant's residence at 924 North 25th Street in the City and County of Milwaukee, State of Wisconsin; they had oral sex and then he gave the man a drink with a sleeping potion in it and then strangled him with a strap while he slept; he dismembered this man and put his head in the freezer and his body in the same blue 57 gallon barrel where he had placed the bodies of the black male and the Puerto Rican male; he kept this man's identification card which identified him as Joseph Bradehoft, date of birth 1/24/66.

AS TO VICTIMS TURNER, LACY AND BRADEHOFT

1) Upon the statement of Dr. Jeffrey Jentzen, Medical Examiner for Milwaukee County, that on July 23rd, 1991 he was called by the Milwaukee Police Department to Apartment 213 at 924 North 25th Street in the City and County of Milwaukee, State of Wisconsin and inside the apartment at that location, among other evidence, he observed a refrigerator with a freezer section; the refrigerator contained a human head and the freezer section

(8)

137

contained human body parts; also there was a floor standing freezer which was found to contain three human heads and other body parts and there was a 57 gallon drum which contained human body parts. Jentzen further stated that at the Milwaukee County Medical Examiner's Office these human body parts were examined and that fingerprints were lifted from hands that had been found at the scene and also efforts at dental identification were made; that Dr. L.T. Johnson, whom he (Jentzen) knows to be a forensic odontologist, did the dental examination and that fingerprint lifts were submitted to the Milwaukee Police Department Bureau of Identification for analysis.

2) Upon the statement of Wayne Peterson, that he (Peterson) is a Bureau of Identification technician and supervisor employed by the City of Milwaukee Police Department and that he (Peterson) made comparisons of fingerprints lifted by the Milwaukee County Medical Examiner's Office from body parts recovered at 924 North 25th Street on July 23rd, 1991 with known prints of various persons and was able to identify the prints of Oliver Lacy, Joseph Bradehoft, and Matt Turner a/k/a Donald Montrell as having been lifted from human body parts discovered in that apartment.

AS TO HABITUAL CRIMINALITY

Complainant further states that he has viewed a certified copy of Judgment of Conviction in Milwaukee County Circuit Court Case No. F-882515 and a copy of that Judgment of Conviction is attached hereto and incorporated herein and the aforementioned Judgment of Conviction indicates that the defendant was convicted of felony offenses in Milwaukee County within five years of the offenses listed in this complaint and that he (the defendant) is therefore a Habitual Criminal.

**** END OF COMPLAINT ****

SUBSCRIBED AND SWORN TO BEFORE ME
AND APPROVED FOR FILING AUGUST 6, 1991

_____   _____
Deputy Ass't. District Attorney   Complaining Witness

(9)

1972   5   110

2412   5   111

PAGE

139

JUDGMENT OF CONVICTION
SENTENCE IMPOSED & STAYED, PROBATION ORDERED

STATE OF WISCONSIN,   Plaintiff   STATE OF WISCONSIN, Circuit Court Branch __16__

v.

Jeffrey L. Dahmer   Defendant   County _Milwaukee_

_5-21-60_ Defendant Date of Birth   Court Case No. _F-88-2515_

The defendant entered his/her plea of ☑ guilty   ☐ not guilty   ☐ no contest:

The ☑ Court ☐ Jury found the defendant guilty of:

Crime(s):	Wis. Statute(s) Violated	Felony or Misdemeanor (F or M)	Class (A-E)	Date(s) Crime Committed
2° Sexual Assault	940.225(2)(a)	F	C	
Enticing Child for Immoral Purposes	944.12	F	C	9/x/88

committed in this County, and

On _May 23, 1989_ , the Court inquired of the defendant why sentence should not be pronounced, and sufficient grounds to the contrary being shown or appearing to the Court, and the Court having accorded the district attorney, defense counsel, and the defendant an opportunity to address the Court regarding sentence; and upon all evidence, records, and proceedings, the Court pronounced findings and judgment as follows:

IT IS ADJUDGED that the defendant on _May 30, 1989_ was convicted as found guilty, and is sentenced the Wisconsin State Prisons for an indeterminate term of not more than _#1 5_ years the County Jail for _# 2, 3 years # indiged concurrent_

IT IS DETERMINED that society will not be harmed and the defendant will benefit by being placed on probation pursuant to Sec. 973.09, Wis. Stats.;

IT IS ADJUDGED that execution of the sentence is stayed and the defendant is placed on probation for the period of _5 years ea. ct._ , in the custody and control of the Wisconsin Department of Health and Social Services, subject to its rules and orders pursuant to Sec. 973.10, Wis. Stats.;
concurrent

IT IS DETERMINED AND ORDERED that the record requires court-imposed conditions as follows:

☐ None   ☑ As ordered below:

That the defendant has the ability to pay within that period the amounts ordered herein. Should his/her financial condition change s/he shall forthwith petition this Court for reconsideration of such conditions.

Fines: ☑ None ☐ $ _____ ; Court Costs: ☐ None ☐ $ _Yes_

Attorney Fees: ☑ None ☐ $ _____ ; Restitution: ☑ None ☐ $ _____

Other: ☑ None ☐ $ _____ ;

Mandatory Victim/Witness Surcharge: ☑ Felony _____ (# counts) @ $30.00   Amount $ _50 + 50_

☐ Misdemeanor _____ (# counts) @ $20.00   Amount $ _____

(Sec. 973.045 Wis. Stats.) Paid ☐ Yes Amount $ _____ ; ☐ No

#1 That the defendant shall be incarcerated in the County Jail for the following periods:

☑ None   ☐ The period of _Re: Abuse of children - Alcohol abuse. In-patient & out-patient alcohol treatment._

IT IS FURTHER ORDERED that the defendant shall pay surcharges pursuant to Sec. 973.09(1)(b), Wis. Stats.; _No contact with anyone under 18 yrs of age_

IT IS ADJUDGED that _____ days sentence credit due pursuant to Sec. 973.155, Wis. Stats., and shall be given by the Department if probation is revoked.

IT IS ORDERED THAT THE Sheriff deliver the defendant into the custody of the Department as it directs and if probation ___ the Sheriff having custody of the defendant shall deliver him/her to the Reception Center designate ___

BY ORDER OF THE COURT / Signature of Judge, Deputy or Clerk of Court

Name of Judge _William D. Gardner_   Date Signed _5/24/89_

Name of Defense Attorney _Gerald Boyle_

Name of District Attorney _Gale Shelton_

IMPORTANT — CLERK OF COURT PLEASE NOTE: Send the following to the local Probation ___

SEC 5 PAGE 112

	INCIDENT HOMICIDE (STABBING)		DATE OF INCIDENT/ACCIDENT 07-23-91		REP CCN #
INCIDENT INFORMATION	VICTIM LACY, Oliver		LOCATION OF INCIDENT/ACCIDENT (Address) 924 North 25th Street, Apt. 213		DIST 3

JUVENILE LAST NAME	FIRST	MID	DATE OF BIRTH	O DETAINED O ORDERED TO MCCC O OTHER

QUAN	TYPE OF PROPERTY	DESCRIPTION	SERIAL #	CODE #	VALUE

Below is a list of the Homicide Victims that Jeffrey DAHMER has confessed to and he states this is the order in which he had killed each individual. Included in this list is his description of the subjects, the approximate time when he killed them, and how he had lured these individuals to his residence, also the identity of each one if they had been identified and what part of the body he kept of the individuals, if any.

1. White male, 25 yoa, 5'6, 130 pds, fair complected, smooth skin, blond shoulder length straight hair. He states he met him approximately 1 week before Thanksgiving, in November, 1987. He states he met him around the 219 Club on 2nd St., and he offered this individual money for sex. He states when he got him to the Ambassador Hotel, where he rented a room, he gave him a drink mixture of rum & coke with approximately 5-7 crushed sleeping pills **20** He states they both went to bed in the nude and when he awoke he observed this individual to have a black & blue chest and blood coming from his mouth. DAHMER also states that his forearms were black & blue, therefore he figured he had killed him by beating him. He then kept the room for another night, proceeded to the Grand Avenue Mall where he purchased a large suitcase at Woolworth's, returned to the Ambassador, placed the victim in the suitcase and took a cab to his grandmother's residence at 2357 S. 57th St., where he was living. He dismembered the victim in the basement, placed him in various garbage bags and threw them in the garbage. He did not keep any remains. As of this time this victim has not been identified.

2. Hispanic male, 16-18 yoa, 6'0, 150 pds, slim build, dark complected, regular cut hair, clean shaven, lives in the vicinity of 10th & National. He states he met this individual in front of the 219 Club on 2nd St., around 1:00 a.m., and the individual was waiting for a bus. He stated he offered him money for sex, he accepted, and they took the bus to his grandmother's house at 2357 S. 57th St. He stated they had light sex, kissing, body rubbing and masturbation. He states he gave him the drink mixture of rum & coke with approximately 5-7 curshed sleeping pills **# 20** states that after the victim fell asleep he strangled him, dismembered him, smashed the bones with his sledge-hammer and disposed of the bones inside garbage bags and into the trash. He viewed a photo array and tentatively picked out I.D. #234356, which is the photo of DOXTATOR, James E, Indian male, 03-01-73, 1010 W. Pierce St., reported missing on 01-16-88 and the report came in on

REPORTING OFFICER 2472 see	5	PAYROLL #	LOC CODE	SUPERVISOR SIGNATURE
		PAGE 118		

DAHMER: Wonders if he's influenced by 'evil force'

He wanted 'excitement, gratification'

MILWAUKEE — Jeffrey Dahmer's sanity trial resumes today in an attempt to explain why he killed.

Key defense witness Fred Berlin, a psychologist who runs the sexual disorders clinic at Johns Hopkins University in Baltimore, is expected to testify that the serial killer suffers from a psychosexual mental disorder.

But a 179-page confession offered Dahmer's first comments about his motives.

Dahmer said he killed for "excitement and gratification" and he must be "thoroughly evil." He spoke of God and Satan; sexual obsessions; and devastating loneliness.

"My consuming lust was to experience their bodies. I viewed them as objects, as strangers. If I knew them, I could not have done it.

"It's hard for me to believe that a human being could have done what I've done, but I know I did it.

"It would be me who has to stand before God and admit my wrongdoing.

"I realize what I have done is my fault, but I have to question if there is an evil force in the world and if I am influenced by it. If I am to be honest with myself, I would have to admit that if I was set up in another apartment and had the opportunity, I probably would not be able to stop.

"A power higher than myself had been fed up with my deeds and decided it was time for me to be stopped."

— *Debbie Howlett*

Art courtesy of Susan Eve Padron.

PO15-8 5-89 SUPPLEMENT REPORT MILWAUKEE POLICE DEPARTMENT	O INCIDENT SUPPLEMENT O ACCIDENT SUPPLEMENT O JUVENILE SUPPLEMENT	PAGE___of_8	DATE OF REPORT 08-02-91	INCIDENT/ACCIDENT # 91-51767/M2472-M2481	
INCIDENT	HOMICIDE (STABBING)		DATE OF INCIDENT/ACCIDENT 07-23-91		REP CON
VICTIM	LACY, Oliver		LOCATION OF INCIDENT/ACCIDENT (Address) 924 N. 25th Street #213		DIS
JUVENILE LAST NAME	FIRST	MID	DATE OF BIRTH	O DETAINED O ORDERED TO MCCC O OTHER	
QUAN	TYPE OF PROPERTY	DESCRIPTION	SERIAL #	CODE #	VALUE

01-18-88. DAHMER states he met this individual in approximately January, 1988. There were also no remains of this victim.

3. Hispanic male, 19-21 yoa, 5'8-5'10, slim build, light complected, short straight black hair, wearing a long knee length coat. DAHMER states he met him in March, 1988, in a bar called the Phoenix, in the doorway, offered him money for sex, at which time they took a taxi to his grandmother's house at 2357 S. 57th St. While there, he gave him the drink mixture of rum & coke and sleeping pills, they had oral sex, the victim fell asleep, he strangled him, dismembered him, broke up the bones, threw them in garbage bags and into the garbage. He did not keep anything on this victim. This victim was subsequently identified by DAHMER, as GUERRERO, Richard, Hispanic male, 12-12-65, 3332 N. 1st St., 263-5512. GUERRERO was missing since 03-29-88.

4. Black male, 21-22 yoa, 5'9, 150 pds, slim build, light complected, short curly hair with a small ponytail, with a rubberband on it. He stated he met this individual the night before Easter, at closing time at the LeCage, on 03-25-89. He states that a friend of this individual, a white female drove them and dropped them off near a tavern by his grandmother's house, the Mai Khi Tavern (phonetic). He states they walked to his grandmother's house, he gave him the drink, and the reason he got him there was money for sex. He states they had sex, he fell asleep, and he killed him. He dismembered him on Easter Sunday, but kept his scalp, genitals, and skull. He subsequently painted the skull and genital area and preserved the scalp. This victim has been identified through photo by the suspect and also through dental records, as last name SEARS, Anthony L, black male, 01-26-65, 1657 N. Astor. Reported missing 03-25-89.

5. Black male, 22 yoa, 5'8-5'9, 140 pds, curly black hair, slight mustache. He states he met this individual in May, 1990. He offered him money for sex and for posing for him and watching videos. He states he met him in the area of the 219 Club, about 2 months after he had been released from the House of Correction. DAHMER states they took a cab from the 219 Club to his apartment. He gave him the drinking potion, and took pictures. After he died, he had oral sex with the vicitm, took photographs of him, dismembered him and subsequently kept his scalp and painted it. This victim was also identified

INCIDENT INFORMATION	INCIDENT HOMICIDE (STABBING) ,		DATE OF INCIDENT/ACCIDENT 07-25-91		REP CON #
	VICTIM LACY, Oliver		LOCATION OF INCIDENT/ACCIDENT (ADDRESS) 924 N. 25th Street #213		DIST
JUVENILE LAST NAME	FIRST	MID	DATE OF BIRTH	O DETAINED O ORDERED TO MCCC O OTHER	
QUAN	TYPE OF PROPERTY	DESCRIPTION	SERIAL #	CODE #	VALUE

by the suspect, as SMITH Raymond L, black male, 08-10-57, a/k/a BEEKS Rickey Lee, black male, 08-10-57, with a nickname of "Cash D", This individual had not been reported missing.

6. Black male, 24 yoa, 6'2, 170 pds, medium build, dark skin, prematurely bald, close cut hair, clean shaven, and he use to dance with the Milwaukee Ballet. He states this victim wore a headband like a Arab. He states he offered this individual money for sex and posing and that he had met him approximately in July, 1990. He states he met him at the Phoenix Bar, they took a cab to his apartment, had oral sex, gave him the drink mixture of rum & coke or coffee, and sleeping pills, strangled him, dismembered him and also took 4 or 5 photos of him, and disposed of the body by placing it in garbage bags and putting it in the trash. He states he also disposed of the pictures of this victim. This victim was identified by the suspect, to I.D. Photo #244654, that being a SMITH Edward W, black male, 08-02-62, 3606 N. 11th St., reported missing on 06-23-90.

7. Black male, 24 yoa, 6'0, 160 pds, medium build, medium complexion, chin whiskers, short black hair. He states he met this individual around September, 1990, in the 800 block of N. 27th St., in front of the bookstore. He states he offered him money for sex and for posing. This individual agreed and they proceeded to his residence where he gave him the drink mixture, had sex, and then when he fell asleep he cut his throat. He photographed the body, cut it up, and kept this individual's skull, his biceps and heart. He states he painted the skull and kept his biceps and heart to eat. He also kept the entire skeleton and bleached it down. He also took numerous photographs of this individual. This individual was identified by the suspect, and through dental records as MILLER Ernest, black male, 05-05-67, of Chicago, IL. He had been missing since 09-03-90.

8. Black male, 25 yoa, 150 pds, slim build, medium to dark complexion, short dark hair. He states he met this individual around October, 1990, on 2nd & Wisconsin, and they walked to his residence. He states he offered him money for sex, to pose for him, and view videos. When he got to his apartment he gave him the mixed drink with the sleeping pills in it, they talked, didn't have sex, because he wasn't his type. He states after the individual fell asleep, he killed him because he had already given him the potion and thought when he woke up he would be "pissed off". He states he took two picture

| REPORTING OFFICER | PAYROLL # | LOC CODE | SUPERVISOR SIGNATURE |
| 2472 SEC 5 PAGE 115 | | | |

PO15-8 5-89 SUPPLEMENT REPORT MILWAUKEE POLICE DEPARTMENT	■ INCIDENT SUPPLEMENT O ACCIDENT SUPPLEMENT O JUVENILE SUPPLEMENT	PAGE 4 of 8	DATE OF REPORT 08-02-91	INCIDENT/ACCIDENT # 91-51767/M2472-M2481	
INCIDENT INFORMATION	INCIDENT HOMICIDE (STABBING)		DATE OF INCIDENT/ACCIDENT 07-23-91		REP CON
	VICTIM LACY, Oliver		LOCATION OF INCIDENT/ACCIDENT (Address) 924 N. 25th Street #213		DI!
JUVENILE LAST NAME	FIRST	MID	DATE OF BIRTH	O DETAINED O ORDERED TO MCCC O OTHER	
QUAN	TYPE OF PROPERTY	DESCRIPTION	SERIAL #	CODE #	VALUE

of this individual, he didn't keep anything because he wasn't his type. The suspect, DAHMER, viewed a photograph of the victim and identified him to this photograph. This victim was subsequently identified by relatives, through photographs. He has been identified as THOMAS David C. black male, 12-21-67, 6432 W. Birch, and has been missing since 09-24-90, I.D. #200484.

9. Black male, 18 yoa, 6'0, 140 pds, slim build, medium complexion, three inch perm, mustache. He states he met this individual approximately February, 1991. He offered him money for posing, sex, and videos, while this individual was waiting for a bus near Marquette. He states they proceeded to his residence, where he gave him the drink mixture containing the sleeping pills. They had oral sex, the victim fell asleep, and then he killed him and photographed him. He then cut him up, kept his skull, hands, and genitals. He states he used a strap to strangle this victim. He also stated this victim was wearing an earring, but he disposed of it. This victim was subsequently identified by the suspect, and by dental records, as STRAUGHTER Curtis, black male, 04-16-73, 3628 N. 19th St., and he has been missing since 02-18-91. He states that he disposed of this individual in two barrels, one for bones and one for flesh and used acid to melt down the bones and flesh. He did take pictures of this victim also.

10. Black male, 20 yoa, 5'9-5'10, 150 pds, short black hair, medium build, medium complexion. He states he met this individual approximately March, 1991, on the corner of 27th & Kilbourn. He states he offered this individual money for posing, and to view videos. He states when they got to his residence, he gave him the drink mixture with the sleeping pills, and when he fell asleep he strangled him, had oral sex after death on the victim, took pictures of him, dismembered him and saved his skull. He also disposed of this individual by putting the bones and the flesh in the two barrels with the acid. This individual was subsequently identified by the suspect, and with dental charts, as being LINDSEY Earl, black male, 03-03-72, 2510 W. Juneau, Apt. 4, I.D. #220831.

11. Black male, 26 yoa, 6'0, 150 pds, and a deaf mute. He states he met him approximately early May, 1991, in front of the 219 Bar on 2nd St. He states the victim was with friends who were also deaf mutes, and these friends drove them to 23rd & Wells,

INCIDENT INFORMATION	INCIDENT HOMICIDE (STABBING)		DATE OF INCIDENT/ACCIDENT 07-23-91		REP COM
	VICTIM LACY, Oliver		LOCATION OF INCIDENT/ACCIDENT (Address) 924 N. 25th Street #213		DIS
JUVENILE LAST NAME	FIRST	MID	DATE OF BIRTH	□ DETAINED □ ORDERED TO MCCC □ OTHER	
QUAN	TYPE OF PROPERTY	DESCRIPTION		SERIAL #	CODE #	VALUE

where they got out and subsequently walked to his apartment. He states he had them drop him off there, so they would not know where he lived. He states he communicated with this victm by writing notes to him and that he offered him $50.00 for sex. He states he does not remember whether or not they had sex, but upon going to his apartment, he gave him the drinking potion and the victim subsequently passed out and so did the suspect. Suspect states when he woke up this victim was dead. He states he dismembered him and kept his head. He states he disposed of the body and flesh in the two barrels of acid. He did not take any photos of this individual. The victim was identified by the suspect, and through dental records, as HUGHES Tony Anthony, black male, 08-26-59, reported missing in Madison, WI., on 05-31-91, and last seen on 05-24-91.

12. Asian male, 18-19 yoa, 5'5, 120 pds, slim build, black hair. He states he met him in late May, 1991, in the Grand Avenue Mall. He states he offered money to take pictures of him and to view videos, but not for sex. He was hoping it would lead to sex. He states they took the bus back to the apartment and the individual posed for two photos while he was alive. He states he gave him the drink mixture and the victim passed out. Suspect states he then had oral sex on him, after he passed out and finished watching a video and then he ran out of beer. He then went to the Care Bear Tavern, in the 900 block of N. 27th St., drank beer until around closing and returned to the apartment. As he was returning to the apartment he saw the victim sitting on the curb at 25th & State in the nude. He was taking him back to the apartment when the Police and Fire Dept., showed up. Someone put a yellow blanket around the victim and he told the Police that the victim always acted like this when he got drunk and that the victim could not speak English, because the victim was not speaking English. Police questioned him, subsequently escorted him back to the apartment, at which time he convinced the Police it was his homosexual lover, the Police left, and later on he subsequently strangled the victim, had oral and anal sex with the victim after death, took numerous photos of the victim, dismembered him and kept his head. He put the bones and the flesh of the victims in the acid barrel. This victim was subsequently identified through photos and dental charts, as SINTHASOMPHONE Konerak, Asian male, 12-02-76, 2634 N. 56th St., and he had been reported missing on 05-26-91.

| REPORTING OFFICER 472 | SEC 5 | PAGE 117 | PAYROLL # | LOC CODE | SUPERVISOR SIGNATURE |

| | INCIDENT HOMICIDE (STABBING) | | DATE OF INCIDENT/ACCIDENT 07-23-91 | | REP CON # |
| INCIDENT INFORMATION | VICTIM LACY, Oliver | | LOCATION OF INCIDENT/ACCIDENT (Address) 924 N. 25th Street #213 | | DIST |

| JUVENILE LAST NAME | FIRST | MID | DATE OF BIRTH | O DETAINED O ORDERED TO MCCC O OTHER |
| QUAN | TYPE OF PROPERTY | DESCRIPTION | SERIAL # | CODE # | VALUE |

13. Black male, 22 yoa, 5'8, 140 pds, medium build, dark complexion, having a high top fade to the left side. He states he met this individual on June 30th, after the Gay Pride Parade, at the Chicago Bus Station. He states he offered him money for sex, posing, and to view videos. This individual accompanied him back to Milwaukee on the Grayhound Bus and then took a cab to his apartment, namely a City Vet Cab. He states he then gave him the drinking potion and they were nude and playing with each other. He states this victim fell asleep, so he strangled him, possibly with a strap, and did not have sex with him. He then took photos, dismembered him, and kept his head in the freezer and the body in the blue 57 gallon barrel which he had purchased a short while before this. The victim was identified by the suspect, through a photo from Chicago. He was also identified by friends from Chicago. This individual has been identified as TURNER Matt, black male, 07-03-70, a/k/a Donald MONTRELL. DAHMER states that he disposed of this individual's flesh in the trash.

14. Puerto Rican male, part Jewish, 23-24, 5'10, 140 pds, slim build, light complexion, short black hair, thin mustache. He states he met this individual around July 6th, at Carol's in Chicago (gay bar). He states they left about 4:00 a.m., returned to Milwaukee with the victim, via the Grayhound, and took a cab to his apartment. He states they spent two days together. He states they had oral sex the first day and on the second day the victim wanted to leave, so the suspect killed him, by giving him the drink mixture with the sleeping pills and when he fell asleep he strangled him, took photos, dismembered him, put his head in the freezer and his body in the 57 gallon barrel. This subject was identified by the suspect, through pictures, as WEINBERGER Jerimiah, Puerto Rican male, 09-26-67, 3404 N. Halsted, Chicago, IL., 929-2478. DAHMER states that he threw the victim's flesh out in the barrel.

15. Black male, 24 yoa, 5'9, 160 pds, muscular build, short hair. He states he met this individual on 27th St., between State & Kilbourn, which would be the 900 block. He states he met this individual about the 2nd week in July. He states that he offered him money to pose for pictures and watch videos with him and have a drink. He states the victim proceeded with him to his apartment, he gave him the drink mixture, they did some body rubbing, the victim fell asleep, and he killed him. He states he had anal sex after

| REPORTING OFFICER 2472 / SEC 5 | PAYROLL # / PAGE 118 | LOC CODE | SUPERVISOR SIGNATURE |

| | INCIDENT HOMICIDE (STABBING) | | DATE OF INCIDENT 07-23-91 | | REP CON |
| INCIDENT INFORMATION | VICTIM LACY, Oliver | | LOCATION OF INCIDENT/ACCIDENT (Address) 924 N. 25th Street #213 | | DIS |

| JUVENILE LAST NAME | FIRST | MID | DATE OF BIRTH | ☐ DETAINED ☐ ORDERED TO MCCC ☐ OTHER |
| QUAN | TYPE OF PROPERTY | DESCRIPTION | | SERIAL # | CODE # | VALUE |

death. He then took photos, kept the victim's I.D., and two other personal photos, because he wanted more pictures of him. He dismembered this individual, placed his head in the bottom of the refrigerator in a box, kept his heart in the freezer to eat later and ate his right bicep. He also put his body in the freezer. He states the victim was wearing a white shirt and bluejeans at the time he met him and that the victim told him he was a Weight Lifter and a Model. The suspect identified the victim to his I.D., which was found in his wallet and he was also identified through dental records and prints, as LACY Oliver, black male, 06-23-67, 3237 N. 24th Pl. The suspect stated that he disposed of the victim's flesh in the trash, but that he kept his head, body, heart, and took photos, and he also ate the bicep. This victim was reported missing on 07-15-91, last seen on 07-12-91.

16. White male, early 20s, 5'9, 140-150 pds, brownish blond hair, short mustache. He states he met this individual approximately 07-19-91, at around Wisconsin Ave., near the Marquette University. This victim was waiting for a bus, with a "6 pack" in his arms. He states he offered this individual money to pose for pictures and to view videos. He agreed and they took a bus to his apartment. He gave this individual the drink mixture, had oral sex before he fell asleep. When he fell asleep he strangled him with a strap, dismembered him, put his head in the freezer, and placed the body in the 57 gallon barrel. He states he disposed of the flesh in the trash. He identified this victim from a photo in his apartment, as BRADEHOFT Joseph, white male, 01-24-66, 426 E. Spring, Lot 11, Greenville, IL.

17. White male, 18-19, 6'0, 150 pds., light hair. This victim was killed in June, 1978. After further questioning he identified him as wearing a necklace with braces on. He states this individual did not have a shirt, but had jeans and shoes. He states he met him hitchhiking on Cleveland Massing (phonetic) Rd., in Ohio, picked him up, took him to his home to drink beer. Once they got there they were drinking beer in his bedroom and the victim wanted to leave. He states he hit him in the head with a barbell and then strangled him with the barbell. He states he did not have sex with the victim. He states he then put him under the crawl space under the house. He subsequently dismembered him, put him in three garbage bags. Two weeks later he broke up the bones and threw them in

| REPORTING OFFICER | PAYROLL # | LOC CODE | SUPERVISOR SIGNATURE |
| 2472 / SEC 5 / PAGE 119 | | | Sgt. Raymond R Crick |

INCIDENT INFORMATION	INCIDENT HOMICIDE (STABBING)		DATE OF INCIDENT/ACCIDENT 07-23-91		REP CO
	VICTIM LACY, Oliver		LOCATION OF INCIDENT/ACCIDENT (Address) 924 N. 25th Street #213		D1

JUVENILE LAST NAME	FIRST	MID	DATE OF BIRTH	O DETAINED O ORDERED TO MCCC O OTHER

QUAN	TYPE OF PROPERTY	DESCRIPTION	SERIAL #	CODE #	VALUE

the woods behind his house. He disposed of the knife he used to dismember him and the victim's necklace in the river. This victim was identified by the suspect, through a photo, and by the suspect recalling his last name, that being HICKS Steve M. white male, 06-22-59, 2993 Pryor Dr., Ohio, 644-5600. He stated he recalls the name HICKS, because he states "you don't forget your first one".

DAHMER states he gave the drinking potion to most of his victims, therefore being easier to control them and he could kill them without having them fight with them. He stated the reason he killed them, because there was excitement and gratification in it and he wanted to keep the victims.

Further investigation pending.

Report dictated by: Detective Dennis MURPHY

DM: hvs 08-02-91

2472 / SEC 5 / PAGE 120

REPORTING OFFICER Det. MURPHY	PAYROLL # 32893 91	LOC CODE	SUPERVISOR SIGNATURE

PO15-B 5-89 SUPPLEMENT REPORT	☒ INCIDENT SUPPLEMENT	PAGE _1_ of _5_	DATE OF REPORT	INCIDENT/ACCIDENT #
MILWAUKEE POLICE DEPARTMENT	☐ ACCIDENT SUPPLEMENT		08/05/91	91-51767/M-2472-248
	☐ JUVENILE SUPPLEMENT			

INCIDENT		DATE OF INCIDENT/ACCIDENT	REP CO
INCIDENT INFORMATION	HOMICIDE	07/23/91	
VICTIM	LACY, Oliver	LOCATION OF INCIDENT/ACCIDENT (Address) 924 N. 25th St., #213	DI

JUVENILE LAST NAME	FIRST	MID	DATE OF BIRTH	☐ DETAINED ☐ ORDERED TO MCCC ☐ OTHER

QUAN	TYPE OF PROPERTY	DESCRIPTION	SERIAL #	CODE #	VALUE

REFER TO FOLLOWUP NUMBER:

NARRATIVE

On Monday, 08-05-91, I, Detective KENNEDY, along with Detective James DEVALKENAERE, proceeded to the 5th floor lock up of the Milwaukee County jail where, after obtaining an order to produce, we met the suspect, Jeffrey DAHMER, and returned with him to the 4th floor CIB where his attorney, Wendy PATRICKUS, was waiting. At this time we all entered into the interview room and conducted the following interview.

Regarding information from the Detroit Police Department and a photograph of Alex Reginald BROWN, who was reported missing from Detroit, DAHMER stated, after viewing the photo, that he has never seen this individual before and denied that he is one of his victims.

Regarding photo #150029 from the ID Division, that being a David Allen LEE, DAHMER stated that this is not one of his victims and he has never seen him before.

Regarding photo #244202 from the ID Division, that being Ronald (nmn) BROWN, DAHMER stated, after viewing the photo, that he has never seen the individual before and denies he is one of his victims.

Regarding information obtained about a white male by the name of Michael J. HEFFNER, DOB 06-23-53, lna 1328 E. Albion and a report that he had, in fact, lived with DAHMER for a period of time at his 25th Street address, DAHMER stated that he has never had a live in companion. He stated that none of his sexual pick ups ever spent more than one night except for the individual later identified as WEINBERGER who he brought home with him from Chicago. He related that at no time while he lived in Milwaukee did he have a roommate and at no time did he have a companion who came and spent several days with him.

Regarding a photo obtained from the family of Marvin Guy BIZELLE Jr, B/M, DOB 01-12-60, DAHMER stated that he has never seen the individual before and denies that he is one of his victims.

Regarding a photo sent from Ashland, Wisconsin of Bobbie MAYOTTE, Indian male, 11yoa, who has been missing since 09-17-88, DAHMER stated that he is not one of his vic-

REPORTING OFFICER	SEC 5 PAGE 1	PAYROLLS # 1	LOC CODE	SUPERVISOR SIGNATURE

| INCIDENT INFORMATION | INCIDENT HOMICIDE (STABBING) | | DATE OF INCIDENT/ACCIDENT 07-23-91 | | REP COM |
| | VICTIM LACY, 'Oliver | | LOCATION OF INCIDENT/ACCIDENT (Address) 924 N. 25th Street #213 | | DIS |

| JUVENILE LAST NAME | FIRST | MID | DATE OF BIRTH | O DETAINED O ORDERED TO HCCC O OTHER |
| QUAN | TYPE OF PROPERTY | DESCRIPTION | | SERIAL # | CODE # | VALUE |

tims and he has never seen him before.

Regarding information from Orlando, Florida stating that a missing juvenile was reported missing on 06-18-85 and a brief description, DAHMER noted that he was living in Milwaukee at the time of this missing juvenile. He stated that he has never been to Orlando, Florida and that he has never made any return trips to visit the Florida area after moving to Milwaukee.

Regarding information from Toledo, Ohio Police Department regarding a black male who had been found on 04-21-80 dismembered in their city DAHMER stated that he has never been to Toledo Ohio and at the time of this offense he was serving time in the Armed Forces in Germany and denies any part of this offense.

At this time we showed family photographs regarding a possible victim of DAHMER'S, that being Steven W. TUOMI, W/M, DOB 12-19-62, lna 1315 N. Cass Street. Mr. DAHMER viewed this photograph and positively identified him as being the individual whom he first murdered in Milwaukee at the Ambassador Hotel.

It should be noted that Detective James DEVALKENAERE will file a detailed supplementry regarding this identification.

At this time the interview was terminated and DAHMER'S attorney, Wendy PATRICKUS, left the building. As I was attempting to take Mr. DAHMER to the 5th floor of the Sheriff's lock up we again began to speak regarding the second victim in Milwaukee and the fact that we have been unable to identify this individual through photographs. Mr. DAHMER stated that the photo that he has viewed, which has been provided by the ID Division, does have similarities of the person who he was with during this offense, however, he stated that he cannot be sure and that it would be helpful if he could receive other family photographs. At this time I advised Mr. DAHMER that the only family photos available of this possible victim would have him considerably younger, approximatley 14 or 15 years old. To this Mr. DAHMER stated that even younger photographs would be of help and stated he would be glad to view them as they came in.

At this time I asked Mr. DAHMER if he would like to again go over the offense regarding the second victim here in Milwaukee and he stated that he did. He stated that to the best of his recollection he remembers him as being an light tanned skined male and he assumed he was 18 to 20 years old as he met him infront of the Phoenix club at approxi-

| REPORTING OFFICER 2472 | SEC 5 | PAGE 122 | PAYROLL # | LOC CODE | SUPERVISOR SIGNATURE |

PO15-B 5-89 SUPPLEMENT REPORT MILWAUKEE POLICE DEPARTMENT	☑ INCIDENT SUPPLEMENT ○ ACCIDENT SUPPLEMENT ○ JUVENILE SUPPLEMENT	PAGE 3 of 5	DATE OF REPORT 08-05-91	INCIDENT/ACCIDENT # 91-51767/M2472-M2481

INCIDENT INFORMATION	INCIDENT HOMICIDE (STABBING)		DATE OF INCIDENT/ACCIDENT 07-23-91	REP COM
	VICTIM LACY, Oliver		LOCATION OF INCIDENT/ACCIDENT (Address) 924 N. 25th Street #213	DIS

JUVENILE LAST NAME	FIRST	MID	DATE OF BIRTH	○ DETAINED ○ ORDERED TO MCCC ○ OTHER

QUAN	TYPE OF PROPERTY	DESCRIPTION	SERIAL #	CODE #	VALUE

mately 1:00am in the morning. He stated that he may have been younger than this, however, because he was out at this hour and infront of a tavern he assumed him to be slightly older. He indicated that he believes he offered him $50.00 to return with him to his apartment, to watch videos and have sex. He related that at this point they took the bus to 57th and National and they then walked to his grandmother's house. He stated that they did not have any conversation on the bus as they sat in separate seats because the bus was slightly crowded. He stated that once at his grandmother's house they sat in the front room and had some light sex which he described as hugging and kissing and that at this time he told the victim that it would be quieter down in the basement. He related that they proceeded to the basement where there was a large easy chair and they continued to hug and kiss and mutually masturbate one another. He indicated that it was around this time that the victim stated that he would have to be home in the morning. Upon hearing this Mr. DAHMER made him a drink of coffee Irish cream and the sleeping pills. He stated that after the individual fell asleep he pulled out a old sheet and layed it on the ground of the basement. He indicated that he did this because the basement floor was chilly. He layed the victim on the sheet and at this time he strangled him. After strangling him he layed on top of the victim and kissed and hugged and held him and then wrapped him up in the sheet and placed him in the fruit cellar. He stated it was approximately 7:00am in the morning at this time and his grandmother awoke. He indicated that he went upstairs and had breakfast with his grandmother and after she left for church he returned to his victim and decided to dispose of his body.

At this time I asked him how he went about disposing of his victims. He stated that he generally placed them near a drain or in a tub, that he took off all of his clothes and took off all of the clothes of his victims if they were not already completly undressed. He stated that he would then take a sharp knife and start at the top of the sternum and make a single cut down the middle of the upper torso of the victims. He stated that once the initial cut was made he would spread the wound and remove all the internal organs. He stated that he would place the internal organs, that he would cut up into fist size pieces, into a plastic bag. He related that then he began to cut the flesh off the victim and he would start stripping the flesh off the arms and biceps, then the chest and then slowly work his way down the leg until he got to the feet. He stated that

INCIDENT INFORMATION	INCIDENT HOMICIDE (STABBING)		DATE OF INCIDENT/ACCIDENT 07-23-91		REP COM
	VICTIM LACY, Oliver		LOCATION OF INCIDENT/ACCIDENT (Address) 924 N. 25th Street #213		DIS
JUVENILE LAST NAME	FIRST	MID	DATE OF BIRTH	O DETAINED / O ORDERED TO MCCC / O OTHER	

QUAN	TYPE OF PROPERTY	DESCRIPTION		SERIAL #	CODE #	VALUE

at this time he would slice up all the strips of flesh into small fist like pieces and place them into approximately 3 bags, that being plastic garbage bags. He indicated that he was careful not to place too much into each bag, approximately 25lbs worth. He would then triple bag the garbage bags. He stated that at this time he rewrapped up the skeleton and head of the victim in the sheet and then used a sledge hammer to smash the bones until they broke into smaller pieces. He related that he would then place the upper part of the torso bones in a plastic bag and the lower part in another bag. He stated that this was his usual pattern and it usually took about five 25lbs bags to dispose of his victims.

He stated that during the time that he was cutting up his victims and attempting to dispose of the bones that he was feeling several different emotions. He indicated that the emotions were a combination of fright, for fear of being caught, and excitement knowing that he had done what he had done. He stated that he also had the feeling that the victims could not leave him anymore because he had complete control over them. He stated that when he would place the plastic bags into the garbage after cutting up his victims he felt an intense sense of loss and stated that as he placed the bags in the garbage he felt that the individuals life was such a complete waste and that at one time they were a full human being and now they were reduced to 4 or 5 bags of plastic garbage which he had placed in the trash. He also stated that at this time he felt deep remorse for his actions, however, it did not last.

He went on to state that he feels that one of the triggers which started him on this path of murder happened shortly after he had moved to Milwaukee and was living with his grandmother. He feels that sometime in 1983 he was attempting seriously to find some religious meaning in his life and he was attending church with his grandmother and doing a lot of religious reading. He related that he did have fantasies of dismemberment and strong homosexual urges, however, he was trying to control his drinking and was not giving into any of these urges. He stated that one time while he was sitting in the West Allis library an individual walked by and threw a note in his lap and continued walking. He stated that upon opening the note he read that if he wanted a blow job he should go to the second level bathroom. He stated that at this time he thought "it's going to take more than this to make me stumble," as he was continually fighting his homosexual urges.

	INCIDENT HOMICIDE (STABBING)		DATE OF INCIDENT/ACCIDENT 07-23-91		REP COM
INCIDENT					
INFORMATION	VICTIM LACY, Oliver		LOCATION OF INCIDENT/ACCIDENT (Address) 924 N. 25th Street #213		DI:

JUVENILE LAST NAME	FIRST	MID	DATE OF BIRTH	☐ DETAINED ☐ ORDERED TO MCCC ☐ OTHER

QUAN	TYPE OF PROPERTY	DESCRIPTION	SERIAL #	CODE #	VALUE

However, he stated that it was shortly after this incident in the library that he again began frequenting the gay book stores, gay bars and gay baths and he feels that this was the catalyst which started him again in his homosexual lifestyle which eventually lead to the killing and dismembering of his victims.

At this time Mr. DAHMER was turned over to the Milwaukee County Sheriffs on the 5th floor.

Report dictated by: Det. Patrick KENNEDY

PK:dls 08-05-91

2472 SEC 5 PAGE 125

| INCIDENT INFORMATION | INCIDENT HOMICIDE | | DATE OF INCIDENT/ACCIDENT 07/23/91 | | REP CON |
| | VICTIM LACY, Oliver | | LOCATION OF INCIDENT/ACCIDENT (Address) 924 N. 25th St., #213 | | DI |

| JUVENILE LAST NAME | FIRST | MID | DATE OF BIRTH | O DETAINED O ORDERED TO MCCC O OTHER |

| QUAN | TYPE OF PROPERTY | DESCRIPTION | SERIAL # | CODE # | VALUE |

REFER TO FOLLOWUP NUMBER:

NARRATIVE

On Monday, 8-5-91, at 2:PM, I, Detective James DEVALKENAERE, along with Detective Patrick KENNEDY, interviewed Jeffery L. DAHMER in an interview room on the fourth floor of the Police Administration Building. Also present at that time was Jeffery DAHMER'S attorney, Attorney Wendy PATRICKUS. By the time of this interview, a photo of a possible homicide victim, namely Steven W. TUOMI, W/M, 12-19-62, of 1315 N. Cass Street, had been obtained from his family.

In previous interviews, Jeffery DAHMER had related to Detectives KENNEDY and MURPHY that he believed he had encountered this individual in November of 1987. Jeffery DAHMER viewed the photos which had been received of Steven TUOMI and he positively identified this as being the person he had encountered in November of 1987.

DAHMER related that at that time he had been in front of the 219 Club, a tavern on South 2nd Street, at about bar closing time. At that time he had encountered TUOMI while TUOMI was waiting at a bus stop. He had already obtained a hotel room at the Ambassador Hotel, which he believes is located around 24th and Wisconsin. He had gotten the room earlier with the plan that - if he had encountered someone he would take him back there for the purposes of having sex with him. He had already purchased some sleeping pills, which he had at the hotel room, for the purpose of rendering anyone he brought back there, helpless, so he could have sex with them. He spoke with TUOMI and asked him if he wanted to spend the night with him at a hotel room. TUOMI agreed. DAHMER does not recall if he offered TUOMI money to come with him, or not.

On arrival at the hotel, both DAHMER and TUOMI got undressed and laid on the bed. At that time they had what DAHMER called "light sex". He described this as hugging, kissing, and mutual masturbation. After about an hour or two, DAHMER made a drink for TUOMI in which he put the sleeping pills. TUOMI drank this and fell asleep. DAHMER kept drinking and eventually fell asleep himself. DAHMER related that when he woke up he was lying on top of TUOMI and DAHMER'S forearms were visibly bruised. He then saw that TUOMI was obviously dead. He was bleeding from the head and his chest was crushed in and some

24 2 SEC 5 PAGE 126

| REPORTING OFFICER | PAYROLL # 44258 | LOC CODE 93 | SUPERVISOR SIGNATURE |

INCIDENT INFORMATION	INCIDENT HOMICIDE (STABBING)			DATE OF INCIDENT/ACCIDENT 07-23-91		REP COM #
	VICTIM LACY, Oliver			LOCATION OF INCIDENT/ACCIDENT (Address) 924 N. 25th Street #213		DIST

JUVENILE LAST NAME	FIRST	MID	DATE OF BIRTH	O DETAINED O ORDERED TO MCCC O OTHER

QUAN	TYPE OF PROPERTY	DESCRIPTION	SERIAL #	CODE #	VALUE

of the bones were broken. DAHMER then carried TUOMI and placed him in a closet in the hotel room. DAHMER sat around the hotel room for a couple of hours, trying to figure out what to do.

At about noon he went to the Grand Avenue Mall. He bought a large suitcase with wheels on it and returned to the Ambassador Hotel. During that time he may have had some beers and he left the hotel room to get a bite to eat. At about 5:PM he returned to the hotel room and placed TUOMI into the large suitcase. DAHMER related that it was a very tight fit, but he was able to get him into the suitcase. DAHMER related that he had purchased the room for another night and he remained in the room that night until 1:AM. At that time he left the room with the suitcase, taking an elevator to the ground floor. He got a cab and upon approaching the cab, had the cab driver help him place the suitcase in the back seat of the cab. He then took the cab to his grandmother's house on S. 57th Street.

Upon arrival at his grandmother's house, DAHMER put the suitcase in the fruit cellar beneath the house. He left the suitcase there for about a week. He said he did this because it was Thanksgiving time and it was cold in the basement and he knew this would slow the decomposition of the body. After about a week he got the suitcase out of the fruit cellar and removed the body from it. After removing the body from the suitcase, DAHMER used a knife to open the body and then stripped the flesh from it. He placed the flesh in plastic bags. DAHMER then used an old sheet which had been in the basement to wrap the bones and he then crushed the bones with a sledge hammer. DAHMER related that he wrapped the bones in a sheet so that when he was crushing them, the splinters and fragments of bones would not fly all over the basement. He then put these items in the trash.

Regarding the Ambassador Hotel, DAHMER related that on four or five times previous to his encounter with TUOMI, he had rented a room at the Ambassador for the purpose of having sex with someone he would meet. He indicated that at no previous time had he killed anyone there and nothing had happened.

On 8-5-91, information was received from the Bath Township, Ohio Police Department that they had recovered a receipt from Don Stricker Guns located at 2465 S. 84th Street, Milwaukee. The receipt showed that Jeffery L. DAHMER had purchased a Colt

REPORTING OFFICER	PAYROLL #	LOC CODE	SUPERVISOR SIGNATURE

156

INCIDENT INFORMATION	INCIDENT HOMICIDE (STABBING)		DATE OF INCIDENT/ACCIDENT 07-23-91	REP CON
	VICTIM LACY, Oliver		LOCATION OF INCIDENT/ACCIDENT (Address) 924 N. 25th Street #213	DI!

JUVENILE LAST NAME	FIRST	MID	DATE OF BIRTH	O DETAINED O ORDERED TO MCCC O OTHER

QUAN	TYPE OF PROPERTY	DESCRIPTION	SERIAL #	CODE #	VALUE

Lawman 357 Magnum revolver, serial #20301U, on 1-23-82. DAHMER was questioned regarding the ownership of this gun. DAHMER related that while working at the Plasma Center he had purchased a 357 snubnose revolver. DAHMER thinks he bought the gun in 1982 or 1983. He related that he only owned this gun for about one year and he used it for target shooting at a range. DAHMER related that he bought this gun at a gun shop in the area of 83rd and Lincoln. He paid about $350. for same. He does not remember the cost for using the range. DAHMER was shown a faxed copy of the receipt which Don Stricker's had given for the purchase of the gun, bearing the signature of Jeffery L. DAHMER. DAHMER identified this as a copy of the receipt he had received when he bought the gun, that the signature at the bottom of the sheet were, in fact, his. DAHMER further related that when his grandmother found out he had a gun in the house, she did not like it. He showed her the gun. Shortly after that his father visited from Ohio and his grandmother told his father that he had a gun and his father took the gun from him. DAHMER believes that his father took the gun back to Ohio and sold it. DAHMER further related that he only bought the gun because he had enjoyed shooting while he was in the Military and felt that it was something he might like to do.

DAHMER also related that he had stated he never owned a gun, in previous interviews, because he did not feel the gun had any connection with any of the victims in the homicides for which he was being talked to. He had never used the gun for anything other than target shooting.

Report per Det. James DEVALKENAERE.

JD: gb 8-5-91

2472 SE. 5 ... 12 A

REPORTING OFFICER DETECTIVE JAMES DEVALKENAERE	PAYROLL # 44258	LOC CODE 93	SUPERVISOR SIGNATURE

INCIDENT INFORMATION	INCIDENT HOMICIDE		DATE OF INCIDENT/ACCIDENT 07/23/91		REP CO
	VICTIM LACY, Oliver		LOCATION OF INCIDENT/ACCIDENT (Address) 924 N. 25th St., #213		O

JUVENILE LAST NAME	FIRST	MID	DATE OF BIRTH	O DETAINED O ORDERED TO MCCC O OTHER

QUAN	TYPE OF PROPERTY	DESCRIPTION	SERIAL #	CODE #	VALUE

REFER TO FOLLOWUP NUMBER:

NARRATIVE

On Wednesday, 08-07-91, I, Detective KENNEDY, was informed by the Milwaukee County Sheriff's Dept., that the suspect in this offense, Jeffrey DAHMER, had requested to speak with me. At this time, after obtaining an order to produce, I went to the 5th fl., Lock Up, of the Milwaukee County Sheriff, and returned with the suspect, DAHMER, to the 4th fl., interview room, of the CIB. At this time we were joined by DAHMER's Attorney, Scott HANSON.

At this time I questioned DAHMER, regarding information we had received from Bath, Ohio Police Department, that while he was staying in Miami, that he in fact had a girlfriend who lived with him and that he had intended to marry her. To this DAHMER stated that while he was in Miami he was working at a submarine shop called Sunshine Submarines. He states he met another employee there. He states she was a white woman, with long curly, thick black hair, and that she was originally from England. He states that she was in this country illegally and that they had become friends. He states that he is unsure, but he thinks her name was Julie. He states he did go out to dinner with her several times and walk along the beach with her, however, he, at no time had any inclination for sexual activity with her, and never felt attracted to her in that way. He states they were merely friends. He goes onto indicate that many times she advised him that she would be willing to marry an American, as a marriage of convenience, in order for her to obtain her naturlized citizenship. He states to the best of his recollection she was attracted to the manager of the Sunshine Submarine Club, however, she did mention to him, DAHMER, several times, that she would be willing to marry him in a marriage of convenience, if he could help her to become a citizen. He states they did talk about that several times, however, he never in fact took it seriously, and because he was not interested in her sexually or as a lifetime partner, he never actually encouraged this conversation. He states after moving back to Ohio, he believes that she did either call him once or twice or write him a letter, however, he did not respond, as he had stated previously he was not interested in pursuing a relationship with her. He denies that at anytime he considered her a girlfriend, or had any relationship with her, other than a

REPORTING OFFICER 2472	SEC 5	PAYROLL # PAGE 120	LOC CODE	SUPERVISOR SIGNATURE Lt. R Manske

158

| | INCIDENT HOMICIDE (STABBING) | | DATE OF INCIDENT/ACCIDENT 07-23-91 | | REP COM |
| INCIDENT INFORMATION | VICTIM LACY, Oliver | | LOCATION OF INCIDENT/ACCIDENT (Address) 924 N. 25th Street #213 | | DIS |

JUVENILE LAST NAME	FIRST	MID	DATE OF BIRTH	☐ DETAINED ☐ ORDERED TO MCCC ☐ OTHER

QUAN	TYPE OF PROPERTY	DESCRIPTION	SERIAL #	CODE #	VALUE

work relationship and he also denies that she ever lived with him in any of the motels that he had while he was staying in Miami.

Regarding information we received that he had an Aunt Unis (phonetic), who lived in the Milwaukee area during the time he stayed with his grandmother, he states that this is true and that he felt he always had a good relationship with his Aunt Unis. He states that he saw her several times during the holidays, as he was living at grandma's house and he felt that it was usually Aunt Unis who reported to his father activities that got him somewhat in trouble while he was living at grandmother's house. He states that he belives that she was the one who informed his father that he had a gun in the home and that several times she complained about the foul smell emanating from the basement at grandma's house. He states that he told grandma and Aunt Unis that the smell was because of the cat that grandma had by the name of Jody, had fowled the kitty litter box, which was located in the basement and it had not previously been emptied. He states one time his Aunt Unis pressed him further, stating that was not a kitty litter smell, and at this time he made up a ploy story stating that he had found a dead racoon and had cut the racoon up in the basement, in order to save the bones. He states he told this because he realized that there was the smell of dismembered bodies that came from the basement. At this time I asked him how this could be. He states that was because several of his vicims, although he cut them up and dismembered them over the drain pipe in the basement, he states after hosing down the basement floor and washing all the blood down the drain he was careful that none of the body parts or chunks of flesh got into the drain. He states after disposing of the body parts and the bones and hosing down the blood, he would pour a full gallon bottle of bleech down the drain in order to try to get rid of the smell, but the dismembered bodies would give off an awful oder and it would linger in the basement for one or two days before it would it go away. He states this is the smell that his Aunt Unis smelled and that she was the one that bought up the foul smell to his grandmother and to his father, however, he was usually able to dissuade them from investigating further, by his explanations of the racoon and the kitty litter box. At this time I showed DAHMER another photo array of several individuals that may be the second victim who is still un-identified and after viewing all of these photos, he stated that none of the photographs shown to him resembles the victim he in fact killed at his grandmother's house.

REPORTING OFFICER 2472	SEC 5	PAGE 130	LOC CODE	SUPERVISOR SIGNATURE H. Kronlew

INCIDENT INFORMATION	INCIDENT HOMICIDE (STABBING)		DATE OF INCIDENT/ACCIDENT 07-23-91		REP COM
	VICTIM LACY, Oliver		LOCATION OF INCIDENT/ACCIDENT (Address) 924 N. 25th Street #213		DI!

JUVENILE LAST NAME	FIRST	MID	DATE OF BIRTH	O DETAINED O ORDERED TO MCCC O OTHER

QUAN	TYPE OF PROPERTY	DESCRIPTION		SERIAL #	CODE #	VALUE

At this time I informed DAHMER that these were all the questions that I had to speak with him about on this ocassion and at this point his Attorney, Scott HANSON left the interview room. I then advised DAHMER that I would be returning him to the Milwaukee County Sheriff's Jail, at which time he requested a cup of coffee and another cigaret. To this request I complied and he asked me to again sit down with him. He stated that he wished to know some of the information regarding the events happening in Milwaukee at this time. At this time I lightly advised him that the News Media was reporting daily bits of information they had received regarding his case. At this time DAHMER started to talk about the movie which we found in his apartment, that being the Exorcist II. I asked him at this time why he in fact purchased the Exorcist II, and he stated that he had seen the movie when it was first released and that he was fascinated by it. He stated that he enjoyed the movie so much, that when it was first released on video cassette he spent approximately $100.00 in order to purchase a copy of it. I asked him what his fascination was with the movie, to which he stated he was unsure, but he knows that he felt a tremendous amount of guilt, because of his actions. He stated he felt evil and throughly corrupted, body & soul, because of the horrible crimes he had committed against people. He stated that everytime he would try to overcome his feelings of wanting to kill and dismember people, they would haunt him and overcome him, almost like an addiction. He states he felt that he could not fight that feeling and wondered if in fact the devil had anything to do with his evil thoughts. He states because of this he watched the movie Exorcist II on almost a weekly basis, for approximately 6 mos., and sometimes 2 and 3 times a week. He states that in the movie he could tell that the devil was angry for being condemned and that he could relate with the devil, because he felt that his life on earth was condemned. He went onto state that the main character in the movie appeared to be driven by evil and that he could relate to this character as felt that his life was driven by evil. At this time I questioned DAHMER regarding the heads which he had kept in his apartment. I asked him how in fact he got the brain matter out of the skulls and why the skulls looked so completely clean and dried when we discovered them. He states after killing his victims and decapitating them, he would use a small drill to drill several holes and various areas of the head and then he would boil the head. He stated during the boiling process he would use a large plastic syringe which he had purchased at an Ace

REPORTING OFFICER 2472	SEC 5	PAGE 181	PAYROLL #	LOC CODE	SUPERVISOR SIGNATURE Lt. R M Mauler

INCIDENT		DATE OF INCIDENT/ACCIDENT	REP COM
INCIDENT INFORMATION	HOMICIDE (STABBING)	07-23-91	
VICTIM	LACY, Oliver	LOCATION OF INCIDENT/ACCIDENT (Address) 924 N. 25th Street #213	DIS

JUVENILE LAST NAME	FIRST	MID	DATE OF BIRTH	O DETAINED O ORDERED TO MCCC O OTHER

QUAN	TYPE OF PROPERTY	DESCRIPTION	SERIAL #	CODE #	VALUE

Hardware Store and that he would fill the syringe with a Soilex cleansing solution and boiling water, and inject that solution into the holes which he had previously drilled into the skulls. He states that this solution would help to turn the brain matter into a mushy substance and that after approximately 1 hr of boiling, the upper vertebra, located in the neck area, would become loose and he could dislodge them. He states at this time he would use a large serving spoon or utensil to dig into the back part of the skull and scoop out the brain matter which had turned into mush. He states after scooping out the brain matter and discarding it in the toilet, he would again place the skull into the boiling water and boil it throughly until it was completely clear of any flesh, hair, mucus, or brain matter. At this time I asked him why he kept the heads, and if in fact he considered them to be a trophy. He stated that he did not consisder them trophys, however, he wanted to keep the skulls of his victims, because to him the skull represented the true essence of his victims. He states that he felt by at least keeping the heads, the death of his victims would not be a total loss, because the heads would be with him. He stated he eventually planned to paint all of the skulls in order to keep them from being detected, however, he never got around to doing that. At this time DAHMER stated to me "it's hard for me to believe that a human being could of done what I done, but I know that I did it, I want you to understand that my questions regarding satan and the devil were not to defuse guilt from me and blame the devil for what I've done, because I realized what I've done is my guilt, but I have to question whether or not there is an evil force in the world and whether or not I have been influnced by it. Although I am not sure if there is a GOD, or if there is a devil, I know that as of lately I've been doing a lot of thinking about both and I have to wonder what has influenced me in my life". To this I again asked DAHMER if there were any other victims that he had neglected to tell me about, to which he stated "Pat, what good would it do for me to admit to just half of my victims or to a few of my victims, or to not tell you of a couple, when I know that in the long run it will be me that has to stand before GOD and admit to my wrong doings and he'll know if I was truthful and honest when I finally was caught, and if I helped to try and clear this whole matter up. I'm telling you the truth now, becuase I want to clear my conscisous and all that I've told you is the truth and I've not left anything out". At this time DAHMER finished his cup of coffee and cigaret and I returned him to the 5th fl.,

REPORTING OFFICER	PAYROLL #	LOC CODE	SUPERVISOR SIGNATURE
2472 SEC 5 PAGE 192			Lt. KMouler

161

| INCIDENT INFORMATION | INCIDENT HOMICIDE (STABBING) | DATE OF INCIDENT/ACCIDENT 07-23-91 | | REP CON # |
| | VICTIM LACY, Oliver | LOCATION OF INCIDENT/ACCIDENT (Address) 924 N. 25th Street #213 | | DIS |

JUVENILE LAST NAME	FIRST	MID	DATE OF BIRTH	O DETAINED O ORDERED TO MCCC O OTHER

QUAN	TYPE OF PROPERTY	DESCRIPTION		SERIAL #	CODE #	VALUE

of the Milwaukee County Jail.

      Report dictated by: Detective Patrick KENNEDY

PK: hvs 08-08-91

2472 SEC 5 PAGE 133

REPORTING OFFICER Det. KENNEDY	PAYROLL # 48171	LOC CODE 93	SUPERVISOR SIGNATURE

INCIDENT INFORMATION	INCIDENT HOMICIDE		DATE OF INCIDENT/ACCIDENT 07/23/91		REP CON
	VICTIM LACY, Oliver		LOCATION OF INCIDENT/ACCIDENT (Address) 924 N. 25th St., #213		DI

JUVENILE LAST NAME	FIRST	MID	DATE OF BIRTH	O DETAINED O ORDERED TO MCCC O OTHER

QUAN	TYPE OF PROPERTY	DESCRIPTION		SERIAL #	CODE #	VALUE

REFER TO FOLLOWUP NUMBER:

NARRATIVE

On Thursday, 8-8-91, I, Detective KENNEDY, along with Lieutenant Richard MUNCEY of the Bath Township Police Department in Ohio, Detective John KARABATSOS of the Summit County Sheriff's Department in Ohio, and the Attorney for the suspect, Wendy PATRICKUS all met in the 4th floor Interview room of the CIB. At this time I retrieved the suspect Jeffrey DAHMER, after obtaining an Order to Produce. I returned with DAHMER from the 5th floor of the Milwaukee County Jail to the interview room.

At this time, I, Det. KENNEDY, sat in on an interview with the two Officers from Ohio as they questioned the suspect, Jeffrey DAHMER regarding the 1970 Homicide which occurred in their jurisdiction. Questions placed to Mr. DAHMER by the two Officers followed closely in line with questioning already placed to Mr. DAHMER earlier in our investigation. A copy of the Bath, Ohio reports are forthcoming and will become a part of this report.

However, during the questioning, several points did arrise which had not been covered previously in our investigation of this matter, regarding a large black traveler's trunk which Mr. DAHMER had kept in the basement, locked, at his grandmother's house in West Allis. Mr. DAHMER related that this was the trunk which he had used from the time he left the Military Service in order to travel by placing all of his worldly goods in it. He related that the reason he kept this trunk locked while at his grandmother's house, was because it was in this trunk that he placed all his pornographic materials, including magazines and video tapes which he had purchased. He related that the trunk was locked because he did not wish his grandmother to discover that he was involved in viewing and reading pornographic material.

Regarding information asked by Officers from Ohio, pertaining to the bar bell which has been mentioned in previous reports that Mr. DAHMER used to choke his victim to death; Bath, Ohio Officers report that they have recovered a bar bell set from the suspect's father. They inquired as to which article of the bar set was used to commit

2472 SEC 5 PAGE 134

REPORTING OFFICER	PAYROLL #	LOC CODE	SUPERVISOR SIGNATURE Lt. KMenle

INCIDENT INFORMATION	INCIDENT HOMICIDE (STABBING)		DATE OF INCIDENT/ACCIDENT 07-23-91		REP COM #
	VICTIM LACY, Oliver		LOCATION OF INCIDENT/ACCIDENT (Address) 924 N. 25th Street #213		DIST

JUVENILE LAST NAME	FIRST	MID	DATE OF BIRTH	O DETAINED O ORDERED TO MCCC O OTHER

QUAN	TYPE OF PROPERTY	DESCRIPTION	SERIAL #	CODE #	VALUE

this offense. At this point Mr. DAHMER related that he used one of the dumb bells, which is a smaller hand held set of bar bells, which you would use independantly of the other bar bells in the set. He related that when the victim told him that he was going to leave, he struck him while he was sitting in a chair, with the bar bells. After striking him he panicked and then used the smaller dumb bell to choke the victim to death. At this point I was advised by Bath, Ohio officials that they had, in fact retrieved and had on inventgory, the dumb bells spoken of by Mr. DAHMER.

It should be noted that at the beginning of this interview with Mr. DAHMER, Lieutenant MUNCY from Bath Township, Ohio, had obtained in writing a letter pertaining to the fact that Mr. DAHMER realized his constitutional rights and that he fully and voluntarily was speaking with Officers from Ohio regarding this Homicide. At this time Mr. DAHMER did date and sign this document. It should also be noted that at the completion of the interview, Lieutenant Richard MUNCY of the Bath Township Police Department noted that Mr. DAHMER'S attorney, Wendy PATRICKUS, had a small portable tape recorder which appeared to be on. At this time Lieutenant MUNCY questioned Miss PATRICKUS as to whether or not she had been tape recording the entire session. At this time Miss PATRICKUS related that she did not feel it was necessary for her to answer this question. It should be noted that I (Det. KENNEDY) also noticed the tape recorder at this time.

On Friday, 8-9-91, I, along with Det. DEVALKENAERE, were informed by Deputies of the Milwaukee County Sheriff's Department that the suspect, Jeffrey DAHMER, had requested to speak with us. After obtaining an Order to Produce, we proceeded to the 5th floor of the Milwaukee County Jail lock-up where we returned with the suspect DAHMER to the 4th floor of the CIB. At this time we again spoke with the suspect regarding the second victim, at his grandmother's house. That victim, as of this date, has not been positively identified. Again, Mr. DAHMER viewed a photo array and picked out #234356, ID photo of James E. DOXTATER. Mr. DAHMER related that this photo is possibly that of the victim in question. He related that the hair is about the same, however the photo appears to show the victim to be a bit too young. At this time I questioned Mr. DAHMER as to whether or not he can remember anything regarding the victim, which would help us in our investigation, that being tattoos or scars. DAHMER related that he is not sure, but the

REPORTING OFFICER 2472, SEC 5, PROC 135	PAYROLL #	LOC CODE	SUPERVISOR SIGNATURE Lt. K Meule

164

INCIDENT		DATE OF INCIDENT/ACCIDENT		REP COM
INCIDENT	HOMICIDE (STABBING)	07-23-91		
INFORMATION	VICTIM LACY, Oliver	LOCATION OF INCIDENT/ACCIDENT (Address) 924 N. 25th Street #213		DIS

JUVENILE LAST NAME	FIRST	MID	DATE OF BIRTH	O DETAINED O ORDERED TO MCCC O OTHER

QUAN	TYPE OF PROPERTY	DESCRIPTION	SERIAL #	CODE #	VALUE

victim could have had a slight and quite faded scar in his stomach or groin area, possibly that of an appendix removal or a hernia operation. He related that although he is not completely positive, that he seems to remember that during the time of this offense, as he cut open his victim, it occurred to him that the victim possibly only had one kidney. He related that he is not completely sure of this, however, he seems to remember that upon removing the internal organs of his victim, that it did not appear that all of his internal organs were there. He further related that he remembers the victim being almost as tall as me (Det. KENNEDY) himself, possibly 5'10-5'11, with dark, curly, medium length hair and he remembers the victim stating he lived in the area of 10th and National. When the victim mentioned that he had to return to his mother's house in that area earlier in the morning, this is when DAHMER decided to kill him.

I questioned DAHMER regarding the possibility that the victim had a tattoo on either one of his arms, to which he related "it is possible that he could have, however I can not really remember". At this time Mr. DAHMER again requested additional photos, possibly family photos of the victim in order to help him make his determination as to a positive identification.

At this time our interview was completed and Mr. DAHMER was returned to the Milwaukee County Sheriff's, 5th floor jail lock-up.

Report per Det. KENNEDY.

PK: gb 8-9-91

2472 SEC 5 136

REPORTING OFFICER DETECTIVE PATRICK KENNEDY	PAYROLL # 48171	LOC CODE 93	SUPERVISOR SIGNATURE

| | | | 8-16-91 | 91-51767/M2472 M2481 |

INCIDENT INFORMATION	INCIDENT	HOMICIDE (STABBING)		DATE OF INCIDENT/ACCIDENT 7-23-91		REP CON #
	VICTIM	LACY, Oliver		LOCATION OF INCIDENT/ACCIDENT (Address) 924 N. 25th St., #213		DIST 3

JUVENILE LAST NAME	FIRST	MID	DATE OF BIRTH	☐ DETAINED ☐ ORDERED TO MCCC ☐ OTHER

QUAN	TYPE OF PROPERTY	DESCRIPTION		SERIAL #	CODE #	VALUE

On Friday, 8-16-91, I, Det. Dennis MURPHY, proceeded to obtain an order to produce for the defendant, Jeffrey DAHMER. At approximately 10 AM, we, Det. Dennis MURPHY, Lt. Kenneth MEULER, West Allis Det. Lt. Ken RISSE, and Det. GUY NOVAK proceeded to the Milwaukee County Jail where we picked up Mr. DAHMER and walked with him over to the Criminal Investigation Bureau where at approximately 10:15 AM, we went with his attorney, Scott HANSON (phonetic) and informed him that we wished to question him regarding identification of the last victim in which the homicide occurred in West Allis.

West Allis officers asked him numerous questions regarding possible identification of the subject, Jamie DOXTATOR (phonetic) and upon viewing the Identification Division photo of James E. DOXTATOR, he stated that he was approximately 75% sure that this was the Hispanic male he met by the bus stop from the 219 sometime in January, 1988. He stated that this Hispanic male informed him that he lived with his mother in the vicinity of 10th and National, and that he had to be home in the morning. He also stated that when he was informed of this, that's when he killed this individual, in the early morning hours.

He stated that he was a complete stranger and when he met him, this individual told him that he was coming from visiting one of his cousins from downtown. He stated that at the time he met him, he was wearing a coat because it was in January, but he wasn't wearing a cap. He stated that he was wearing some type of sweater and an undershirt. He doesn't remember him wearing any suspenders, but stated that the sweater was yellowish. He also stated that he thinks this individual was circumcised. He stated that he may have had an appendix scar, but he doesn't remember seeing any scar on his face. He also stated that he did not recall anything wrong with his teeth, nor does he recall any tattoos, but he stated that there could have been.

He did recall that this individual had two scars, one about each nipple and about the same circumference of his cigarette. He stated that he does not know if there were burn scars or not, but that they were in fact scars and he does recall this. He stated that he thinks this individual had a slight mustache, but he can not be sure. He also stated that after he had dismembered the body and taken out the organs, he recalls that this individual was possibly missing a right kidney.

He again stated that he decided to kill this individual in the morning, but did not

REPORTING OFFICER 2472/ SEC 5	PAYROLL #	LOC CODE	SUPERVISOR SIGNATURE
/ PAGE 137			

PO15-B 5-89 SUPPLEMENT REPORT   ✓ INCIDENT SUPPLEMENT | PAGE _2_ of _6_ | DATE OF REPORT 8-16-91 | INCIDENT/ACCIDENT # 91-51767/M2472-M2481
MILWAUKEE POLICE DEPARTMENT   O ACCIDENT SUPPLEMENT
   O JUVENILE SUPPLEMENT

	INCIDENT	HOMICIDE (STABBING)		DATE OF INCIDENT/ACCIDENT 7-23-91		REP CON
INCIDENT INFORMATION	VICTIM	LACY, Oliver		LOCATION OF INCIDENT/ACCIDENT (Address) 924 N. 25th St., #213		DIS

JUVENILE LAST NAME	FIRST	MID	DATE OF BIRTH	O DETAINED O ORDERED TO MCCC O OTHER

QUAN	TYPE OF PROPERTY	DESCRIPTION	SERIAL #	CODE #	VALUE

keep anything from him. He stated that he did not keep anything from any of his individuals until victim number four, Anthony SEARS, at which time he decided to keep the skulls
for rememberance. He stated that when he did keep more items of these individuals, it was
because he liked them more or they appealed to him more.

The officers from West Allis then asked his attorney, Scott HANSON, if they could ask
him questions regarding the incident with Mr. FLOWERS (phonetic) who had reported a theft
complaint on 4-8-88 and who had been in Jeffrey DAHMER'S grandmother's house at 2357 S.
57th St. with him and had been dopped, but had not been killed. At this time, Mr. HANSON
requested that we leave the conference room so that he could talk to his client.

We left the conference room for approximately five minutes and we were called in by
Mr. HANSON at which time he informed us that he had advised his client not to talk about
the FLOWER'S incident or other incidences other then the identification of victim number
17 and Mr. DAHMER informed Mr. HANSON that he wanted to talk to the Police about anything.

At this time, the officers questioned Mr. DAHMER about the FLOWER'S incident, and he
informed them that when he met Mr. FLOWERS, Mr. FLOWERS told him that he was a councilor
for the retarded. He also told them that he had had car problems at which time Jeffrey
stated they could take a cab back to his grandmother's house where he would get his grandmother's car and come back to give him a jump. He stated that they went into the house.
After he turned off the alarm, he gave him a cup of coffee in the basement and the coffee
had the #10 in it.

Mr. DAHMER stated that he had told Mr. FLOWERS that they were going into the basement
so that he would not wake up his grandmother. They agreed on light sex. Mr. FLOWERS had
taken his shirt off when the pills started to take affect. Mr. DAHMER stated that he gave
FLOWERS as many as # 20 in the coffee and that he passed out about a half hour
after he arrived at the residence. He stated that they had been doing body rubbing before
he drank the coffee. He stated that Mr. FLOWERS passed out at which time he pulled his
pants down. He does not recall if he had oral sex with him or not, but in the morning his
grandmother saw him, at which time, he figured that Mr. FLOWERS was to big and didn't want
to cause a commotion and his grandmother saw him so he did not kill him.

He stated that he walked him to the bus stop on 57th and Lincoln and gave him $1 to
get on the bus. He did admit to taking $80 from Mr. FLOWERS but stated that he left other
monies in his wallet. He denied taking any jewelry and he stated that if any jewelry had

REPORTING OFFICER 2472	SEC 5	PAGE 138	PAYROLS #	LOC CODE	SUPERVISOR SIGNATURE

Official says fear of loneliness helps explain Dahmer killings

MILWAUKEE — An intense fear of loneliness that goes back to his parents' divorce led Jeffrey Dahmer to kill homosexual men he lured to his apartment and keep their dismembered remains, a police investigator said Saturday.

That intense fear of being alone apparently surfaced each time one of the men wanted to leave his apartment, causing Dahmer to kill and dismember the victim, the investigator told The Associated Press.

"He didn't want anybody else to leave him," said the source, speaking on condition of anonymity. "His childhood situation contributed a lot."

The source, a key investigator in the case, said he was paraphrasing things Dahmer told him in interviews.

Police allege Dahmer, a 31-year-old Army veteran and former chocolate factory worker, has admitted killing 17 people over 13 years, including one in Ohio and three at his grandmother's apartment in suburban Milwaukee.

Dahmer, who records show told his probation agent he felt guilty

'His childhood situation contributed a lot.'

—Investigator

about being homosexual, did not hate the gay men he killed, as some people have suggested, the source said.

"They were the easiest to get into his apartment," the officer said.

Police are investigating the possibility Dahmer had killed more than 17 people, the source said. "It is possible he just doesn't remember any more. We are looking at it in that vein. We haven't stopped looking for victims, I will tell you that."

Dahmer has admitted eating the body part of one victim and having sex with at least one victim after death because of "gratification, reliving the experience of knowing these people," the investigator said.

Dr. Dave Busby, a Milwaukee psychiatrist, said the investigator's explanation "makes sense"

based on cases he's seen of intense fear of loneliness.

"They are very, very insecure and dependent and it just goes all to pieces when they are abandoned," he said.

Dr. John Liccione, a psychologist at the Milwaukee County Mental Health Complex, was somewhat skeptical about the observations of an investigator with no formal psychological or psychiatric training.

Dahmer could be making everything up or saying things in an "eagerness to please," Liccione said.

"Anything is possible, but it sounds more like a third-rate playwright script in Hollywood. It sounds so simplistic and unprofessional," Liccione said. "The strange part of it is, it might be true."

Summoned by a man running down a street with a handcuff on one hand July 22, police went to Dahmer's apartment and found the remains of 10 mutilated men and one boy.

A criminal complaint charging Dahmer with four counts of murder said he had sex with one victim after killing him and kept one man's heart "to eat later."

PO15-B 5-89 SUPPLEMENT REPORT MILWAUKEE POLICE DEPARTMENT	☒ INCIDENT SUPPLEMENT O ACCIDENT SUPPLEMENT O JUVENILE SUPPLEMENT	PAGE 3 of 6	DATE OF REPORT 8-16-91	INCIDENT/ACCIDENT # 91-51767/M2472-M24.	
INCIDENT	INCIDENT HOMICIDE (STABBING)		DATE OF INCIDENT/ACCIDENT 7-23-91		REP CO
INFORMATION	VICTIM LACY, Oliver		LOCATION OF INCIDENT/ACCIDENT (Address) 924 N. 25th St., #213		D
JUVENILE LAST NAME	FIRST	MID	DATE OF BIRTH	O DETAINED O ORDERED TO MCCC O OTHER	
QUAN	TYPE OF PROPERTY	DESCRIPTION	SERIAL #	CODE #	VALUE

fallen off him or had been left by him, he threw them away.

Mr. DAHMER also stated that Mr. FLOWERS wasn't his type and that was another reason why he did not kill him. He stated that he disappeared on Sat. night or early Sunday morning. He stated that he did not drug him in the kitchen and drag him in the basement, nor did he attempt to choke him while he was in the basement. He stated that he does not know how Mr. FLOWERS obtained any marks on his body because he did not inflict any on him. Further reports will be called in by the West Allis detectives regarding their part in the investigation.

I then questioned Mr. DAHMER regarding various incident requests that we obtained through telephone calls from various agencies regarding having possible knowledge of Mr. DAHMER or articles of Mr. DAHMER. Some of the requests were from Bath, Ohio in which they were inquiring as to whether or not he had returned to Ohio any other time other then when he stated that he went with his grandmother. He stated that was the only time he could recall returning was on Thanksgiving of 1982.

He also stated that he did remember having a seance and that it could have occurred the night of the Prom or the night after. He stated that present at the seance were a Mike COSTLOW who he stated was his idea to have the seance, a Jeffrey SIX (phonetic), possibly a Wally (phonetic) SCHOEFF and maybe Bridget (phonetic) GIEGER or BEHAM. He stated that he does not recall whether or not a Lynn SOQUEL was there. He stated that they attempted to contact a white female that had killed herself in the woods behind her house. He stated that this female had shot herself and that they all held hands and tried to make contact with the spirits. He again stated that it was not his idea, it was Mike COSTLOW'S idea.

He was also asked as the whether or not they had gone to the cemetery and anyone had sat on the tombstone and he had stated that they did drive by the cemetery the night of the seance, but to his knowledge, no one sat on the tombstone, and no one was in the nude.

He was also questioned regarding whether or not he went to a Ted NEWGENT (phonetic) concert with Jeffrey SIX and he stated that he did go and they both were together. He was then asked questions relative to other calls we had received, namely whether or not he had any relatives in Newport Beach, California, and he stated that he does not have any relatives in California other then his mother who lives somewhere in the northern part of

INCIDENT	HOMICIDE (STABBING)		DATE OF INCIDENT/ACCIDENT 7-23-91		RE
INFORMATION VICTIM	LACY, Oliver		LOCATION OF INCIDENT/ACCIDENT (Address) 924 N. 25th St., #213		

JUVENILE LAST NAME	FIRST	MID	DATE OF BIRTH	☐ DETAINED ☐ ORDERED TO MC ☐ OTHER

QUAN	TYPE OF PROPERTY	DESCRIPTION	SERIAL #	CODE #	VAL

California and that he, himself, has never been in California. He also stated that he h
never been in Racine nor at the Regincy Mall in Racine nor has he carved his initials in
any benches. He also stated that he has never attended any Gay Pride parades in Milwauke
and the only time he has attended one was in Chicago on 6-30-91.

He was questioned again regarding the Ohio incidents as to when he went to Prom and
he stated that in his Junior year, he went to the Prom and he did go in to the Prom with
his date, but his Senior year he went to the Prom but they wouldn't let him in because
they were drunk.

The call we received on Tuesday, 8-6-91 from a citizen named John GEIS, that he had
personal contact with DAHMER in July or August of 1984, which Jeffrey DAHMER denied this.
He stated that he does not know any individuals that were named by Mr. GEIS, namely a Gar
BLOOR or Lloyd BLOOR, or Mark HOHNER. Mr. DAHMER stated that he does not know these indi
viduals nor does he know Mr. GEIS nor has he ever been at the residence of 3120 W.
Michigan.

He also stated that he has never been in a fight other then one time when he was in
the service and that was when he was stationed in Germany. Regarding the inquiry that we
had received from a Kim BROCK (phonetic) who stated that DAHMER may have seen Corpus
Christi, Texas with her, he stated that he has never been in Corpus Christi, Texas, nor
does he know Kim BROCK or her sister Sue KRIBBS. A follow up report has been called in
regarding this inquiry by myself.

He was also questioned regarding an inquiry from a Carlo GRACEFFA indicating that he
had seen Mr. DAHMER'S name on 5-6-89 carved in a picnic bench in Racine. Mr. DAHMER
stated that he has never been in Racine, nor has he ever been in any parks in Racine.
Also referring to an inquiry from a Kay ROUSE indicating that she had seen Mr. DAHMER in
the Regincy Mall in Racine, he again denied ever being in the Regincy Mall or in the
Racine area.

Regarding an inquiry from an Iris YOKOI requesting information as to whether or not
Mr. DAHMER has any relatives in Newport Beach, California, Jeffrey stated that he has
never been in California and the only relative he has in California is his mother who
lives somewhere in northern California. Further investigation revealed Fresno,
California.

Regarding an inquiry from Cathy (phonetic) KOLLER indicating that in 1983 she might

REPORTING OFFICER 2472	SEC 5	PAYROLL # PAGE 140	LOC CODE	SUPERVISOR SIGNATURE A/X 17.Cn. mind A.c...l

INCIDENT INFORMATION	INCIDENT HOMICIDE (STABBING)			DATE OF INCIDENT/ACCIDENT 7-23-91		REP CON #
	VICTIM LACY, Oliver			LOCATION OF INCIDENT/ACCIDENT (Address) 924 N. 25th St., #213		DIST
JUVENILE LAST NAME	FIRST		MID	DATE OF BIRTH	O DETAINED O ORDERED TO MCCC O OTHER	
QUAN	TYPE OF PROPERTY	DESCRIPTION		SERIAL #	CODE #	VALUE

have seen Mr. DAHMER in a laundromat in the vicinity of 82nd and Oaklahoma, Jeffrey stated that he has never been around that area or in any laundromat around that area.

Regarding an inquiry received from a Lt. Reena (phonetic) FABBIO regarding whether or not Mr. DAHMER knows a Cassandra (phonetic) N. KERNS, I asked him and he denied ever hearing this name or knowing this individual.

Regarding an inquiry from Det. Paul MARAWAY from Pittsburgh, Pennsylvania Police Department regarding the homicide in their city two years ago, Jeffrey stated that he has never been in Pittsburgh, Pennsylvania and that he denied any knowledge of any homicides in that area.

Regarding an investigation where a citizen brought a small suitcase into the Detective Bureau indicating that this was the suitcase that DAHMER had used to dispose of victim number one from the Ambassador Hotel, I questioned him and he stated that the size of the suitcase that he had purchased was approximately 3'x3'x1', that it had wheels on, and that after he disposed of the body of Steven TUOMI, he ripped up the suitcase, cut it up and threw it in the trash so that it could not be used again.

I also questioned him regarding telephone calls that he had placed to various agencies, including Chicago and Milwaukee Police Departments and he stated that on July 3rd and 4th of 1991, he place calls to the Chicago Police Department to report his wallet stolen or missing so that he could obtain an excuse for Ambrosia Chocolate because he missed work.

He stated that regarding the call placed in May of 1991 to the Milwaukee Police Department, he stated that because he wanted to report a robbery of $5. He does admit to calling several barrel companies in the area and also a barrel company in Chicago to get information regarding the barrels. He stated that he subsequently purchased a barrel in Milwaukee so that he could dispose of the body parts of his victims.

Regarding calls placed to J&R News or in other bookstores in the City, he stated that he did place calls to these various bookstores and that he did in fact purchase videos from the Dead Mark Bookstore, J&R News, The Ram Bookstore in Chicago, and the Paradise Bookstore in Milwaukee. He stated that he also purchased a set of handcuffs from the Army Surplus Store around 6th and Wisconsin.

We questioned him regarding his activities in the bookstore, and he stated that it

| REPORTING OFFICER | PAYROLL # | LOC CODE | SUPERVISOR SIGNATURE |
| SEC 5 PAGE 141 | | | |

171

| INCIDENT
INFORMATION | INCIDENT
HOMICIDE (STABBING) | | DATE OF INCIDENT/ACCIDENT
7-23-91 | | REP COI |
| | VICTIM
LACY, Oliver | | LOCATION OF INCIDENT/ACCIDENT (Address)
924 N. 25th St., #213 | | D |

JUVENILE LAST NAME	FIRST	MID	DATE OF BIRTH	☐ DETAINED ☐ ORDERED TO NCCC ☐ OTHER

QUAN	TYPE OF PROPERTY	DESCRIPTION		SERIAL #	CODE #	VALUE

then it continued on to meeting people in the back room of the bookstores, having sex, and then going into the bath houses. He stated that he did spend a lot of time at these bookstores until recently when he began killing his victims.

Regarding the chemicals used in his disposal of bodies or onces that were found at his residence, he stated that he bought formaldehyde approximately two months ago from Laal on 27th and Kilbourne, and he also bought the ether and the clorophene there about four months ago. He stated that he would get his prescriptions filled at Walgreens and that he would obtain the soilex from the hardware store. He stated that he called Ace Hardware regarding what chemical to use to remove the skin from the skull of a rabbit and at which time they suggested Soilex and that's when he started using it. He stated that he also called taxidermy places to find out what they use. He stated that he bought the Soilex from Ace Hardware on 4th St. and Walnut and that he also bought his muridic acid from Ace Hardware and True Value Hardware, even the one on 43rd and Oklahoma.

We questioned Mr. DAHLMER as to whether or not he has let anyone go or in fact had any sex with individuals without killing them during this killing spree, and he stated that other then the ones that got away, there were possibly no more then ten that he had sex with and not killed due to the fact that he did not like them that much or he did not have any #10 left. He stated that most of time it was because he did not like them and did not want to keep them around. The most recent one that he had sex with without harming the individual or attempting to drug him or kill him was a big black male truck driver and they had a normal relationship during this killing spree. He also stated that earlier on when he first started killing, he would shop around and find someone that he liked but near the end, compulsion took over and he would find someone and then just keep them.

During this interview, Mr. DAHMER was given coffee, cigarettes, and soda and he again stated that he wished to cooperate fully in our investigation to answer any questions that we had and to help identify the last victim and to ease the pain of their families. Mr. DAHMER was then taken back to the Milwaukee County Jail at approximately 12:32 PM and turned over to the Sgt. TYLKE.

Report dictated by Det. Dennis MURPHY.

DM/rc 8-16-91 **5** SEC **-142**

REPORTING OFFICER Det. Dennis MURPHY	PAYROLL # 32893	LOC CODE 91	SUPERVISOR SIGNATURE

	INCIDENT HOMICIDE			DATE OF INCIDENT/ACCIDENT 07/23/91		REP CON #
INCIDENT INFORMATION	VICTIM LACY, Oliver			LOCATION OF INCIDENT/ACCIDENT (Address) 924 N. 25th St., #213		DIST 3

JUVENILE LAST NAME	FIRST	MID	DATE OF BIRTH	O DETAINED O ORDERED TO MCCC O OTHER

QUAN	TYPE OF PROPERTY	DESCRIPTION	SERIAL #	CODE #	VALUE

REFER TO FOLLOWUP NUMBER:

NARRATIVE

On Friday, 08-16-91, just prior to taking Mr. Jeffrey DAHMER back to the Milwaukee County jail from the CIB, we, Detective Dennis MURPHY, Lieutenant Kenneth MEULER, Lieutenant RISSE of the West Allis Police Department and Detective Guy NOVAK, asked Mr. DAHMER is he missed drinking since he has been locked up. At this time he stated that he did not drink everyday, only when he committed the offenses. We informed Mr. DAHMER that he did not have to say anything regarding this due to the fact that his attorney had already left and he stated that it didn't make any difference, that he would cooperate with with us and has cooperated and has made statments against his interest without his attorney not being present therefore he would be willing to talk about his drinking.

He stated that when he killed these individuals he was always drunk and the drinking helped him get into the frame of mind and made it easier for him. He indicated that he didn't drink everyday but when he planned to get someone he would start drinking after he planned and then he was usually drunk when he killed them. He related that he even drank when he was cutting up the bodies. He again stated that it helped to make it easier when he was doing this. He related that he feels that he is not an alcoholic and the reason he was drinking was due to the fact that he committed these terrible offenses.

Further investigation was conducted after Mr. DAHMER had informed us that the Hispanic male that he had picked up from the 219 Club, namely victim #1 in West Allis, who he stated had two possible scars above his nipples. Investigation revealed that he did, in fact, injure himself when he was child with a bicycle and his mother stated he had two scars above his nipples at which he would state he had. four nipples. This information was obtained from her on today's date, 08-16-91. West Allis will conduct follow up in regards to this investigation

Report dictated by: Det. Dennis MURPHY

DM:dls 08-16-91

2472 SEC 5 PAGE 143

REPORTING OFFICER Det. Dennis MURPHY	PAYROLL # 32893	LOC CODE 91	SUPERVISOR SIGNATURE Det.Lt.Raymond 2 Such

	INCIDENT HOMICIDE		DATE OF INCIDENT/ACCIDENT 07/23/91		REP CON #
INCIDENT INFORMATION	VICTIM LACY, Oliver	.	LOCATION OF INCIDENT/ACCIDENT (Address) 924 N. 25th St., #213		DIST

JUVENILE LAST NAME	FIRST	MID	DATE OF BIRTH	○ DETAINED ○ ORDERED TO MCCC ○ OTHER
QUAN	TYPE OF PROPERTY	DESCRIPTION	SERIAL #	CODE #	VALUE

REFER TO FOLLOWUP NUMBER:

NARRATIVE

On Wednesday, 8-21-91, we, Detectives Patrick KENNEDY and Dennis MURPHY, were contacted by the Milwaukee County Sheriff's Department and were informed that the suspect, Jeffrey DAHMER wished to speak with us. At this time we were also advised by the Defense Attorney for the suspect, Gerald BOYLE, that he wished to sit in on the interview with Jeffrey DAHMER.

At this time the suspect was conveyed from the 5th floor of the Milwaukee County Sheriff's Department to the 4th Floor CIB and placed into an interview room where several questions, pertaining to this investigation were asked by Detective MURPHY. A detailed supplementary report will be filed relative to that interview.

At this time I questioned Jeffrey DAHMER regarding the muriatic acid which was found in his apartment on the night of his arrest, that being approximately 16 gallons of muriatic acid. DAHMER related that he bought the muriatic acid at Ace Hardware. He took a City Vet Cab to the hardware store in order to purchase it. DAHMER related that he intended to use the muriatic acid in the 57 gallon industrial strength drum which he had previously purchased in order to dispose of the body parts which he had in his apartment. At this time he realized that because of the loss of his job and the fact that he was out of money, he would soon have to leave his apartment. Therefore, he decided that he would completely destroy all the evidence of his deeds by mixing water and muriatic acid in the 57 gallon drum and thereby placing all the body parts which he had in his apartment, in the drum at one time, including all the skulls which he had saved and boiled, the complete torsos which he had saved and boiled from his victims, and the victims who were recently killed and were already placed in the drum. He felt that by doing this he would completely rid himself of any evidence of his crimes and after the bones and flesh had decalcified, he would be able to pour them down the toilet, completely destroying all evidence. He felt he would be thrown out of his apartment because of lack of funds and he would start a new life by going to the Salvation army where he could stay, he thought for

2475 -
SEC _____ PAGE 144

REPORTING OFFICER	.	PAYROLL #	LOC CODE	SUPERVISOR SIGNATURE Lt. KMManler

| INCIDENT INFORMATION | INCIDENT HOMICIDE (STABBING) | | DATE OF INCIDENT/ACCIDENT 07-23-91 | | REP COM |
| | VICTIM LACY, Oliver | | LOCATION OF INCIDENT/ACCIDENT (Address) 924 N. 25th Street #213 | | DIS |

| JUVENILE LAST NAME | FIRST | MID | DATE OF BIRTH | ☐ DETAINED ☐ ORDERED TO MCCC ☐ OTHER |

| QUAN | TYPE OF PROPERTY | DESCRIPTION | | SERIAL # | CODE # | VALUE |

about a month, until he could find another job and get on his feet.

At this time I questioned him as to whether he truly believed that by destroying all the evidence and starting over again, if he would be able to stop committing the Homicides which he had been involved in. At this time DAHMER related "If I am to be honest with myself, I would have to admit that if I again was set up in another apartment and had the opportunity, I probably would not be able to stop. I feel that it is almost a driving compulsion to commit these acts and I probably would have started up again, after sometime". Mr. DAHMER stated "obviously a power higher than myself had been fed up with my deeds and decided it was time for me to be stopped".

Regarding the fact that the flesh on the feet of several of the victims found in his apartment seemed to have been cut off, the Medical Examiner had inquired as to why this was done. Upon being asked this question, Mr. DAHMER related that by cutting the flesh off the sole and heel of the foot of his victims, it was easier for the muriatic acid to work on the bones of the foot, to decalcify and turn it to a sludgy substance. He related that the skin on the bottom of the foot was extremely tough and that it took more time for the muriatic acid to work though that and that was the reason why he cut the flesh off the feet of his victims.

At this time we were requested by Attorney BOYLE and his assistant, Wendy PATRICKUS, if they could have some time with the suspect, Jeffrey DAHMER, so that they could question him regarding the preliminary hearing which is to be held on 8-22-91. At this time an allotted period of time was granted for them to use the Milwaukee Police interview room. Following that, Mr. DAHMER was returned to the 5th floor of the Milwaukee County Sheriff's jail.

Report per Det. KENNEDY.

PK: gb 8-21-91

2472 SEC 5 PAGE 145

| REPORTING OFFICER DETECTIVE PATRICK KENNEDY | PAYROLL # 48171 | LOC CODE 93 | SUPERVISOR SIGNATURE Lt. K/Meuler |

	INCIDENT		DATE OF INCIDENT/ACCIDENT	REP COM
INCIDENT	HOMICIDE		07/23/91	
INFORMATION	VICTIM		LOCATION OF INCIDENT/ACCIDENT (Address)	DIS
	LACY, Oliver		924 N. 25th St., #213	

JUVENILE LAST NAME	FIRST	MID	DATE OF BIRTH	☐ DETAINED ☐ ORDERED TO MCCC ☐ OTHER

QUAN	TYPE OF PROPERTY	DESCRIPTION	SERIAL #	CODE #	VALUE

REFER TO FOLLOWUP NUMBER:

NARRATIVE

On Wednesday, 8-21-91, we obtained an Order to Produce for the defendant, Jeffrey DAHMER. At about 12:30PM, we picked up DAHMER at the Milwaukee County Jail. Present were: Detectives Dennis MURPHY, Patrick KENNEDY, William STAWICKI and Lieutenant Kenneth MEULER. DAHMER was taken to the CIB, Room 411, where we met with his attorney, Wendy PATRICKUS. We questioned DAHMER regarding some background information and other information, from previous statements, which needed to be cleared up.

Mr. DAHMER related that when he moved into the residence at 924 N. 25th Street, he picked that area because it was low rent and it was close to work. He related that he had no idea as to who was living in the apartment complex at the time and thought it was mostly family members. He did state that he knew most of the tenants were black, due to the area. He related that he is not prejudice nor does he dislike the blacks. He related that he was harrassed by blacks in the neighborhood and those people, who made remarks to him, he did not care for, but personally he did not feel he was prejudice.

He also related that the security items in his apartment, namely a Brown alarm, which was on the door, was purchased from Radio Shack in the Grand Avenue Mall. He related that he also purchased a Black and Decker Alarm at the Black and Decker Distribution Center across from the Zoo and a fake video camera at another store. He does not recall which store. He related that he purchased all of these items about one year ago.

Regarding chemicals he purchased, which were recovered in his residence, he related that he went to Laabs on 27th and Kilbourn. He went into the back room and bought one gallon of formaldehyde. He also bought a pint of ether and a pint of chloroform at this location. He was given a handwritten receipt and he paid cash for these items. He related that he does not recall who sold him these items, only that it was one of the workers. He also admitted buying the muriatic acid at Ace Hardware on 4th Street. He related that when he picked up the gallons of acid, he went by cab.

2472 sec 5 146

REPORTING OFFICER	PAYROLL #	LOC CODE	SUPERVISOR SIGNATURE
			Lt. KMeuler

PO15-8 5-89 SUPPLEMENT REPORT MILWAUKEE POLICE DEPARTMENT	■ INCIDENT SUPPLEMENT O ACCIDENT SUPPLEMENT O JUVENILE SUPPLEMENT	PAGE 2 of 3	DATE OF REPORT 08-21-91	INCIDENT/ACCIDENT # 91-51767/M2472-M2481	
INCIDENT INFORMATION	INCIDENT HOMICIDE (STABBING)		DATE OF INCIDENT/ACCIDENT 07-23-91		REP COM #
	VICTIM LACY, Oliver		LOCATION OF INCIDENT/ACCIDENT (Address) 924 N. 25th Street #213		DIST
JUVENILE LAST NAME	FIRST	MID	DATE OF BIRTH	O DETAINED O ORDERED TO MCCC O OTHER	
QUAN	TYPE OF PROPERTY	DESCRIPTION		SERIAL #	CODE #	VALUE

We then questioned him regarding an article which appeared in the Thursday morning Sentinel on 8-15-91 which indicated that he had a nickname of the Chop Chop Man and that he had spoken to inmates in the jail. Mr. DAHMER denies hearing of any nicknames or of being called any nicknames. He related that the prisoners walk by and state "There's DAHMER, the murderer" but no one ever called him by any nicknames, which he heard. He also related that he was housed in a regular cell, as were the other prisoners, except there was no one directly next to his cell. He related that he did not get any special meals nor was he allowed to smoke in the jail. He also related that none of the guards read the paper to him, nor would they talk to him. He related that they asked if he would like a paper and he would state no, or they would say Good Morning and he would respond good morning, but he never talked with any guard, nor did he talk with any inmates regarding his situation. He related that he did not receive any special treatment or any special meals, nor did he have special rules.

He related that when prisoners would hurl taunts at him and homosexual remarks, he did not reply to any of them. He related that he did not talk to anyone about what had occurred at his residence nor during this investigation. He also related that he did not make any statements to anyone that it was his business as to what occurred.

DAHMER also denies that he talked to any prisoners about the individual known as Tracy EDWARDS, who is the man who got away wearing the handcuffs. DAHMER related that he did not talk to anyone regarding him nor did he make any statements that it was all EDWARDS' fault. He also denies having a dislike for blacks and using the word "nigger".

Mr. DAHMER also related that the only visitors he has received are his attorneys, his father and members of the Milwaukee Police Department.

DAHMER related that he is quiet and he will not talk to anyone regarding this investigation, other than his attorney and ourselves, Detectives MURPHY and KENNEDY.

During this interview, DAHMER'S attorney, Wendy PATRICKUS was present. After the interview, Dr. Ken SMAIL and Attorney Gerald BOYLE were allowed to interview Mr. DAHMER in the room, outside of our presence. They finished their interview at 2:25PM and Attorney BOYLE requested that we let Mr. DAHMER had a couple of cigarettes before conveying him back to the County Jail. Mr. DAHMER was given several more cigarettes and a cup of cof-

REPORTING OFFICER	5	PAYROLL # 142	LOC CODE	SUPERVISOR SIGNATURE Lt. K.M.

INCIDENT			DATE OF INCIDENT/ACCIDENT	REP CON
INCIDENT INFORMATION	HOMICIDE (STABBING)		07-23-91	
	VICTIM LACY, Oliver		LOCATION OF INCIDENT/ACCIDENT (Address) 924 N. 25th Street #213	DIS

JUVENILE LAST NAME	FIRST	MID	DATE OF BIRTH	○ DETAINED ○ ORDERED TO MCCC ○ OTHER

QUAN	TYPE OF PROPERTY	DESCRIPTION		SERIAL #	CODE #	VALUE

fee. He was allowed to finish these before being transported back to the jail.

Report per Det. MURPHY.

DM: gb 8-21-91

2472   5   148

REPORTING OFFICER DETECTIVE DENNIS MURPHY	PAYROLL #	LOC CODE 91	SUPERVISOR SIGNATURE Lt. K. Menler

| INCIDENT INFORMATION | INCIDENT HOMICIDE | | DATE OF INCIDENT/ACCIDENT 07/23/91 | | REP CON # |
| | VICTIM LACY, Oliver | | LOCATION OF INCIDENT/ACCIDENT (Address) 924 N. 25th St., #213 | | DIST 3 |

| JUVENILE LAST NAME | FIRST | MID | DATE OF BIRTH | □ DETAINED □ ORDERED TO MCCC □ OTHER |

| QUAN | TYPE OF PROPERTY | DESCRIPTION | SERIAL # | CODE # | VALUE |

REFER TO FOLLOWUP NUMBER:

NARRATIVE

On Thursday, 8-22-91, I received information that Jeffrey DAHMER wished to speak to me (Det. MURPHY) and Detective KENNEDY. At this time we obtained an Order to Produce, with the approval of Attorney Gerald BOYLE. At approximately 1:45PM, Mr. DAHMER was brought to the CIB and was questioned in room 411 regarding various calls that came into our Department. Mr. DAHMER also related that he had a few other things he wished to tell us.

We questioned Mr. DAHMER in regard to a call which came in from Todd TINKER, W/M, 10-3-52, who related that he was employed at the Adult Toy Store in Lomira, Wisconsin. Mr. TINKER stated that DAHMER had come in and tried to purchase "knock out" pills. Mr. DAHMER related that he has never been in Lomira, Wisconsin, nor does he know about the Adult Bookstore.

We also questioned him regarding **# 47**, who related that he was in love with DAHMER and had been in his apartment twice and actually had seen heads in the refrigerator on his first visit to the apartment, but did not call the police and had returned to the apartment a second time. Regarding this, Mr. DAHMER related that he does not know this subject and this never did happen.

We then questioned him regarding a person he had drugged in one of the bathhouses, possibly Richard BURGER. DAHMER related that he did not recall the names of the individuals he met in the bathhouses, but he did recall drugging one of the individuals in the bathhouse on 7th and Wisconsin. When the subject did not awake after a couple of hours, he became concerned and had the people in the bathhouse call the paramedics, who took this subject to the hospital thinking that he had overdosed.

We then asked him if he was experiencing any withdrawals, not only from alcohol but from not using **#10** He related that he has not experienced any withdrawals from alcohol nor from the use of **#20** because he does not take the pills regularly. He related that he would take one pill about every six months and that was only when he could

2472 SEC 5 PAGE 149

| REPORTING OFFICER | PAYROLL # | LOC CODE | SUPERVISOR SIGNATURE _Lt. RMenke_ |

Dahmer trial: made-for-TV horror, but is it too much?

MILWAUKEE (AP) - The prospective jurors who will decide whether Jeffrey Dahmer is insane are being asked if they like horror movies. A macabre question, but fitting.

The trial, after all, will put real-life horror onto TV screens around the country. By all indications, it will be gruesome stuff.

"Judge, I just don't have the stomach for it," one prospective juror said Monday before she was excused from the case.

By the end of the trial, some television viewers may be saying the same thing.

Dahmer, a 31-year-old former chocolate factory worker, has confessed to 17 killings and pleaded guilty but mentally ill to the 15 with which he is charged in Wisconsin.

A jury will decide whether he was insane at the time of the slayings. The verdict will mean the difference between life in prison and an indefinite stay in a mental hospital.

One Milwaukee TV station plans gavel-to-gavel live coverage beginning Wednesday, and Court TV plans extensive live coverage on cable once the trial gets under way. CNN plans regular live reports but doesn't intend to broadcast live testimony at length, as it did at the William Kennedy Smith rape trial in Florida.

Like the Smith trial, however, the Dahmer case promises to push the boundaries of what is considered acceptable television.

Just as the Smith trial exposed viewers to unprecedented frankness in its testimony about sexual organs and functions, the Dahmer case will offer more than most people care to know about dismemberment, necrophilia and cannibalism.

Already broadcasters have agreed to limit their camera views of the many photographs that are expected to be shown to the jury.

WDJT, the Milwaukee station that plans live coverage, said it may cut into some of the most gruesome testimony and have reporters provide toned-down descriptions.

"We don't want to homogenize this trial, but when it gets extremely graphic we're going to have to make a decision," said WDJT general manager, Bill LeMonds. "It's going to be extremely difficult."

WDJT and another local station, WITI, also plan to use a small symbol in the corner of the screen to warn viewers of potentially graphic testimony.

WITI decided not to provide gavel-to-gavel coverage but agreed to have its own reporters and camera crews feed full coverage to WDJT.

Court TV has no plans to delete any testimony but may reconsider once the trial gets under way, senior producer Andy Regal said.

He said he didn't anticipate any testimony so offensive that it couldn't be aired. Still, he added, "I wouldn't say I'm not concerned about it."

Dahmer belongings

Relatives of Jeffrey Dahmer's victims have accepted a plan intended to avoid a public auction of the serial killer's belongings, including items he used for murder and dismemberment.

Lawyer Thomas Jacobson said an auction would raise $1 million. But he said Tuesday his clients would accept $407,225 from donors who want the items destroyed.

Jeffrey Dahmer takes the blame

NEW YORK — Jeffrey Dahmer said he alone was to blame for the series of dismemberment killings for which he's serving life in prison and said he still feels "those old compulsions" that led him to commit those crimes.

"The only person to blame is the person sitting right across from you," Dahmer said in his first interview since he was convicted in February 1992. "That's the only person — not parents, not society, not pornography."

Dahmer

On July 22, 1991, police discovered severed heads, refrigerated skulls and preserved genitalia in Dahmer's Milwaukee apartment. He confessed the next day to killing and dismembering 17 young men and boys.

The 32-year-old Dahmer was interviewed Jan. 12 at Columbia Correctional Facility in Portage, Wis., where he's serving 15 consecutive life terms.

Parts of the interview, scheduled to air this week on the syndicated television show "Inside Edition," were released to reporters Sunday.

Dahmer said that if he had not been caught, he would probably still be committing similar crimes.

PO15-B 5-89 SUPPLEMENT REPORT MILWAUKEE POLICE DEPARTMENT	☑ INCIDENT SUPPLEMENT O ACCIDENT SUPPLEMENT O JUVENILE SUPPLEMENT	PAGE 2 of 5	DATE OF REPORT 8-22-91	INCIDENT/ACCIDENT # 91-51767/M2472-M2481	
INCIDENT INFORMATION	INCIDENT HOMICIDE (STABBING)		DATE OF INCIDENT/ACCIDENT 07-23-91		REP CON #
	VICTIM LACY, Oliver		LOCATION OF INCIDENT/ACCIDENT (Address) 924 N. 25th Street #213		DIST
JUVENILE LAST NAME	FIRST	MID	DATE OF BIRTH	O DETAINED O ORDERED TO MCCC O OTHER	
QUAN	TYPE OF PROPERTY	DESCRIPTION	SERIAL #	CODE #	VALUE

not sleep. He related that the main reason he had #20 was to use on the people he brought to his apartment or the ones he met in the bathhouses. He related that he first started to experiment by using three pills on the people and then used as many as seven on some of them. He related that he would bluff the doctors into prescribing the pills for him because he would tell them that he could not sleep but he never used them. He figures that the last time he did take one of the pills was about six months ago.

DAHMER related that he did have a black male over to his residence, about one month before his incident with the victim whom he described as CASH D. He related that at this time he had mixed a drink for this black male, but he mixed up the cups and he subsequently drank the drink. He passed out and when he awoke the next morning he was missing $300 and this black male was missing from his residence. He related that he never reported this incident to the police. He also related that the only drugs or any other pills he took were vitamins. He also denies ever going into O'Connor's Bar on E. Wells Street. He related that he was only in Carol's Bar in Chicago once, that being on 7-6-91 or 7-5-91 when he picked up WEINBERGER.

We then asked DAHMER if he recalled what his home phone number was. He related that he could not recall it, therefore he was unable to have given his phone number to anyone.

We then questioned him as to whether his father had ever come to his grandmother's residence, on S. 57th Street, and if he ever found any bones in the garbage. He related that his father did come up there regarding the smell which was in the garage. Upon checking the garbage his father did find some smashed up bones but Jeffrey told him they were from a raccoon. Jeff related that these bones were actually the backbone and the arm bones of one of his victims.

We questioned DAHMER regarding two hispanic males who had called our Department and related that Jeff had approached them on approximately 7-21-91 at the Grand Avenue Mall. Jeff related that he did remember asking two hispanic males at the mall, to come to his place to be photographed and offered them about $100. Jeff related that he did stop at the liquor store, bought some beer and then they all got into the cab. He thought the hispanic males were 18 years old. While they were in the cab proceeding to his residence,

REPORTING OFFICER	PAYROLL	LOC CODE	SUPERVISOR SIGNATURE
72	5 150		

INCIDENT INFORMATION	INCIDENT HOMICIDE (STABBING)		DATE OF INCIDENT/ACCIDENT 07-23-91		REP CON #
	VICTIM LACY, Oliver		LOCATION OF INCIDENT/ACCIDENT (Address) 924 N. 25th Street #213		DIST
JUVENILE LAST NAME	FIRST	MID	DATE OF BIRTH	O DETAINED O ORDERED TO MCCC O OTHER	
QUAN	TYPE OF PROPERTY	DESCRIPTION	· SERIAL #	CODE #	VALUE

they jumped out of the cab around 22nd and Wisconsin (or in that vicinity) and walked away fast. He related that they had changed their minds. DAHMER related that on that occasion he was just interested in taking their pictures because there were two subjects.

Mr. DAHMER related that if we recalled the victim, whom he met on 27th and Kilbourn, that it was sometime after the winter and that this was the victim who he had skinned. He stated that it took him approximately two hours to do that. We asked him why he wanted to skin this subject and he related that he wanted to try it and he wanted to keep the skin. He stated that when he started to cut it, he cut it from the rear of the back of the neck area and then kind of peeled it away. He related that it was like skinning a chicken. He stated that when he pulled off the face, he had to be careful, but when it came off, it was just like a mask. He then used two items to try to preserve the skin. He used a box of borax and about seven boxes of salt. He related that he mixed these together in water and placed the skin which he had removed from the victim in the solution, with the intention of saving it, but he left it in too long and it became mushy and he had to dispose of it.

Mr. DAHMER stated that he had more to tell us but at this time, Dr. Ken SMAIL, a Psychiatrist for the defense, arrived and he interviewed Mr. DAHMER from about 2:50PM until 3:50PM.

After Dr. SMAIL finished his interview, Jeff DAHMER went on to relate that he had originally told us that he had only eaten a bicep of one of his victims. He related that there were other times in which he had eaten part of the victim. The first time was the person he identified as CASH D (Raymond SMITH - Victim #5). He related that he eat this victim's heart. He related that it tasted kind of spongy. He indicated that the next victim was the person he met by the bookstore, (Victim #7 - Ernest MILLER). He related that this was a person he really liked. He indicated that he had fileted his heart and had kept it in the freezer and also kept his bicep. He indicated that he had eaten the thigh muscle of this subject, but it was so tough he could hardly chew it. He then purchased a meat tenderizer and used it on the bicep. He stated that it tasted like beef or a filet mignon. The next person who he was going to eat, and in fact tried, was victim #15 - Oliver LACY. He stated that on this victim he ate his bicep. This also tasted

REPORTING OFFICER	PAYROLL # St. 3 ~AGE 1.51	LOC CODE	SUPERVISOR SIGNATURE Lt. AMeule

INCIDENT INFORMATION	INCIDENT HOMICIDE (STABBING)		DATE OF INCIDENT/ACCIDENT 07-23-91		REP CON #
	VICTIM LACY, Oliver		LOCATION OF INCIDENT/ACCIDENT (Address) 924 N. 25th Street #213		DIST

JUVENILE LAST NAME	FIRST	MID	DATE OF BIRTH	O DETAINED O ORDERED TO MCCC O OTHER	

QUAN	TYPE OF PROPERTY	DESCRIPTION	SERIAL #	CODE #	VALUE

like Filet mignon. He stated that he would tenderize it first. He stated that he did keep this individual's heart and bicep. We asked him if he had eaten the body parts, just plain. He stated that he would use salt, pepper and A-1 Steak sauce on them. He stated that the reason he ate these parts was because he was curious but then it was because he wanted to make them a part of him. He stated that this way he could keep these people with him. He stated that he ate only the people that he really liked and wanted them to be a part of him or with him all the time.

Mr. DAHMER related that he did not try to eat any other of the victims. He stated that the two hearts in the freezer and the bicep muscles recovered in the freezer would have been eaten by him had he not been arrested by the police.

Mr. DAHMER related that he does not think there is anything else that he could recall to tell us at this time. We asked him why he had not informed us of eating the various body parts when he first stated that he only ate the bicep. He stated that he did not want to talk about it, because it was not very appealing and he did not want us to think less of him.

We advised Mr. DAHMER that we had spent enough time with him where we would be willing to sit down and talk with him regarding any of his activities relative to this investigation or any other activities which he can recall and wishes to tell us about. Mr. DAHMER related that there was nothing else that he can recall relative to this investigation, nor is he involved in any other homicides, sexual assaults or attacks on anyone. He stated that if some individuals do come forward, indicating that he had made requests to them to pose for him, he states that that is true because he had approached many other people but he has not killed anyone else, nor has he had any other sexual relations with anyone, without their consent. He stated that the other individuals whom he had had sexual relations with or sexually touched or rubbed, was done with mutual consent and those were the individuals whom he did not desire and he let them leave his apartment.

Mr. DAHMER related that if he does recall anything, he will contact the Sheriff and inform them to contact us so he could give us this information.

We informed Mr. DAHMER that he should contact his attorney prior to contacting us so his attorney can be aware of the situation. Mr. DAHMER was then returned to the

REPORTING OFFICER		PAYROLL #	LOC CODE	SUPERVISOR SIGNATURE
	-5	752		Lt. K Meuler

	INCIDENT	DATE OF INCIDENT/ACCIDENT		REP COM #
INCIDENT	HOMICIDE (STABBING)	07-23-91		
INFORMATION	VICTIM LACY, Oliver	LOCATION OF INCIDENT/ACCIDENT (Address) 924 N. 25th Street #213		DIST

JUVENILE LAST NAME	FIRST	MID	DATE OF BIRTH	O DETAINED O ORDERED TO MCCC O OTHER

QUAN	TYPE OF PROPERTY	DESCRIPTION	SERIAL #	CODE #	VALUE

Sheriff's Department.

Report per Det. MURPHY.

DM: gb 8-22-91

2472 SEC. 5 PAGE 153

REPORTING OFFICER	PAYROLL #	LOC CODE	SUPERVISOR SIGNATURE
DETECTIVE DENNIS MURPHY	32893	91	

INCIDENT INFORMATION	INCIDENT HOMICIDE		DATE OF INCIDENT/ACCIDENT 07/23/91		REP CON #
	VICTIM LACY, Oliver		LOCATION OF INCIDENT/ACCIDENT (Address) 924 N. 25th St., #213		DIST 3

JUVENILE LAST NAME	FIRST	MID	DATE OF BIRTH	O DETAINED O ORDERED TO MCCC O OTHER

QUAN	TYPE OF PROPERTY	DESCRIPTION	SERIAL #	CODE #	VALUE

REFER TO FOLLOWUP NUMBER:

NARRATIVE

On Thursday, 8-22-91, I, Detective KENNEDY, along with Detective MURPHY, after obtaining an Order to Produce, and retrieving the suspect, Jeffrey DAHMER from the Milwaukee County Sheriff's Department, did interview him in the 4th floor CIB Interrogation room. During the interview, several questions were asked regarding outside jurisdiction investigations. The following are the answers given by the suspect, DAHMER.

Regarding information received from Chicago, Illinois - a hispanic male by the name of ERIC (who does not wish to give any further information regarding his identity) related that he was frequenting a bar located in the gay area of Chicago, known as the Vortex. While he was in the Vortex Bar he met the suspect, DAHMER, who offered to pay him $800 if he would accompany him back to Milwaukee via Greyhound bus and allow him to take nude photos of him and have him spend the night with him. He related that this occurred on a Sunday evening and he believes that it happened during the Gay Pride Parade, which was on approximately 7-30-91. He related that the suspect DAHMER told him, "I'm not leaving tonight until I find someone". He refused to go with DAHMER, however he is positive that it is the suspect DAHMER who approached him.

When questioned regarding this, DAHMER admits that he does recall talking to a white or hispanic male at the tavern known as the Vortex in Chicago. He stated that he was extremely drunk that day, however he does recall that he offered an individual $800 to have him return with him. He related that although the subject did not accompany him, he did meet one of his victims, Matt TURNER, at the Greyhound Bus Station in Chicago before returning home.

Regarding information received from Thomas LAMBROS of Schaumburg, Illinois. He related that about one week before Christmas of 1990, he was approached by DAHMER who asked him about his mobile telephone. He states that DAHMER told him he was on his way to Albuquerque, New Mexico for a couple of weeks and asked him to accompany him.

When questioned regarding this, DAHMER denied ever meeting this subject and

4 12 SEC 5 PAGE 154

REPORTING OFFICER	PAYROLL #	LOC CODE	SUPERVISOR SIGNATURE Lt. KMenla

INCIDENT INFORMATION	INCIDENT HOMICIDE (STABBING)		DATE OF INCIDENT/ACCIDENT 07-23-91		REP CON #
	VICTIM LACY, Oliver		LOCATION OF INCIDENT/ACCIDENT (Address) 924 N. 25th Street #213		DIST

JUVENILE LAST NAME	FIRST	MID	DATE OF BIRTH	0 DETAINED 0 ORDERED TO MCCC 0 OTHER

QUAN	TYPE OF PROPERTY	DESCRIPTION	SERIAL #	CODE #	VALUE

related that he has never taken the AmTrak Train, which the subject LAMBROS stated he was on during the time of this incident.

Regarding information from the Oak Park, Illinois Police Department - regarding a child molestor known as Michael KAUSMAN and wondering if the suspect DAHMER could be this subject.

DAHMER denied knowing any subject by the name of Michael KAUSMAN and related that he has never used an alias, in particular the name Michael KAUSMAN.

Regarding information from Officer MEAD of Abingdon, Police Department in Illinois - inquiring into the possibility that the suspect DAHMER was involved in a homicide where the victim was dismembered in that jurisdiction.

DAHMER denies being involved in this incident and related that he was never in Abingdon, Illinois.

Regarding information from an unidentified caller, only known as TERRY, - who stated he met the suspect DAHMER while at Carol's Speak Easy Tavern in Chicago. Terry related that DAHMER offered him $300 to return with him to Milwaukee to pose for photos. He also related that DAHMER was with his friend, whom he described as a white male in his early 30's or 40's.

DAHMER related that he never accompanied any friends while he was in Chicago and always acted alone. He related that he does not remember offering any individual $300 or any white male fitting the description of the caller TERRY. He denies this incident.

Regarding information from Detective KUSJAWA of the DuPaige County, Illinois Sheriff's Department - relative to the homicide of Patrick DENESEVICH, W/M, whose body was found strangled and left floating in the Des Plaines River in Illinois.

DAHMER denies any involvement in this incident and related that he has never been in DuPaige County, Illinois.

Regarding contacts that the suspect DAHMER had with police -
I questioned DAHMER regarding the fact that many times throughout his criminal

REPORTING OFFICER	PAGE	PAYROLL # 155	LOC CODE	SUPERVISOR SIGNATURE Kt. Menter

PO15-B 5-89 SUPPLEMENT REPORT MILWAUKEE POLICE DEPARTMENT	☐ ● INCIDENT SUPPLEMENT ☐ ACCIDENT SUPPLEMENT ☐ JUVENILE SUPPLEMENT	PAGE 3 of 5	DATE OF REPORT 08-22-91	INCIDENT/ACCIDENT # 91-51767/M2472-M2481	
INCIDENT INFORMATION	INCIDENT HOMICIDE (STABBING)		DATE OF INCIDENT/ACCIDENT 07-23-91		REP CON #
	VICTIM LACY, Oliver		LOCATION OF INCIDENT/ACCIDENT (Address) 924 N. 25th Street #213		DIST
JUVENILE LAST NAME	FIRST	MID	DATE OF BIRTH	☐ DETAINED ☐ ORDERED TO MCCC ☐ OTHER	
QUAN	TYPE OF PROPERTY	DESCRIPTION	SERIAL #	CODE #	VALUE

activities, he was, in fact, contacted by authorities, namely police, his parents, superintendants of apartment buildings he had lived in and the fact that they had questioned him regarding certain aspects of activities.

He related that the first time he was stopped by the police was while living in Ohio and attempting to dispose of his first victim. A Police Officer stopped him and he was able to convince the Officer that all was right and he in fact eluded detection.

He states that while at his grandmother's house, his grandmother questioned him many times regarding the foul smells emanating from the basement which were the results of the victims which he had murdered and cut up. He related that he was able to convince her that the foul smells were because of her cat Jody.

He also was questioned by his father, while at his grandmother's house, when his father did, in fact, find some of the broken up bones of one of his victims in a garbage bag placed in the garbage of his grandmother's house. To this, he stated that he told his father that those were the broken bones of a racoon which he had found and cut up. He convinced his father that this activity was similar to the activity he had experimented with while he was back in Ohio, at an early age in his teenage years. He stated that his father was unable to tell that they were human bones as he had used a sledge hammer and had smashed them up into such small fragments that they were undetectable.

He was confronted by Mr. SOPA, who is the Building Supervisor of the Oxford Arms Apartment where he was staying on N. 25th Street relative to the foul smell. He related that on the several occasions that Mr. SOPA confronted him, at one time he showed him some rotten meat which he had in the freezer, stating that the freezer had gone out and the rotten meat was what was causing the foul smell.

Regarding another time when he was confronted by the Building Supervisor regarding the foul smell, he showed him a plastic garbage container which he had been using in order to dissolve human bones and flesh with muriatic acid. However, upon

REPORTING OFFICER

LOC CODE

SUPERVISOR SIGNATURE

INCIDENT INFORMATION	INCIDENT HOMICIDE (STABBING)		DATE OF INCIDENT/ACCIDENT 07-23-91		REP CON #
	VICTIM LACY, Oliver		LOCATION OF INCIDENT/ACCIDENT (Address) 924 N. 25th Street #213		DIST
JUVENILE LAST NAME	FIRST	MID	DATE OF BIRTH	O DETAINED O ORDERED TO MCCC O OTHER	
QUAN	TYPE OF PROPERTY	DESCRIPTION		SERIAL #	CODE #	VALUE

showing him the garbage container, it was ~~still~~ empty and although it emitted a foul odor, he stated that he advised Mr. SOPA that he used the garbage container in order to change the water from his fish tank and that at times dead fish were left in there. He related that this seemed to appease him and he was advised by Mr. SOPA to get rid of the bucket, which he did, promptly.

Regarding the incident with the police and the Asian boy, Konerak SINTHASOMPHONE, he related that although he was extremely nervous during the time of the questioning by police, he put on a very calm attitude and felt he was able to convince the police that it was a lover's problem between two homosexuals. He related that due to the fact that he was able to convince all these people, in positions of authority, his parents and neighbors who questioned him regarding his activities, it gave him a feeling that he could get away with his crimes. He felt that he had the ability to make people see a phase of him that only he wished them to see and that this encouraged him to continue on with his crimes, feeling that he would never be caught.

We asked him if he shared with anyone his activites, or felt the need ever to tell anyone. Mr. DAHMER stated no, stating that these ideas were all his own. He related that he did not get these ideas, for cutting up people or killing people from movies, TV, books or magazines. He stated that they were strictly out of his head. He related that he liked the fact that these ideas were his own and that they were uniquely his own. He felt power in the fact that they were his own private thoughts and that while he was doing this he felt it was his own private world that belonged to no one else. Due to the fact that he states he was always a loner, he took pleasure in the fact of knowing that he had a private world of his own that no one else knew about.

When questioned further regarding the subject who was completely skinned - DAHMER related that the skin of the human being was easily detached; he states much the way you would detach skin from a chicken which you are planning to cook. He stated that after the initial incision, he could pull on the skin and it would pull off the muscle tissue of the body easily. The only time it was difficult was when he was pulling the skin off around

| REPORTING OFFICER
2/ S 5 | PAYROLL #
157 | LOC CODE | SUPERVISOR SIGNATURE
H. KJMeuler |

PO15-8 5-89 SUPPLEMENT REPORT MILWAUKEE POLICE DEPARTMENT	⊕ INCIDENT SUPPLEMENT 0 ACCIDENT SUPPLEMENT 0 JUVENILE SUPPLEMENT	PAGE _5_ of _5_	DATE OF REPORT 08-22-91	INCIDENT/ACCIDENT # 91-51767/M2472-M2481	
INCIDENT INFORMATION INCIDENT	HOMICIDE (STABBING)		DATE OF INCIDENT/ACCIDENT 07-23-91		REP COM #
VICTIM	LACY, Oliver		LOCATION OF INCIDENT/ACCIDENT (Address) 924 N. 25th Street #213		DIST
JUVENILE LAST NAME	FIRST	MID	DATE OF BIRTH	0 DETAINED 0 ORDERED TO MCCC 0 OTHER	
QUAN	TYPE OF PROPERTY	DESCRIPTION	SERIAL #	CODE #	VALUE

the joints and at this time he would use a small paring knife to carefully cut the skin around the joint portion of the body.

Regarding the fact that the skin was completely taken off the head of the subject, DAHMER related that he would start an incision in the lower portion of the back of the neck and slice up to the top (or crown of the head). He related that at this time he could pull on either side of the skin from the incision and it would completely pull right off the skull of the individual. He related that the only time he needed to do any real cutting would be around the facial features, that being the eyes, nose, lips and mouth. He related that the entire skull portion of the skin came off in one complete piece and while it was off it actually looked somewhat like a mask you can buy at a party store. He related that he kept the skin and the mask-like facial features of this subject and planned to treat them with a solution he made up of salt and borax. He stated that he soaked them in a salt, borax and water solution for several weeks and then planned to take them out and dry them to preserve them. He wanted to keep the skin and the mask-like portion of the individuals head, however he underestimated the powerful mixture of borax and salt. After several weeks in the solution, the skin turned to a mushy like substance and was unable to be kept and it had to be thrown out.

There were also several questions, regarding the victims, which were asked by Det. MURPHY. Det. MURPHY will file a separate supplementary report regarding that part of the interview.

Report per Det. KENNEDY.

P:; gb 8-22-91

2472 M_____, SEC__5__, PAGE 158

REPORTING OFFICER		PAYROLL #	LOC CODE	SUPERVISOR SIGNATURE
DETECTIVE PATRICK KENNEDY		48171	93	Lt. KJMeuler

Kile M-2472 Lt.KJMeuler

CIRCUIT COURT
STATE OF WISCONSIN   CRIMINAL DIVISION   MILWAUKEE COUNTY

- -

STATE OF WISCONSIN, Plaintiff   AMENDED CRIMINAL COMPLAINT

           vs.   CRIME(S):
                                       See Charging Section Below
Jeffrey L. Dahmer   05/21/60   STATUTE(S) VIOLATED
924 N. 25th St.   See Charging Section Below
Milwaukee, WI   COMPLAINING WITNESS:
                                       Donald Domagalski
           Defendant.   CASE NUMBER:
                                       F-912542

- -

THE ABOVE NAMED COMPLAINING WITNESS BEING DULY SWORN SAYS THAT THE ABOVE
NAMED DEFENDANT IN THE COUNTY OF MILWAUKEE, STATE OF WISCONSIN

COUNT 01: FIRST DEGREE MURDER

in January of 1988, at 2357 South 57th Street, City of West Allis, County
of Milwaukee, did cause the death of another human being, James E.
Doxtator, with intent to kill that person contrary to Wisconsin Statutes
section 940.01.

COUNT 02: FIRST DEGREE MURDER

in March of 1988, at 2357 South 57th Street, City of West Allis, County of
Milwaukee, did cause the death of another human being, Richard Guerrero,
with intent to kill that person contrary to Wisconsin Statutes section
940.01.

COUNT 03: FIRST DEGREE INTENTIONAL HOMICIDE

on or about March 26, 1989, at 2357 South 57th Street, City of West Allis,
County of Milwaukee, did cause the death of another human being, Anthony
Sears, with intent to kill that person contrary to Wisconsin Statutes
section 940.01(1).

COUNT 04: FIRST DEGREE INTENTIONAL HOMICIDE

during the Spring or early Summer of 1990, at 924 North 25th Street, City
and County of Milwaukee, did cause the death of another human being,
Raymond Smith a/k/a Ricky Beeks, with intent to kill that person contrary
to Wisconsin Statutes section 940.01(1).

COUNT 05: FIRST DEGREE INTENTIONAL HOMICIDE

during the Summer of 1990, at 924 North 25th Street, City and County of
Milwaukee, did cause the death of another human being, Edward W. Smith,
with intent to kill that person contrary to Wisconsin Statutes section
940.01(1).

2472 SEC 5 PAGE 159

COUNT 06: FIRST DEGREE INTENTIONAL HOMICIDE

on or about September 3, 1990, at 924 North 25th Street, City and County of Milwaukee, did cause the death of another human being, Ernest Miller, with intent to kill that person contrary to Wisconsin Statutes section 940.01(1).

COUNT 07: FIRST DEGREE INTENTIONAL HOMICIDE

on or about September 24, 1990, at 924 North 25th Street, City and County of Milwaukee, did cause the death of another human being, David Thomas, with intent to kill that person contrary to Wisconsin Statutes section 940.01(1).

COUNT 08: FIRST DEGREE INTENTIONAL HOMICIDE

on or about February 18, 1991, at 924 North 25th Street, City and County of Milwaukee, did cause the death of another human being, Curtis Straughter, with intent to kill that person contrary to Wisconsin Statutes section 940.01(1).

COUNT 09: FIRST DEGREE INTENTIONAL HOMICIDE

on or about April 7, 1991, at 924 North 25th Street, City and County of Milwaukee, did cause the death of another human being, Errol Lindsey, with intent to kill that person contrary to Wisconsin Statutes section 940.01(1).

COUNT 10: FIRST DEGREE INTENTIONAL HOMICIDE

on or about May 24, 1991, at 924 North 25th Street, City and County of Milwaukee, did cause the death of another human being, Tony Anthony Hughes, with intent to kill that person contrary to Wisconsin Statutes section 940.01(1).

COUNT 11: FIRST DEGREE INTENTIONAL HOMICIDE

on or about May 27, 1991, at 924 North 25th Street, City and County of Milwaukee, did cause the death of another human being, Konerak Sinthasomphone, with intent to kill that person contrary to Wisconsin Statutes section 940.01(1).

COUNT 12: FIRST DEGREE INTENTIONAL HOMICIDE

on or about June 30, 1991, at 924 North 25th Street, City and County of Milwaukee, did cause the death of another human being, Matt Turner a/k/a Donald Montrell, with intent to kill that person contrary to Wisconsin Statutes section 940.01(1).

(2)

172 SEC 5 PAGE 160

193

COUNT 13: FIRST DEGREE INTENTIONAL HOMICIDE

on or about July 7, 1991, at 924 North 25th Street, City and County of Milwaukee, did cause the death of another human being, Jeremiah Weinberger, with intent to kill that person contrary to Wisconsin Statutes section 940.01(1).

COUNT 14: FIRST DEGREE INTENTIONAL HOMICIDE

on, or about July 15, 1991 at 924 North 25th Street, City and County of Milwaukee, did cause the death of another human being, Oliver Lacy, with intent to kill that person contrary to Wisconsin Statutes section 940.01(1).

COUNT 15: FIRST DEGREE INTENTIONAL HOMICIDE

on or about July 19, 1991 at 924 North 25th Street, City and County of Milwaukee, did cause the death of another human being, Joseph Bradehoft, with intent to kill that person contrary to Wisconsin Statutes section 940.01(1).

HABITUAL CRIMINALITY

on January 30, 1989, Jeffrey L. Dahmer was convicted in the Circuit Court of Milwaukee County in Circuit Court Case Number F-882515 of the felony offenses of Second Degree Sexual Assault and Enticing a Child for Immoral Purposes in violation of 940.225(2)(e) and 944.12 of the Wisconsin Statutes and that said convictions remain of record and unreversed and therefore defendant is a repeater pursuant to Wisconsin Statutes 939.62, and is subject to a total sentence of not more than ten (10) years on each count recited in addition to the mandatory life sentence for each count of First Degree Intentional Homicide and First Degree Murder.

Upon conviction of each count of First Degree Intentional Homicide and each count of First Degree Murder, Class A Felonies, the penalty is life imprisonment.

Complainant states that he is a Captain of Police with the City of Milwaukee Police Department and bases this complaint upon the following:

VICTIM JAMES DOXTATOR, DOB: 3/1/73

1) Upon the statement of the defendant, which statement is against his (the defendant's) penal interest that in January of 1988 he met a young male he thought was Hispanic who was waiting for a bus in front of the 219 Club on 2nd Street in the City and County of Milwaukee, State of Wisconsin; he (the defendant) approached him and asked him if he would like to make some money by posing in the nude, viewing videos, and having a drink at his (the defendant's) residence; at this time he (the defendant) lived at 2357 South 57th Street in the City of West Allis, County of Milwaukee, State of Wisconsin; the two of them went to that location by bus and they had sex

(3)

2472 SEC. 5 PAGE 161

and then he gave the young male a drink with sleeping potion and after he
passed out killed him by strangling him; he dismembered him and smashed the
bones with a sledgehammer and disposed of them; he did not keep any portion
of this individual; further he remembers that the young male told him that
he lived with his mother in the vicinity of 10th and National; he further
recalls that the young male had two scars close to each of his (the young
male's) nipples that were approximately the circumference of a cigarette;
the defendant viewed a copy of a booking photo of James E. Doxtater, DOB:
3/1/73, that had been taken on September 23, 1987 and indicated that he was
75% sure that this was the male that he met by the bus stop, although he
remembered him as looking somewhat older and heavier.

    2) Upon the statement of Debra Vega, an adult citizen, that she (Vega)
in January of 1988 lived at 1010 East Pierce in the City and County of
Milwaukee, State of Wisconsin and that her son is James E. Doxtator, DOB:
3/1/73; she reported her son missing on January 18, 1988 and has never seen
him since or been contacted by him since; further her son had two small
scars in the area of his nipples that looked like cigarette burns; also
that her home in 1988 at 1010 East Pierce was approximately one block from
10th and National; also that her son was a Native American.

VICTIM RICHARD GUERRERO, DOB: 12/12/65

    1) Upon the further statement of the defendant, that in approximately
March of 1988 he (the defendant) met a Hispanic male in the Phoenix Bar
located on 2nd Street near the 219 Club in the City and County of
Milwaukee, State of Wisconsin; he (the defendant) asked this man to come to
his residence which at that time was his grandmother's house located at
2357 South 57th Street in the City of West Allis, County of Milwaukee,
State of Wisconsin; he asked the man to come to look at videos and take
photos or engage in sex and the man came with him; they had oral sex at the
house and then he drugged the man; while the man was drugged he killed him
and dismembered the body and disposed of it completely without keeping any
parts; he recalls that he later saw in the personal section of a local
newspaper a photo of this victim and a report that he was missing; further
the defendant viewed a photograph from the January 7, 1989 Milwaukee
Journal of Richard Guerrero, DOB: 12-12-65, and identified this as the
person he killed in this incident.

    2) Upon the statement of Pablo Guerrero, an adult citizen, that he
(Guerrero) is the father of Richard Guerrero and that he has not seen his
son since mid March, 1988; at that time he (Pablo Guerrero) reported his
son as missing to the Milwaukee Police Department; further that
advertisements with his son's picture were placed in local newspapers
indicating that his son was missing.

VICTIM ANTHONY SEARS, D.O.B.: 1/28/65

    1) Upon the further statement of the defendant, that he met Anthony
Sears (whom he identified in a photograph) at a club called LaCage; that a
friend of Anthony Sears drove him (the defendant) and Anthony Sears to the
area of his (the defendant's) grandmother's house in the City of West
Allis, County of Milwaukee, State of Wisconsin; that his grandmother's
house is 2357 South 57th Street; that after they arrived at that residence,

(4)

195

they had sex and he gave Anthony Sears a drink with sleeping pills in it; that he strangled him and dismembered the body; that he kept Anthony Sears' head and boiled it to remove the skin; further, that he kept the skull and painted it.

2) Upon the statement of Jeffrey Connor, an adult citizen, that he (Connor) was with Anthony Sears on the evening of March 25th, 1989 and on that evening they were at a bar on 6th and National; they closed the bar and that Anthony Sears had met a white male named Jeff who said that he was here from Chicago and was visiting his grandmother who lived at 56th and Lincoln; that he (Connor) then gave Jeff and Anthony Sears a ride to the vicinity of 56th and Lincoln where they (Jeff and Sears) got out of the car and walked southbound.

3) Upon complainant's personal knowledge of addresses in Milwaukee County and that the intersection of 56th and Lincoln is north of and in close proximity to the address 2357 South 57th Street in the City of West Allis.

4) Upon the statement of Dr. Jeffrey Jentzen, Milwaukee County Medical Examiner, that during the early morning hours of July 23rd, 1991 he (Jentzen) with Milwaukee police officers and other members of the County of Milwaukee Medical Examiner's Office was present at 924 North 25th Street in the City and County of Milwaukee, State of Wisconsin in Apartment 213; that he was present at that location when seven human skulls (three of which were painted) four human heads, and numerous other body parts were recovered; that all the human remains recovered were transported to the Milwaukee County Medical Examiner's Office.

5) Upon the statement of Dr. L.T. Johnson, a Forensic Odontologist, that he (Johnson) made a comparison of the painted human skulls recovered from 924 North 25th Street in the City and County of Milwaukee, State of Wisconsin during the early morning hours of July 23rd, 1991 with known dental records of Anthony Sears and determined that one of the painted skulls is that of Anthony Sears.

VICTIM RAYMOND SMITH A/K/A RICKY BEEKS, D.O.B.: 8/10/57

1) Upon the further statement of the defendant that approximately two months after he (the defendant) moved into Apartment 213 at 924 North 25th Street in the City and County of Milwaukee, State of Wisconsin he met a black male at the 219 Club and offered him money to be photographed and have a drink and watch videos; that the man agreed and came with him (the defendant) to 924 North 25th Street, Apartment 213; that at that location he (the defendant) gave the man a drink which was drugged and the man fell asleep; that he (the defendant) then strangled the man and removed the man's clothing and had oral sex with him; further, that he dismembered the body but kept the skull and later painted it; further, that he (the defendant) identified photographs of Raymond Lamont Smith as being photographs of the man to whom he had done this.

2) Upon the further statement of Dr. L.T. Johnson that he (Johnson) examined the painted skulls recovered at 924 North 25th Street in the City and County of Milwaukee, State of Wisconsin during the early morning hours of July 23rd, 1991 with known dental records of Raymond Lamont Smith and determined that one of the aforementioned skulls is that of Raymond Smith.

3) Upon your complainant's personal observation of a copy of the defendant's rental application for the living premises at 924 North 25th Street, Apartment 213; that the aforementioned rental agreement has an initial lease date of May 13th, 1990.

VICTIM EDWARD SMITH, DOB: 8/2/62

1) Upon the further statement of the defendant, that during the Summer of 1990, approximately in July, he met a person whom he identified through a photograph as Edward W. Smith, DOB: 8-2-62, at the Phoenix Bar on 2nd Street in Milwaukee and offered him money for sex and to pose for pictures; they took a cab to his (the defendant's) apartment at 924 North 25th Street in the City and county of Milwaukee, State of Wisconsin; they had oral sex and he gave Smith a drink which contained sleeping pills and then strangled him; he dismembered Smith and took four or five photos of him; he completely disposed of Edward Smith's body by placing it in garbage bags and at a later time he also got rid of the photos of Edward Smith; he further recalls that Smith wore a headband like an Arab.
2) Upon the statement of Carolyn Smith, an adult citizen, that she (Carolyn Smith) is the sister of Edward W. Smith and that she has had no contact with him since June 23, 1990; further that her brother was called "the Sheik" because he frequently wore a turban-like wrap on his head.

VICTIM ERNEST MILLER, D.O.B.: 5/5/67

1) Upon the statement of Vivian Miller, an adult citizen, that she (Miller) is the aunt of Ernest Miller and that on September 1st, 1990 Ernest Miller came from his home in Chicago to Milwaukee to visit for the Labor Day weekend and that he left her home during the early morning hours of September 3rd, 1990 and she has not seen him or heard from him since.
2) Upon the further statement of the defendant that during the summer of 1990 he met a black male (whom he identified through a photograph of Ernest Miller as being Ernest Miller) in front of a book store in the 800 block of North 27th Street in the City and County of Milwaukee, State of Wisconsin and that he offered the man money to return to his (the defendant's) apartment at 924 North 25th Street in the City and County of Milwaukee, State of Wisconsin; that when they returned to his apartment they had sex and then he (the defendant) drugged Ernest Miller and killed him by cutting his throat; further, that after taking photos of him, he dismembered the body and disposed of the flesh except for the biceps which he kept in the freezer; he also kept the skull which he painted after the skin was removed, and he kept the skeleton which he bleached.
3) Upon the further statement of Dr. L.T. Johnson that he (Johnson) has compared the painted skulls recovered on July 23rd, 1991 from the defendant's apartment at 924 North 25th Street in the City and County of Milwaukee, State of Wisconsin with known dental records of Ernest Miller and determined that one of the aforementioned painted skulls is that of Ernest Miller.

(6)

197

VICTIM DAVID C. THOMAS, D.O.B.: 12/21/67

1) Upon the further statement of the defendant that he in the Autumn of 1990 met a black male in the vicinity of 2nd and Wisconsin in the City and County of Milwaukee, State of Wisconsin and offered the man money to come to his apartment at 924 North 25th Street; when they got to his apartment they drank and talked but he had no sex with this man because the man wasn't his type; that he gave the man a drink with a sleeping potion in it and killed him even though he did not want to have sex with him because he thought the man would wake up and be angry; that he dismembered the body but did not keep any of the body parts because the man wasn't his type; further, that he photographed the man while he was in the process of dismembering him.

2) Upon the statement of Chandra Beanland, an adult citizen, that she (Beanland) is the girlfriend of David C. Thomas and that she reported him missing on September 24th, 1990 to the Milwaukee Police Department.

3) Upon the statement of Brian O'Keefe, a City of Milwaukee Police Detective, that he (O'Keefe) contacted the family of David C. Thomas in the course of this investigation and specifically spoke with Leslie Thomas who identified herself as David C. Thomas' sister and that he (O'Keefe) showed Leslie Thomas the facial portion of the photograph which the defendant identified as having been taken during the course of dismembering David Thomas; further, that the facial portion showed no injuries at the time it was shown to Leslie Thomas and that Leslie Thomas identified the person in the photograph as being her brother, David Thomas; that the Thomas family supplied a photograph of David Thomas sleeping which they had; further that the face in this family photograph appeared to him (O'Keefe) to depict the same individual as in the photograph the defendant had taken while dismembering this victim.

VICTIM CURTIS STRAUGHTER, D.O.B.: 4/16/73

1) Upon the statement of Katherine Straughter, an adult citizen, that she (Straughter) is the grandmother of Curtis Straughter and that she last saw her grandson on February 18th, 1991.

2) Upon the further statement of the defendant that in February of 1991 he observed Curtis Straughter (whom he identified through a photograph) waiting for a bus by Marquette University and offered him money to come back to his apartment at 924 North 25th Street in the City and County of Milwaukee, State of Wisconsin; that Straughter did accompany him back and at the apartment he (the defendant) gave Curtis Straughter a drugged drink and had oral sex with him; the defendant then strangled him with a strap and dismembered the body; he also took photos and kept the man's skull.

3) Upon the further statement of Dr. L.T. Johnson that he (Johnson) compared the unpainted skulls recovered from the defendant's apartment with known dental records of Curtis Straughter and determined that one of the unpainted skulls was that of Curtis Straughter.

(7)

2 4 2 SEC 5 / PAGE 165

198

VICTIM ERROL LINDSEY, D.O.B.: 3/3/72

1) Upon the statement of Yahuna Barkley, an adult citizen, that she (Barkley) is the sister of Errol Lindsey and that she last saw him on April 7th, 1991 when he went to the store and that she has not seen him since that time.

2) Upon the further statement of the defendant that in the Spring of 1991 he met Errol Lindsey (whom he identified by photograph) on the corner of 27th and Kilbourn in the City and County of Milwaukee, State of Wisconsin and that he offered Errol Lindsey money to return with him (the defendant) to his apartment at 924 North 25th Street in the City and County of Milwaukee, State of Wisconsin; that after they returned to his apartment he gave Lindsey a drugged drink and after he fell asleep he strangled Lindsey and then had oral sex with him; he then dismembered the body and saved the skull.

3) Upon the further statement of Dr. L.T. Johnson that he (Johnson) compared the unpainted skulls recovered from the defendant's apartment on July 23rd, 1991 with known dental records of Errol Lindsey and determined that one of the unpainted skulls is that of Errol Lindsey.

VICTIM TONY ANTHONY HUGHES, D.O.B.: 8/26/59

1) Upon the further statement of the defendant that in May of 1991 he met Tony Anthony Hughes (whom he identified through a photograph) who was deaf and mute in front of the 219 Bar on Second Street in the City and County of Milwaukee, State of Wisconsin; that he communicated with Hughes by writing and it appeared that Hughes could read lips; that he offered Hughes $50 to come to his (the defendant's) apartment at 924 North 25th Street in the City and County and Milwaukee, State of Wisconsin to take photos and view videos; further, that he gave Hughes a drink with a sleeping potion and then killed him and dismembered his body and kept his skull.

2) Upon the further statement of Dr. L.T. Johnson that he (Johnson) has compared the unpainted skulls found in the apartment of the defendant with known dental records of Tony Hughes and determined that one of the unpainted skulls is that of Tony Hughes.

3) Upon the statement of Shirley Hughes, an adult citizen, that she (Hughes) is the mother of Tony Hughes and that Tony Hughes came to Milwaukee from Madison during the late afternoon or evening of May 24th, 1991 and that she has not seen him since and further that her son, Tony Hughes, is deaf and mute.

VICTIM KONERAK SINTHASOMPHONE, D.O.B.: 12/2/76

1) Upon the statement of Sounthone Sinthasomphone, an adult resident, that he is the father of Konerak Sinthasomphone who was 14 years of age and that during the afternoon of May 26th, 1991 his son left home and did not return and he has not seen him since.

2) Upon the further statement of the defendant that he (the defendant) in late May of 1991 met a young Oriental male (whom he identified by photograph as Konerak Sinthasomphone) in front of Grand Avenue Mall in Milwaukee and that they went back to his (the defendant's) apartment at 924

(8)

199

North 25th Street in the City and County of Milwaukee, State of Wisconsin; that Sinthasomphone posed for two photographs while he was alive and that he (the defendant) gave Sinthasomphone a drink laced with a sleeping potion and that they then watched videos and while they were watching videos, Sinthasomphone passed out; that he (the defendant) then had oral sex with Sinthasomphone and then he (the defendant) went to a bar to get some beer because he had run out; that while he was walking back from the bar located on 27th just North of Kilbourn, he saw Sinthasomphone staggering down the street and he (the defendant) went up to Sinthasomphone and then the police stopped him; that he told the police that he was a friend of this individual and that the individual had gotten drunk and done this before; that the police escorted them back to his (the defendant's) apartment and he told the police he would take care of Sinthasomphone because he was his friend; that they went into the apartment and after the police left, he killed Sinthasomphone by strangling him and then had oral sex with him and then he took more photographs and dismembered the body and kept the skull.

3) Upon the further statement of Dr. L.T. Johnson that he (Johnson) compared the unpainted skulls recovered from the apartment at 924 North 25th Street with known dental records of Konerak Sinthasomphone and determined that one of the skulls which was recovered from that location is that of Konerak Sinthasomphone.

VICTIM MATT TURNER A/K/A DONALD MONTRELL, D.O.B.; 7/3/70

1) Upon the further statement of the defendant that on June 30th, 1991 after the Gay Pride Parade in Chicago, he met a black male at the Chicago Bus Station and offered him money to pose nude and also view videos at his apartment back in Milwaukee; he (the defendant), with this black male, returned to Milwaukee on a Greyhound Bus and then took a City Vet cab to his (the defendant's) residence in Apartment 213 at 924 North 25th Street, in the City and County of Milwaukee, State of Wisconsin; he (the defendant) gave the black male something to drink which had been drugged and the man passed out and he (the defendant) used a strap to strangle the man and then dismembered him and kept his head and put it in the freezer in his apartment and placed his body in a 57 gallon barrel that he had in his residence; further that he (the defendant) looked at a photograph supplied by the Chicago Police Department of Matt Turner a/k/a Donald Montrell and indicated that he thought this was the person that he had killed in this incident.

VICTIM JEREMIAH WEINBERGER, D.O.B.: 9/29/67

1) Upon the further statement of the defendant that on or about July 5th, 1991 he met a Puerto Rican male at Carol's Gay Bar on Wells Street in Chicago and that he offered the man money to come with him to Milwaukee to pose for him and to view videos; they took a Greyhound Bus from Chicago to Milwaukee and then took a cab to the defendant's apartment at 924 North 25th Street in the City and County of Milwaukee, State of Wisconsin; this man stayed with him for two days and on the first day they had oral sex and on the second day the man indicated that he wanted to leave and he (the defendant) didn't want the man to leave so he gave him a drink with a sleeping potion in it and strangled him manually and then took photos of

(9)

200

him and dismembered the body; he then took more photos and kept the man's head in the freezer and body in the 57 gallon drum; he (the defendant) looked at a photo supplied by the Chicago Police Department of Jeremiah Weinberger and indicated that this was the man that he had killed in this incident.

2) Upon the statement of Dr. L.T. Johnson that he (Johnson) at the Milwaukee County Medical Examiner's Office compared one of the human heads recovered from the freezer at 924 North 25th Street with known dental records of Jeremiah Weinberger and determined that the severed human head that he examined in comparison with those records was the head of Jeremiah Weinberger.

VICTIM OLIVER LACY, D.O.B.: 6/23/67

1) Upon the further statement of the defendant that on or about July 15th, 1991 he met a black male on 27th Street between State and Kilbourn in Milwaukee and that the man stated he was going to his cousin's house; he invited the man to his residence to pose for photos and the man agreed to come and model; when they got to the residence at 924 North 25th Street in the City and County of Milwaukee, State of Wisconsin, they removed their clothes and did body rubs and he gave the man a drink which had sleeping potion in it; when the man fell asleep, he strangled him and then had anal sex with him after death; he dismembered the body and placed the man's head in the bottom of the refrigerator in a box and kept the man's heart in the freezer to eat later; he also kept the man's body in the freezer; he kept the man's identification which identified the man as Oliver Lacy, date of birth 6/23/67.

VICTIM JOSEPH BRADEHOFT, D.O.B.: 1/24/66

1) Upon the further statement of the defendant that on or about July 19th, 1991 he met a white male on Wisconsin Avenue near Marquette University; the man was waiting for a bus and had a six pack under his arm; he (the defendant) got off a bus at that location and approached the man and offered him money to pose and view videos and the man agreed; they returned to the defendant's residence at 924 North 25th Street in the City and County of Milwaukee, State of Wisconsin; they had oral sex and then he gave the man a drink with a sleeping potion in it and then strangled him with a strap while he slept; he dismembered this man and put his head in the freezer and his body in the same blue 57 gallon barrel where he had placed the bodies of the black male and the Puerto Rican male; he kept this man's identification card which identified him as Joseph Bradehoft, date of birth 1/24/66.

AS TO VICTIMS TURNER, LACY AND BRADEHOFT

1) Upon the statement of Dr. Jeffrey Jentzen, Medical Examiner for Milwaukee County, that on July 23rd, 1991 he was called by the Milwaukee Police Department to Apartment 213 at 924 North 25th Street in the City and County of Milwaukee, State of Wisconsin and inside the apartment at that location, among other evidence, he observed a refrigerator with a freezer section; the refrigerator contained a human head and the freezer section

(10)

201

contained human body parts; also there was a floor standing freezer which was found to contain three human heads and other body parts and there was a 57 gallon drum which contained human body parts. _Jentzen_ further stated that at the Milwaukee County Medical Examiner's Office these human body parts were examined and that fingerprints were lifted from hands that had been found at the scene and also efforts at dental identification were made; that Dr. L.T. Johnson, whom he (Jentzen) knows to be a forensic odontologist, did the dental examination and that fingerprint lifts were submitted to the Milwaukee Police Department Bureau of Identification for analysis.

2) Upon the statement of Wayne Peterson, that he (Peterson) is a Bureau of Identification technician and supervisor employed by the City of Milwaukee Police Department and that he (Peterson) made comparisons of fingerprints lifted by the Milwaukee County Medical Examiner's Office from body parts recovered at 924 North 25th Street on July 23rd, 1991 with known prints of various persons and was able to identify the prints of Oliver Lacy, Joseph Bradehoft, and Matt Turner a/k/a Donald Montrell as having been lifted from human body parts discovered in that apartment.

AS TO HABITUAL CRIMINALITY

Complainant further states that he has viewed a certified copy of Judgment of Conviction in Milwaukee County Circuit Court Case No. F-882515 and a copy of that Judgment of Conviction is attached hereto and incorporated herein and the aforementioned Judgment of Conviction indicates that the defendant was convicted of felony offenses in Milwaukee County within five years of the offenses listed in this complaint and that he (the defendant) is therefore a Habitual Criminal.

**** END OF COMPLAINT ****

SUBSCRIBED AND SWORN TO BEFORE ME
AND APPROVED FOR FILING August 21, 1991

E. Michael McCann
Deputy/Asst. District Attorney

Donell Domozalski
Complaining Witness

(11)

STATE OF WISCONSIN }
Circuit Court, Milwaukee County } SS

I, GARY J. BARCZAK, Clerk of the Circuit

Court, Director of Court Services, do hereby certify that I have compared the foregoing copy _____ with the original _____

Judgment of Conviction in case F-882515; State of Wisconsin Vs. Jeffrey L. Dahmer

entered in the action therein entitled, that it is a correct transcript therefrom and of the whole thereof as the same remains of record in my office.

IN TESTIMONY WHEREOF, I have hereunto set my hand and affix

the Seal of said Court, on ___ July 25, 1991 ___
(Month, Day, Year)

Gary J Barczak

Clerk of the Circuit Court
Criminal Division

2472 SEC 5 PAGE 170

203

Division of Corrections
DOC-19 (Rev. 7/85)
JUDGMENT OF CONVICTION
SENTENCE IMPOSED & STAYED, PROBATION ORDERED
STATE OF WIS.
Division of
Section

STATE OF WISCONSIN, Plaintiff

STATE OF WISCONSIN, Circuit Court Branch ___

v.

Jeffrey L. Dahmer _____ Defendant   County _Milwaukee_

_5-21-60_ Defendant Date of Birth   Court Case No. _F-882515_

The defendant entered his/her plea of ☒ guilty   ☐ not guilty   ☐ no contest;

The ☒ Court ☐ Jury found the defendant guilty of:

Crime(s)	Wis. Statute(s) Violated	Felony or Misdemeanor (F or M)	Class (A-E)	Date(s) Crime Committed
2° Sexual Assault	940.225(2)(e)	F	E	
Enticing Child for Immoral Purposes	944.12	F	C	9/26/88

committed in this County; and

On _July 23, 1989_, the Court inquired of the defendant why sentence should not be pronounced, sufficient grounds to the contrary being shown or appearing to the Court, and the Court having accorded the district attorney, defense counsel, and the defendant an opportunity to address the Court regarding sentence; and upon the evidence, records, and proceedings, the Court pronounced findings and judgment as follows:

IT IS ADJUDGED that the defendant on _Jan. 30, 1989_ was convicted as found guilty, and is sentenced to the Wisconsin State Prisons for an indeterminate term of not more than # 1 _5_ years the County Jail for _#2, 3 years # Dodge - consecutive_

IT IS DETERMINED that society will not be harmed and the defendant will benefit by being placed on probation pursuant to Sec. 973.09, Wis. Stats.;

IT IS ADJUDGED that execution of the sentence is stayed and the defendant is placed on probation for the period of _5 years ea. ct._ _concurrent_, in the custody and control of the Wisconsin Department of Health and Social Services, subject to its rules and orders pursuant to Sec. 973.10, Wis. Stats.;

IT IS DETERMINED AND ORDERED that the record requires court-imposed conditions as follows:
☐ None   ☒ As ordered below:
That the defendant has the ability to pay within that period the amounts ordered herein. Should his/her financial condition change s/he shall forthwith petition this Court for reconsideration of such conditions.

Fines: ☒None ☐$ _____ ; Court Costs: ☐None ☐$ _Yes_

Attorney Fees: ☒None ☐$ _____ ; Restitution: ☒None ☐$ _____

Other: ☒None ☐$ _____ ;

Mandatory Victim/Witness Surcharge ☒Felony _____ (# counts) @ $30.00   Amount $ _50 + 50_
☐Misdemeanor _____ (# counts) @ $20.00   Amount $ _____
(Sec. 973.045 Wis. Stats.) Paid ☐ Yes Amount $ _____ ; ☐ No

#1 That the defendant shall be incarcerated in the County Jail for the following periods:
☐None ☐ The period of _1 yr Huber / Work Release - Black Release. In-patient out-patient alcohol treatment / No contact with anyone under 18 yrs of age_

IT IS FURTHER ORDERED that the defendant shall pay surcharges pursuant to Sec. 973.09(1)(b), Wis. Stats.

IT IS ADJUDGED that _____ days sentence credit pursuant to Sec. 973.155, Wis. Stats., shall be given by the Department if probation is revoked. _2472_ SEC _3_ PAGE _171_

IT IS ORDERED THAT THE Sheriff deliver the defendant into the custody of the Department as it directs if probation is _____; the Sheriff having custody of the defendant shall deliver him/her to the Reception Center designated _____.

BY ORDER OF THE COURT. Signature of Judge, Deputy or Clerk of Court

Mark P. Geraci

Name of Judge _William Gardner_   Date Signed _5/24/89_

Name of Defense Attorney _Gerald Boyle_   Name of District Attorney _Gale Shelton_

[SEAL - CIRCUIT COURT MILWAUKEE WISCONSIN]

IMPORTANT: ...

Artwork Courtesy of Stanislav.

Artwork Courtesy of Stanislav.

PO15-B 5-89 SUPPLEMENT REPORT MILWAUKEE POLICE DEPARTMENT	☒ INCIDENT SUPPLEMENT ☐ ACCIDENT SUPPLEMENT ☐ JUVENILE SUPPLEMENT	PAGE _1_ of _4_	DATE OF REPORT 08/26/91	INCIDENT/ACCIDENT # 91-51767/M-2472-2482	
INCIDENT INFORMATION INCIDENT	HOMICIDE		DATE OF INCIDENT/ACCIDENT 07/23/91		REP CON #
VICTIM	LACY, Oliver		LOCATION OF INCIDENT/ACCIDENT (Address) 924 N. 25th St., #213		DIST
JUVENILE LAST NAME	FIRST	MID	DATE OF BIRTH	☐ DETAINED ☐ ORDERED TO MCCC ☐ OTHER	
QUAN	TYPE OF PROPERTY	DESCRIPTION	SERIAL #	CODE #	VALUE

REFER TO FOLLOWUP NUMBER:

NARRATIVE

On Monday, 08-26-91, at approximately 11:30am, I was informed by Captain Donald DOMAGALSKI that he had received a phone call through Attorney Gerald BOYLE's office indicating that Jeffrey DAHMER wanted to speak to us. Captain DOMAGALSKI requested that we obtain an order to produce for Mr. DAHMER and bring him to the CIB where he could be interviewed by ourselves and then interviewed by Dr. Ken SMAIL for Attorney BOYLE.

At approximately 2:30pm we picked up Jeffrey DAHMER at the Milwaukee County Jail and conveyed him to the CIB where we asked him various follow up questions relative to our investigation.

We asked him whether or not he knew an individual by the name of Kevin Paul BYRNE, W/M, DOB 01-25-63, who owns and operates a fitting room out of his residence and who he may have met at the bath house on 7th and Wisconsin and may have had sex with. We had information that Kevin may be a bartender at the Phoenix right now. We asked Jeff this and he stated that he did not recall the individual's name but stated that he had sex at the bath house on Wisconsin with several individuals. I then asked Jeff if he had ever told anyone that he had shaved the hair off his body to look younger at which time he stated he did. This is the information that we had received from Kevin BYRNE. Mr. DAHMER stated that he does not recall this individual but he does recall telling this to someone who he had been with in the bath house.

I then questioned him regarding information we received from James Patrick FETZER, W/M, DOB 09-15-51, who is employed at Ambrosia Chocolate who worked with, and ate lunch with Mr. DAHMER. James stated that Jeff would tell him that he had a good time when he went to Chicago and also that he had a good time when he went to Florida on vacation. I asked Mr. DAHMER if he did, in fact, go to Florida on vacation and he stated "no" that he couldn't afford it. He stated that he only went to Chicago on his vacations but he did recall telling James that he had a good time in Chicago and that he would like to live in Florida again because he had lived there in the past. He again stated that he hasn't been to Florida since his return from Miami in 1981.

172

REPORTING OFFICER	SEC 5 PAGE	PAYROLL #	LOC CODE	SUPERVISOR SIGNATURE Lt. KM ___

	INCIDENT	HOMICIDE		DATE OF INCIDENT/ACCIDENT 07-23-91		REP CON #
INCIDENT INFORMATION	VICTIM	LACY, Oliver		LOCATION OF INCIDENT/ACCIDENT (Address) 924 N. 25th Street #213		DIST
JUVENILE LAST NAME	FIRST	MID	DATE OF BIRTH		O DETAINED O ORDERED TO MCCC O OTHER	
QUAN	TYPE OF PROPERTY	DESCRIPTION		SERIAL #	CODE #	VALUE

We then asked Mr. DAHMER who helped him move into his residence at 924 N. 25th Street in May of 1990 and he stated that he hired the Atlas moving company to help him move his large cedar chest, a wood pedestal, and various other items from his grandmother's residence to the 25th Street address. He stated that he paid $100.00 for the move.

I then asked Mr. DAHMER if he was ever at the Red Carpet Lanes in Pewaukee in May of 1991 and he stated that the only Red Carpet Lanes he was ever at was the one around 76th and Oklahoma and this was around Christmas of 1990 when he went there with his father and brother.

We then asked him whether or not he had ever asked a cab driver, namely E.C. FITZPATRICK, W/M, DOB 08-18-65, to come into his apartment for a drink after he had taken the cab home. The cab driver stated that he didn't drink but he would smoke a joint and DAHMER stated to the cab driver that he did have marijuana in his apartment but the cab driver declined stating that he had to work. Upon mentioning this, DAHMER stated that this did happen but it was just a cab that he had taken home and he asked the driver to come in for a sociable drink. He related that he did not intend to kill this person only hope that it might lead to some type of sex.

Regarding supplementry report #177 which indicated that Jeffrey DAHMER had been involved in an altercation on the third floor at the Grand Avenue in the bathroom. It was reported that he was in the bathroom and two white males entered at which time he bent down to look at one of the white males' penis. Mr. DAHMER denied this and stated that he never approached anyone in the bathroom nor did he ever follow anyone out of the bathrooms. He stated that he only approached them when they were in the mall area itself.

In regards to supp #184 in which it stated that Jeffrey was observed coming in to the United Military supply store on Saturday, 07-20-91, with a black male, looking at knives around 3:00pm he stated that this was totally untrue. He related that he has not been in that store since a week or two prior to the date he was arrested. He related that he had pawned the knife he used to cut up his victim's at the Military store across from the Dunkin Donuts about four months ago for $10.00 but then he picked it up about two weeks after pawning it sometime in April or May of 1991.

Regarding supplementry report #296 and #297 indicating that Jeff may have gone by

| REPORTING OFFICER 2472 | 5 | PAYROLL # PAGE 173 | LOC CODE | SUPERVISOR SIGNATURE Lt. K M Mentler |

JUVENILE LAST NAME	FIRST	MID	DATE OF BIRTH	O DETAINED O ORDERED TO MCCC O OTHER	
QUAN	TYPE OF PROPERTY	DESCRIPTION	SERIAL #	CODE #	VALUE

the name of John and had been sucked off," in Juneau Park, by an individual by the name of "Dee," Jeff denied this and stated that he has never been in Juneau park. He related that does not know this individual nor has he ever met anyone in that vicinity.

Regarding follow up #422 which was a photo of a missing white male, Michael L. LIMESAND, W/M, DOB 09-26-58, who was also known as "Miranda." We received this photo from Freeport, Illinois. This person was gay and has been missing since Saturday, 05-25-85, Jeff looked at the photo and stated that he doesn't know him, never saw him and he also stated that he has never been in Madison other than driving through it with his father and brother years ago.

We then questioned Mr. DAHMER in regards to a phone call placed at his residence on 02-17-91 to an individual known as Michael LISOWSKI, who is the director of the Milwaukee AIDS project. We had also received information that victim #9, Curtis STRAUGHTER, had been living with Michael LISOWSKI around this time. We asked Mr. DAHMER if he allowed any of the people that he lured to his residence use his phone and he stated he did. He stated that he never called Mr. LISOWSKI and he said that it was probably Curtis STRAUGHTER who made the call due to the fact that he let several people use his phone once he got them into his residence. A check of the records showed that the phone call was placed to Michael LISOWSKI on 02-17-91 at 6:40pm.

We also questioned Mr. DAHMER as to the night clubs he had visited in Chicago and he stated they were the Bistro 2, Carole's, the Vortex, Christopher's Street, the Lucky Horseshoe, Little Jim's and Roscoe's. He also stated that he visited Ram's (phonetic) book store, including the back viewing room, the Unicorn and the Man's country bath clubs.

In regards to gay bars he frequented or stopped at in Milwaukee stated they were the 219 Club, the Phoenix, C'est La Vie, LaCage, the Boot Camp, which was once or twice, the M&M Lounge, which was once, Partners, which was once, the Triangle and the Ballgame. He related that there may be one or two others but he could not recall the names of these at this time.

During this interview process, at approximately 3:25pm, Dr. Ken SMAIL arrived and he interviewed Jeffrey DAHMER until approximately 4:50pm at which time he left and Mr. DAHMER was given a couple more cigarettes, a cup of coffee, and was questioned regarding the nightclubs he had visited. Mr. DAHMER was then conveyed back to the Milwaukee County

REPORTING OFFICER M 472, SEC 5 / PAGE	PAYROLL # 174	LOC CODE	SUPERVISOR SIGNATURE H. KMeuler

PO15-8 5-89 **SUPPLEMENT REPORT**
MILWAUKEE POLICE DEPARTMENT
O INCIDENT SUPPLEMENT
O ACCIDENT SUPPLEMENT
O JUVENILE SUPPLEMENT
PAGE 4 of 4
DATE OF REPORT 08-26-91
INCIDENT/ACCIDENT # 91-51767/M2472-M2482

	INCIDENT	HOMICIDE		DATE OF INCIDENT/ACCIDENT 07-23-91		REP COM #
INCIDENT						
INFORMATION	VICTIM	LACY, Oliver		LOCATION OF INCIDENT/ACCIDENT (Address) 924 N. 25th Street #213		DIST 3

JUVENILE LAST NAME	FIRST	MID	DATE OF BIRTH	O DETAINED O ORDERED TO MCCC O OTHER

QUAN	TYPE OF PROPERTY	DESCRIPTION	SERIAL #	CODE #	VALUE

Jail at 5:35pm by myself, Detective Dennis MURPHY, Patrick KENNEDY and Lieutenant Ray SUCIK.

    Report dictated by: Det. Dennis MURPHY

DM:dls 08-26-91

2472 SE 5 PAGE ►175

REPORTING OFFICER	PAYROLL #	LOC CODE	SUPERVISOR SIGNATURE
Det. Dennis MURPHY	32893	91	Lt. KMeuler

| | INCIDENT HOMICIDE | | DATE OF INCIDENT/ACCIDENT 07/23/91 | | REP CON # |
| INCIDENT INFORMATION | VICTIM LACY, Oliver | | LOCATION OF INCIDENT/ACCIDENT (Address) 924 N. 25th St., #213 | | DIST 3 |

| JUVENILE LAST NAME | FIRST | MID | DATE OF BIRTH | O DETAINED O ORDERED TO MCCC O OTHER |

| QUAN | TYPE OF PROPERTY | DESCRIPTION | | SERIAL # | CODE # | VALUE |

REFER TO FOLLOWUP NUMBER:

NARRATIVE

On Wednesday, 08-28-91, I received a phone call from Attorney Wendy PATRICKUS, indicating that her client, Jeffrey DAHMER, wish to speak with us, requesting that we obtain orders to produce, so that we can speak with him, and that she and Dr. SMAIL, could also converse with him at the CIB. *DET. PATRICK KENNEDY & MYSELF*

At approximately 1:15 we obtained an order, produced, picked up DAHMER, and conveyed him to the CIB. At that time I showed DAHMER a photograph we had received from the Chicago Police Dept., indicating a black male, who went by the name of Farley TELLADO. Upon DAHMER viewing this photo, he stated he does not know this individual, nor has he ever seen him. This individual has been missing since 06-29-91, and was last seen in his residence. DAHMER stated he has never heard the name, nor seen this individual.

DAHMER was then asked which moving company had moved him to his residence, at 924 N. 25th St., in May, 1990, because he originally stated that it was Atlas Moving Van. A check with Atlas showed that they had not moved him. DAHMER states that it might have been Allied, but he is not sure, but he believes the moving company began with an "A". We will attempt to question Allied Moving Co., to ascertain whether or not they have any records on their computer.

I then questioned DAHMER in regards to his stay in Miami, Florida, in 1981, when he was staying in the Bimini Bay Motel, and asked him what landmarks or other hotels were in the area, and he stated that the Bimini Bay Hotel was approximately ¼ mile from the ocean, and about ¼ mile down Collins Ave., was the Newport Hotel, and the Castaway Hotel. He stated that the Submarine Shop, where he worked, was approximately five blocks away from these hotels. He also stated that the Fountain Blue Hilton was three miles away on Collins Ave. He stated that the Sunshine Submarine Shop was located in like a mini mall, in a semi circle, off of Collins Ave., and you could get breakfast, dinner, or lunch, at this location. He states he does not know if this restaurant is still presently there, he could only recall what was there at the time he was there.

At approximately 1:45, Dr. SMAIL arrived to interview DAHMER, along with Attorney Wendy PATRICKUS. At approximately 2:25, Dr. SMAIL, and Attorney PATRICKUS remained until

| REPORTING OFFICER 2472, SEC 5 PAGE 176 | PAYROLL # | LOC CODE | SUPERVISOR SIGNATURE Lt. KMenle |

INCIDENT INFORMATION	INCIDENT HOMICIDE (STABBING)		DATE OF INCIDENT 07-28-91		REP CON #
	VICTIM LACY, Oliver		LOCATION OF INCIDENT 924 N. 25th Street #P13		DIST

JUVENILE LAST NAME	FIRST	MID	DATE OF BIRTH	O DETAINED O ORDERED TO MCCC O OTHER

QUAN	TYPE OF PROPERTY	DESCRIPTION	SERIAL #	CODE #	VALUE

around 4:00 p.m.

　　After Attorney PATRICKUS left, we again interviewed DAHMER regarding other correspondence we received regarding "missings", and we showed him a photograph of a white male who was known as Grant HOWELL, 09-19-63, and he was from Lake Station, Indiana. HOWELL was last seen in 1982, and his brother, Garnet HOWELL, was requesting assistance to ascertain whether or not DAHMER had in fact known his brother, or had seen him, or had associated with him. We showed DAHMER the photograph we had obtained from the HOWELL family, along with several other family photos, and he stated that he has never seen this individual, and he does not know him. Grant HOWELL will be contacted regarding this investigation, and informed of our results.

　　I then asked DAHMER whether or not he ever ate pizza at Giuseppi's Restaurant, located on Bluemound Ave., and Mayfair Rd., due to a letter that was received by Chief ARREOLA, from a citizen name David PETZOLD. PETZOLD stated that he believes he was confronted by DAHMER at Giuseppi's, on a Friday or Saturday night, during baseball season. He believes DAHMER attempted to persuade him to go with him. Upon questioning DAHMER regarding this, he stated he has never been at Giuseppi's, and the only pizza place he went to in that location was Pizza Hut, and he went there around March, because it was still cold out. He stated that he only had one of the five minute pan pizza's and then left. He stated he was waiting for a bus to go to Mayfair Mall, so he could buy fish supplies for his fish tank. DAHMER was then returned to the Milwaukee County Jail.

　　Report dictated by: Detective Dennis MURPHY

DM: hvs 08-28-91

2472 SEC. 5 PAGE 177

REPORTING OFFICER Det. MURPHY	PAYROLL # 32893	LOC CODE 91	SUPERVISOR SIGNATURE

| | INCIDENT
HOMICIDE | | DATE OF INCIDENT/ACCIDENT
07/23/91 | | REP CON # |
| INCIDENT
INFORMATION | VICTIM
LACY, Oliver | | LOCATION OF INCIDENT/ACCIDENT (Address)
924 N. 25th St., #213 | | DIST |

| JUVENILE LAST NAME | FIRST | MID | DATE OF BIRTH | □ DETAINED
□ ORDERED TO MCCC
□ OTHER |
| QUAN | TYPE OF PROPERTY | DESCRIPTION | SERIAL # | CODE # | VALUE |

REFER TO FOLLOWUP NUMBER:

NARRATIVE

On Wednesday, 08-28-91, I, Detective KENNEDY, along with Detective Dennis MURPHY, obtained a order to produce for the subject Jeffrey DAHMER, and conveyed him from the 5th fl., Sheriff's Dept., Lock Up, to the 4th fl., CIB interrogation room, where we met with the suspect, along with his Defense Attorney Wendy PATRICKUS.

At this time the suspect was asked a series of questions by Det. MURPHY, regarding information received from outside jurisdiction. His answers will be found in a detailed supplement filed by Det. MURPHY. At the end of the interview Attorney PATRICKUS left the building, and before taking the suspect back to the Milwaukee County Sheriff's Dept., he requested another cup of coffee, and a cigaret, at which time I complied, and he stated "is there anything else you wish to ask me regarding the offense?"

At this time I began to question DAHMER regarding the way in which he would decide which individuals to approach. This is related to individuals that eventually became victims of his. He stated that before going out for the evening, he generally would know whether or not he planned to commit a Homicide, and before going out he would prepare the #10 by powderizing it, and leaving it in a glass on the counter top of his kitchen. He states once at the bar he would generally drink by himself, and observe the diffrent individuals in the gay establishment. He states that it did not matter the color, race, or ethnic heritage of any of his victims, as long as they met, what he would call, the physical profile. He stated this was generally from mid to late teens, to mid 20s, males with a medium height, slinder build, and generally smooth skin. He stated upon sitting in the taverns and drinking, he would notice one, maybe two or three, who fit this profile, and who he found attractive. He also stated that he generally looked for individuals that were alone, or not with a tight knit group. He states upon deciding which victim he found attractive, he would generally wait until approximately bar time, which would be the closing of the tavern, and then as the patrons were filing up, he would approach the victims, and ask them if they wish to accompany him home for either pictures, sexual contact, or for cocktails, many of the times offering them money. He states this was his general routine, except for times when he met some of his

| REPORTING OFFICER
2472 | SEC 5 | PAYROLL #
178 | LOC CODE | SUPERVISOR SIGNATURE
Lt. Menken |

| INCIDENT HOMICIDE (STABBING) | | | DATE OF INCIDENT/ACCIDENT 07-27-91 | | REP CON |
| INFORMATION VICTIM LACY, Oliver | | | LOCATION OF INCIDENT/ACCIDENT (Address) 924 N. 25th Street #213 | | DI |

| JUVENILE LAST NAME | FIRST | MID | DATE OF BIRTH | O DETAINED O ORDERED TO MCCC O OTHER |

| QUAN | TYPE OF PROPERTY | DESCRIPTION | | SERIAL # | CODE # | VALUE |

victims on the street, in front of the bookstores, and then the same routine as far as offering money for sex, photographs, or cocktails.

Regarding the indivdual picked up in the mall, that being the victim, Konerak SINTHASOMPHONE. He states that he had been hanging around the Grand Avenue Mall that day, and was leaving the mall, exiting the Wisconsin Ave., exit, and as he was walking out, the victim, SINTHASOMPHONE, was entering the mall. He states upon seeing the individual he was immediately attractive to him, and struck up a conversation. It was at this time that he offered the individual money to return with him to his apartment for photographs. He states regarding other times in the mall, that there were several times that he walked throughout the mall, and would look for individuals that fit his physical profile, and he would approach them, and offer them money, however, many of the people who he talked with and offered money to, returned to his apartment with him refused, some even were hostile towards him. At this time the interview was terminated and Det. MURPHY, and myself, returned the suspect to the 5th fl., Sheriff's Dept., Lock up.

Report dictated by: Detective Patrick KENNEDY

PK: hvs 08-28-91

2472 SEC 5 / PAGE 179

Jury: Dahmer sane

Killer gets life for each murder

MILWAUKEE — Jeffrey Dahmer was sane when he killed and dismembered 15 men and boys in a horrifying quest for sexual gratification, a jury ruled yesterday.

The decision means that Dahmer, who had pleaded guilty to the murders, will receive a mandatory life sentence for each count. A hearing is scheduled tomorrow.

"Dahmer knew at all times that what he was doing was wrong," said District Attorney E. Michael McCann. "This is not the case of a psychotic man."

Dahmer, as he has throughout the three-week sanity trial, sat stone-faced as Judge Laurence Gram calmly read through the jury's verdict on each of 15 murder counts.

The grim roll call of Dahmer's prey sent a shudder of emotion rolling through several victims' families seated behind the man who claimed to have eaten parts of their loved ones.

Some shouted in pain. Others rocked with sobs.

"God bless you, I love you, my brother," one relative called to McCann as he walked out of the courtroom. Others hugged and thanked the prosecutor.

'Powerful argument'

"They gave a powerful, powerful argument," said Teresa Smith, sister of victim Edward Smith. "They brought back the faith I'd lost in the justice system."

Her sister Carolyn said she felt some sympathy for Dahmer "because I am Catholic."

"At times I have hatred like anyone would, but you have got to love all," she said.

McCann said jurors realized Dahmer, 31, could have controlled himself, and 10 of the 12 jurors — the minimum required by law — agreed.

"His whole conduct showed he was a con artist ... above-average in intelligence, and that's all we went by," said juror Karl Stahle.

Defense attorney Gerald Boyle said he warned Dahmer to expect the worst, and Dahmer had thanked him for trying.

"He wants to close the book on it and just live out the rest of his life as he knows it's going to be," Boyle said.

After the verdicts were read, Boyle held a 10-minute meeting with Dahmer and Dahmer's parents.

Few crimes compare for sheer horror, and Dahmer's sanity trial provided an in-depth study of the mind of a killer who — sane or insane — had strayed over 12 years as far outside the bounds of civilized behavior as most people could imagine.

Even his own lawyer said he was not there to excuse Dahmer's behavior, but to explain it.

He insisted that Dahmer's craving for sex with dead males and his fear of loneliness drove him out of control — to kill again and again, unable to stop.

"This was not an evil man. This was a sick man whose sickness rose to the level of mental illness," Boyle said, arguing Dahmer suffered from necrophilia, a sexual attraction to corpses.

Dahmer, a former chocolate-factory worker, probably will be imprisoned in a high-observation, one-man cell at the Columbia Correctional Institution.

Verdict put jurors to the test

MILWAUKEE — Jurors who yesterday found Jeffrey Dahmer sane when he admittedly killed and dismembered 15 men and boys had to consider a two-pronged test in deciding his sanity.

To find him insane, they would have had to rule he had a mental disease or defect.

Then they would have had to decide that the disease kept him from knowing right from wrong, or kept him from being able to stop himself.

A finding of insanity would have meant confinement in a state mental institution, but he could have petitioned for release every six months.

But having been found sane yesterday, Dahmer will get a mandatory life prison sentence for each slaying.

Ten of the 12 jurors had to agree on each of 15 verdicts — the exact margin retained as two jurors dissented on each finding of sanity.

JEFFREY DAHMER prepares to leave courtroom yesterday.

Dahmer killed at Portage prison

First murder case at CCI since it was built

PORTAGE — Serial killer Jeffrey Dahmer was murdered during an attack early Monday morning, apparently by another inmate, in the gymnasium at the Columbia Correctional Institution in Portage.

Columbia County Sheriff Jim Smith said Dahmer died from severe head trauma.

Authorities said Dahmer and another inmate, Jesse Anderson, were transported to the Divine Savior Hospital in Portage, where Dahmer was pronounced dead at 9:11 a.m. Authorities with the state Department of Corrections said inmate Christopher J. Scarver, who was working with the other two, allegedly carried out the attack. Scarver currently is serving a life sentence for murder.

Throughout the day, since the Portage Police Department received a request for an ambulance to respond to the prison at 8:26 a.m. Monday, officials didn't say much about the incident. Smith said Dahmer's body was transported to the University of Wisconsin Hospital in Madison for an autopsy. The cause of death should be determined by the pathologist who performs the autopsy, the sheriff said.

Anderson was treated at the Portage hospital for injuries he suffered in the attack and then he was transported to UW Hospital where he was in critical condition Monday night. Anderson was serving a life sentence for stabbing and bludgeoning his wife to death in Milwaukee.

Sheriff Smith said the Department of Corrections released all the information on the suspect. Scarver's name was released late Monday evening.

"I don't know why some of this was released," Smith said. "I don't think it's necessary.

"Investigators are still doing interviews out there," he said at about 10:30 p.m. Monday. "I didn't want to release anything until our investigation was completed."

Michael Sullivan, secretary of the Department of Corrections, said the three men were on janitorial duty at the time of the attack. Dahmer's body was found in a bathroom and shower area for prison staff at 8:10 a.m. Anderson was found in a bathroom for prisoners.

A bloody broom handle was found in the gymnasium area, but Sullivan wouldn't say if it was the murder weapon. Scarver allegedly was found with blood on his clothes. There also was a great deal of blood in the area of the attack.

Sullivan also commented on the brutality of the attack.

Serial killer Jeffrey Dahmer was murdered during an attack early Monday at the Columbia Correctional Institution in Portage.

Dahmer's body cremated

■ MILWAUKEE — Serial killer Jeffrey Dahmer's remains were cremated Sunday, although his brain was preserved while his parents argue over whether to give it to scientists for study. His father, Lionel Dahmer, of Akron, Ohio, claimed his half of the ashes Sunday, while arrangements were being made for his mother, Joyce Flint, of Fresno, Calif., to receive the rest. Flint wants her son's brain examined to determine whether biological factors influenced his actions. Lionel Dahmer has objected, saying he wishes to put his son's actions behind him. After police found body parts in Dahmer's Milwaukee apartment in 1991, he admitted killing 17 young men and boys, mutilating and sometimes cannibalizing his victims. Dahmer was beaten to death in a Wisconsin prison in 1994.

LETTERS AND CORRESPONDENCE

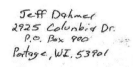

Jeff Dahmer
2925 Columbia Dr.
P.O. Box 900
Portage, WI. 53901

Protect the Environment

29
USA

Rick Staton
P.O. Box 45888
Baton Rouge, Louisiana.
70895-4888

Save the Rain Forests

1.   6·2·93

Dear Rick,

Hi, I hope that this letter finds you in good health and spirits. From your letter, it sounds as if you have friends in far away places.

I do have a job now. I sweep, mop, and clean windows in the prison gym. I earn about $25.00 per month. After I pay for my cigarettes, I have almost nothing left for writing materials. The prison will not allow anyone to send in envelopes, stamps, paper, or books. However, they do allow money to be sent in, money orders are preffered.

I've been wanting to buy a word
                                            over →

Courtesy of Rick Staton.

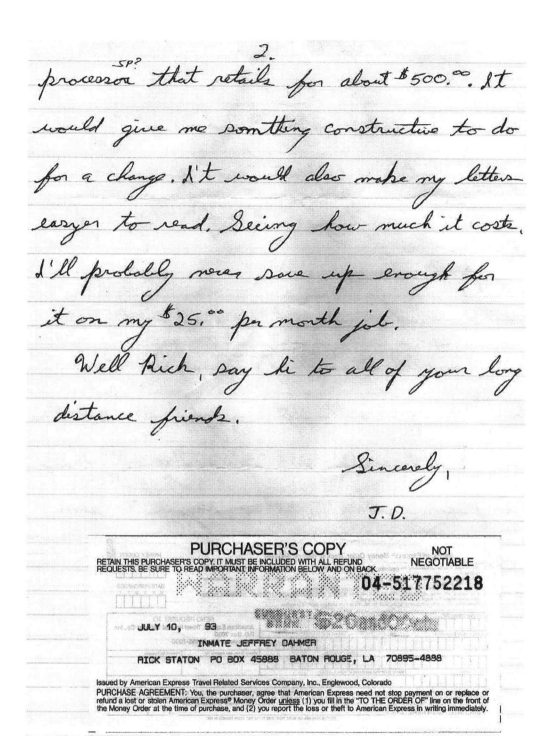

2.

processor [sp?] that retails for about $500.⁰⁰. It would give me something constructive to do for a change. It would also make my letters easier to read. Seeing how much it costs, I'll probably never save up enough for it on my $25.⁰⁰ per month job.

Well Rick, say hi to all of your long distance friends.

Sincerely,

J.D.

Courtesy of Rick Staton.

Tommy G. Thompson
Governor

Patrick J. Fiedler
Secretary

Mailing Address
Columbia Correctional Institution
Post Office Box 950
Portage, WI 53901-0950
Telephone (608) 742-9100

State of Wisconsin
Department of Corrections

July 29, 1993

Mr. Rick Staton
P.O. Box 45888
Baton Rouge, LA 70895-4888

Dear   Mr. Staton:

Jeff Dahmer

has requested to have your name placed on his/her list of approved visitors. If you are interested in visiting the above-named inmate, it is necessary for you to answer the questions on the back of this letter. All questions must be answered. Any omission or falsification of information will be considered sufficient reason for denial of visiting privileges. Please include any other information that you feel would be helpful to us in evaluating your interest in being considered for visiting.

If you do not wish to visit with the inmate, we would appreciate being advised of this also.

Any person under 18 years of age must be accompanied by an adult who is on the approved list, unless the visitor is the spouse of the inmate. Minors are also required to have the written approval of their parent or guardian to visit. A space has been provided on the back of this letter for such approval.

If you are approved for visiting and are over the age of 16, you will be required to show identification upon arrival at the institution. Only the following forms of identification will be accepted:

1. State Driver's License
2. Military I.D. (if a member of the military).
3. Department of Transportation (Motor Vehicle Department) Picture Identification Card (SS 343.50 provides for the issuance of an identification card to all qualified applicants over the age of sixteen by the Department of Transportation).
4. County Welfare Department Picture Identification Card
5. State Picture I.D.
6. Passport (current)

For those visitors visiting from out-of-state, driver's licenses and picture identification cards from those states will be accepted.

Failure to return this questionnaire within 30 days will result in an automatic disapproval of visiting privileges.

Sincerely,

Mark Kohn, Social Worker

DOC-21 (Rev. 10/91)
MK/em

Administrative Code
Chapter DOC 309

Courtesy of Rick Staton.

...a day to dream <u>on</u>
...a day to <u>enjoy</u>
...a day to <u>remember</u>!

Happy Birthday !!!

My Dearest Barbara,
    May your special day be filled with joy and every good thing!
        All my Love,
        and many Hugs,
        Jeff
XOXOXO!

Courtesy of Stephen J Giannangelo.

12-4-93

Dear Barbara,

Hello dear friend, how are you this week? Thanks a lot for that great card with the ducks on it. I know that you'll be happy to finish school! Two more weeks - Wow! Hang in there and it will all be over soon! I know that you'll do just great!

My Thanksgiving wasn't so good; I hope that yours was. I answered a staff phone call while I was working in the gym, and got into trouble. Now for the rest of December, I have to stay in the DS-1 disciplinary cell. In here, all I'm allowed to have is toiletries, 1 book, paper and a pen. I won't be able to write to you again until January 94, because my →

writting supplies are restricted in here. I wanted to send you a nice christmas card this year, but I can't because they won't even let me order cards in this DS-1 cell.

Well, have a very Merry Christmas, and a Happy New Year Barbara!

Sincerely, Your friend,

Jeff

P.S.— Money is the only "gift" item that they will allow to be sent in and kept. Thanks for asking!

My Dearest Barbara,   10-23-94

Hello, and how is my special and most Beautiful friend? Thanks so much for your card! I hope that things are still going well for you at school.

Did you know that my cell has "jumping" spiders in it? I killed one two nights ago. I don't like them because I'm afraid that one will crawl into my ear, or up my nose, while I'm sleeping! Oh well, soon winter will be here, and I won't have to worry about creepy insects anymore.

The judge still hasn't decided about my garnishment. This is the second time that he's said he would decide by a certain date, and then changed his mind. You can't even trust the judges to stick by their word these days! But at least the prison has started to let me buy canteen each week again. It's nice to be able to buy stamps, cigarettes, and coffee each week like the other inmates. I've finally been able to pay back the other inmates too.

It was raining for most of the day yesterday. It finally stopped around 6:00p, and I looked out my window and saw this huge solid Pink rainbow! I've never seen a Pink rainbow before.

Barbara, I love you, and I keep you in my thoughts and prayers!

OXOXOX...!!!

All My Love & Many Hugs, Jeff

10-23-94

My Dearest Mary,

Hello and how is my most Beautiful and Lovely friend, my exotic Summer Orchid? Thank you so much for continuing to write to me while I've been unable to. The cards that you've picked out are just great! About has everything been going at home? Have you been on any more interesting adventures, or are you just relaxing? I'm wishing you a belated "Sweetest Day," because you are the Sweetest!

The Judge still hasn't decided about my garnishment. This is the second time that he said he would decide by a certain date and then changed his mind! You can't trust even the judges to stand by their word now-a-days! But at least the prison has started letting me buy from canteen each week now. It's nice to be able to get a steady supply of stamps, cigarettes and coffee each week again! I've finally been able to pay back the other inmates.

Mary did you know that I have "Jumping" spiders in my cell? I killed one two nights ago. I don't like them because I'm afraid that one will crawl in my ear, or up my nose while I'm sleeping!

It was raining for most of the day, but it finally stopped by 6:00 PM. I looked out of my window and I was surprised to see a Huge solid Pink rainbow! I've never seen a Pink rainbow before!

You really do know how to make a guy feel loved! I cherish you, and am keeping you in my thoughts and prayers.

All My Love & Many Hugs, Jeff

Courtesy of Ryan Almighty.

June 28, 1996

Rick Staton
P.O. Box 45888
Baton Rouge, LA 70895-4888

     Re: Estate of Jeffrey Dahmer

Dear Mr. Staton:

     Thank you for your expression of interest in purchasing property from the Estate of Jeffrey Dahmer. As you may be aware, the Estate has recently concluded its transaction with the Milwaukee Civic Pride Fund, which has not only provided compensation to the families of Mr. Dahmer's victims, but has also destroyed all of the property of the Estate. As a result, there will be no auction, and no catalogue has been produced.

     I do, however, wish to thank you again for your interest in this matter. It was sincerely appreciated.

               Very truly yours,

               Robert K. Steuer
               Successor Personal Representative

RKS:mrk

AND AN EYE FOR AN EYE?
"Something has to be done even if we have to auction off this stuff. I don't care if we have to auction his tooth."
—JANIE HAGEN, SISTER OF A JEFFREY DAHMER VICTIM, IN THE NEW YORK *TIMES*. THE KILLER'S PERSONAL EFFECTS MAY BE SOLD TO BENEFIT HIS VICTIMS' SURVIVORS

Courtesy of Rick Staton.   228

ARTIST GALLERY

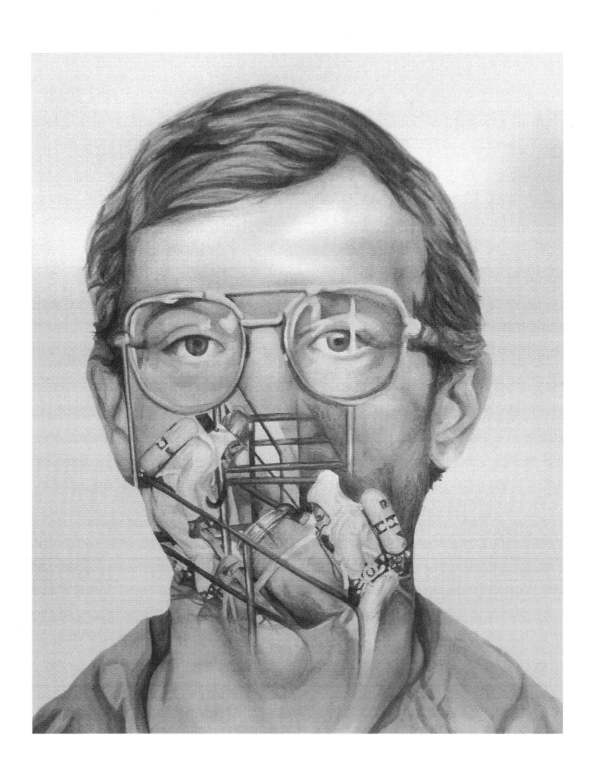

Dahmer

Watercolor, 15 in x 18 in (2016)
Artist: Annie Clift
annieclift.com

Artist Statement

This painting superimposes a photograph of the acid vat being removed from Dahmer's apartment with his mug shot. The relationship of the two images encompasses his crimes, from the cannibalism to his arrest and the depravity discovered at the crime scene. It comments on how its notoriety dehumanized him as crimes overshadow the identities of those involved. They become flattened and indistinguishable from what they've done or had done to them. The rest of the person falls away and they fail to be seen as human or to have a voice that is separated from what happened. Dahmer became a mythologized boogeyman because we want evil to be recognizable when, in reality, it isn't. He was just a man; dehumanizing him reassures us that we are not like him because he is inhuman.

Human Blood Portrait Painting, 2017
Artist: Ryan Almighty, Professional weirdo/human blood painter.

Let me introduce myself... I am a human blood painter and have been using human blood as an artistic medium for performance and later painting for almost 25 years. I also am a collector of oddities /murderbillia and own the *Museum of the Macabre* in Alameda CA.

I am drawn to serial killer/crime portraiture and have already painted Manson, Ramirez, Gacy, Gein, Panzram and many other notable and infamous characters. When I received a letter written by Dahmer to a penpal named Mary I knew I had to add his portrait to the collection.

I found the letter quite intriguing as it was quite flirtatious and seemed that it was an individual Jeff was quite close to. While painting the portrait I had this letter in mind and tried to capture the tragic and frightening multifaceted personality of Jeff. While trying to capture the madness, chaos and even loneliness, all personality traits that made Dahmer the iconic, legendary and infamous individual that we all know and love.

If you wish to visit the letter and human blood portrait it is on display at my museum located in *Tigers Blood Social Club*: 2319 Santa Clara Ave, Alameda CA 94501. If you wish to see more of my human blood painting it can be found on facebook (Human Blood Artwork by Ryan Almighty HBA) Instagram: ALMIGHTY 666 and website: ryan-almighty.pixels.com

235

The Unseen Shrine of Jeffrey Dahmer

Artist: Shane a.k.a Samhane
artgrinder.com

Artist Statement

The image of what Dahmer had as the sketch of the shrine he wanted to build always fascinated me. I wanted to re-create the image in almost real form and give depth to the scene he had in his mind. I have never seen anyone attempt this as it has always remained in sketch form so I wanted to be the first to re-create the shrine as close to colours and look as possible. A copy of the original picture sketch is in the hand of one of the skeletons and also I mounted the picture of Dahmer overlooking the built shrine in tribute to him overlooking his vision.

Wicked Vibes Jeffrey Dahmer Postcard

Artist: Richie Murry, ©Dillon Hallen

Artist Statement

This piece was originally done to promote a "weirdo-art" comic book that Dillon Hallen and myself were working on at the time called *Wicked Vibes*. The stories in the comic were mainly sci-fi and horror related so we were looking to make a promo postcard that gave the impression of something recognizably off-beat and creepy. Since we're both from Milwaukee, the home of arguably one of the most infamous serial killers ever known (Dahmer), we used the "Milwaukee Monster'"as our subject. There are also little details in the image that relate directly to the methods of his madness. On the flip-side of the postcard we included a creepy tourism tagline that read "Wisconsin, We'd love to have you for Dinner!". In my mind it's a little nod to the strange fascination Wisconsin has with its famous native serial killers.

Jeffrey Dahmer

Black ink on paper
Artist: Stanislav
standarkart.bigcartel.com

Artist Statement

I think that for every dark artist it is important to understand the nature of evil and come close to the source. Serial killers and maniacs have always been part of the urban nightmare and of dark art in general, and the Jeffrey Dahmer story is one of the most frightening for me.

Dahmer

Medium: Acrylics on 9x12 stretched canvas (2017)
Artist: Sydney Walton
facebook.com./sydneywaltoniii

Artist Statement

I have been a fan of horror most of my life, and nothing is more horrific than the serial killer and the acts they have committed. Serial killers have always intrigued me, and yes, actually frightened me....because they are real. They unfortunately do exist. Researching what they have done and trying to figure out why they did what they did has always fascinated me. Jeffrey Dahmer has always been at the top of the list for me, as he was headline news as I was going through high school. I've read many books about him, watched many documentaries about him.....all of which I hope has helped me capture the man in this painting.

243

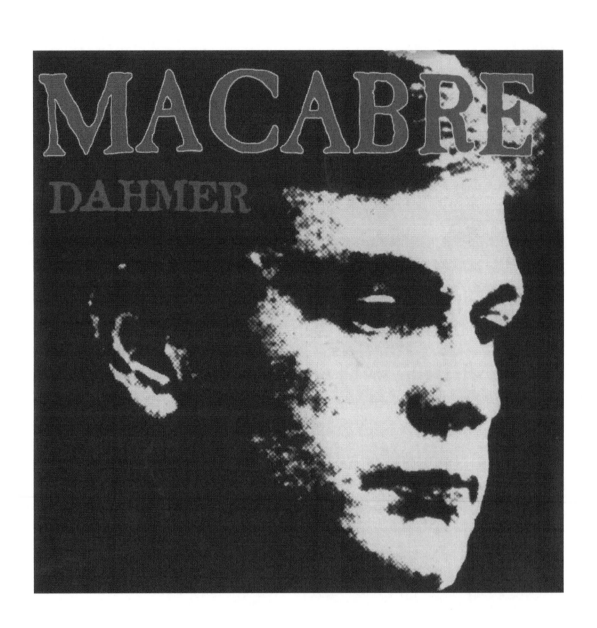

DAHMER ALBUM

Artist: Macabre

Track Listing:

Dog Guts
Hitch Hiker
In the Army Now
Grandmother's House
Blood Bank
Exposure
Ambassador Hotel
Cup of Coffee
Bath House
Jeffrey Dahmer & The Chocolate Factory
Apartment 213
Drill Bit Lobotomy
Jeffrey Dahmer Blues
Mc Dahmers
Into the Toilet with You
Coming to Chicago
Scrub a Dub Dub
Konerak
Media Circus
Temple of Bones
Trial
Do the Dahmer
Baptized
Christopher Scarver
Dahmer's Dead
The Brain

Human Appetite

Artist: Laz Gein
@Laz_tattoo

Artist Statement

I created this piece to be in a serial killer inspired art gallery I did in Sydney in 2010 called "Gallery Forensic." I hired out a shop front, and set the whole place up like a crime scene, police tape, fake limbs, fake blood, it was super fun and got a massive turnout. You can't have a serial killer gallery without Dahmer, to me, he represents everything that frightens people about murderers, he was calm, unassuming, polite, but did some of the most grotesque things we've ever seen, worse than you'll see in any movie or any fiction. The work is a story, his hands putting the tablets in the water, the way he made his victims unconscious, and then holding the skull with that daft expression he has in a lot of photos as if it's not a big deal.

248

Dahmer

Red and black pencil, 8 in x 11 in (2017)
Artist: Bob Ashbaugh

Artist Statement

To me, Jeffery Dahmer was and still is, one of the most fascinating deviant minds of my generation. He was the catalyst for my interest in serial killers and their behavior.

17

Watercolor, 15 in x 18 in (2016)
Artist: Bradley the Dark

Artist Statement

I started painting as a way to deal with my own anxiety and depression. My work naturally takes its turns towards the dark side. I recently decided to do a series of serial killer portraits and Jeffery Dahmer was my very first choice when starting that series. The piece features an acrylic color portrait of Dahmer's Mugshot and two jars, one filled with a heart and one with a severed penis.

Jeffrey Dahmer

AKA: The Milwaukee Monster
Born: May 21, 1960
Died: Beaten to death
with a broom handle by inmates
on November 28, 1994
Victims: 17
Span of Killings: 1978 - 1991
Apprehended: July 22, 1991

Minimalistic Serial Killer Poster

Artist: Dimitri

Artist Statement

In this particular poster I did a series of Serial Killers, in minimalistic form. Just showing the hair or parts that are recognizable from the face and some information about the killer. Simple and to the point.

Dahmer 1 & 2

Artist: Nicolas Castelaux

Artist Statement

As an artist, I have always been struck by the length of Jeffrey Dahmers neck. No real
shoulders, just a long neck. Makes me wonder if he kept the human meat in his throat
for a while before swallowing it. Like some kind of cannibal pelican.

255

The Milwaukee Cannibal

Artist: Adam Crutchfield
Personal Collection of Brandy Williamson

Artist Statement

I have always been very passionate about collecting true crime. Since I was a child, I have always had a huge interest in the darker side of human behavior. Each time I paint a serial killer, after hours of staring at their face, I tend to see behind "the monster". I really start to see the human side of them. It's something that's hard to explain, but when you stare at a face for hours at a time, after a while, I forget the bad person they were, and see them just as human as anyone else. The stories that relate to these subjects are so hard to grasp for any rational thinker. Which in turn, sparks endless amounts of interest, and turns these people into folklore celebrities. Kind of like driving past a really bad car accident. No one wants to look, but everyone slows down to get a glimpse of the macabre that they are being exposed to.

Tom Bombo and Jeff Dahmer

Artist: Mikael Ekström, Cartoonist, Sweden.

Artist Statement

My cartoon character Tom Bombo has meet killers before, but never a serial killer. Jeff Dahmer is notorious, even in Sweden where Tom and I live, so it felt naturally to include Jeff in Tom's world, even though it is debatable if its ok to give a serial killer space in a cartoon.

Class Clown

Artist: Susan Eve Padron
Marker on paper 18"x 11" 2016

Artist Statement

This artwork exemplifies young teenage Dahmer's attempt to fit in with his classmates during high school years by mimicking a man with cerebral palsy. This act had won him a group of friends for a few years.

Dahmer, Party of One

Artist: Josh Cullen
facebook.com/HeythisGuyDoesArt

Artist Statement

When I was in fourth or fifth grade I used to head down to the local library and besides the classics like *Superfudge* and *Dear God, it's Me Margret* I always found myself in the true crime, biography, history, or macabre horror sections. I would get lost in the backgrounds of some of the darkest times and people in history. As I got older, I found it interesting that these serial killers could have been your next door neighbor, your local delicatessen, or a party clown. They committed unspeakable crimes in the most mundane of towns and, eventually, through media, reached almost pop culture icon status. Books, movies, and TV show references put people like Jeffrey Dahmer and Ted Bundy right up there in the ranks of Wheel of Fortune and Oprah.

Over the last few years I have taken my love for pop culture and horror and have combined them into little love letters addressed to pieces of my childhood. Recently, I had the idea to take this same approach; this over the top, so bright that it hurts your eyes, pop art style and apply it to those who went from violent murderers to those who will end up being a Jeopardy answer. I started with Dahmer, the former "Milwaukee Cannibal" turned Katy Perry lyric. The reason I went with the colors in the original piece was a homage to the neon mess that was the 1980's and early 90's. It's fluorescent, yet distorted at the same time. His face, taken from his mugshot, is broken by intricate blade work in reference to the precise way he would clean and dispose of some of his victims. I found that black suited his demeanor and how he almost seems to look back at you, mocking you for your unintelligent nature.

Wolf

Artist: Benjamin Prince
Artwork provided via The House of Liquid Mercury

Artist Statement

Although drawing has always come naturally to me, it's not always necessarily easy. This one challenged me because it made me think back to when I was a child and how this news story made me feel. I also thought of all of the pain and horror he caused. I gathered photographs of not only him, but also of predators in nature. One of a wolf really popped out at me. The angle and the gaze were an eerie match. Taking a peek inside the mind is part of and helps a lot in capturing someone's likeness down on paper. I usually mix materials but decided to do keep this one entirely in graphite pencil to unify the idea and not lose it behind layers of inks and paints.

Artist: Herlaka Rose

Artist Statement

This art was done in pencil. I created it at work while I was frustrated! Note: The 213 drawn so many times over and over. I find Dahmer's essence to be more complicated than any other I have drawn. 213 is a number that is similiar to 911, Emergency! In a way, it is like a black cat crossing your path when you see that number.

As far as creating the art...I am an artist...I draw serial killers...I am an "underground" artist...My work is about the macabre. Growing up as a child, I always read about killers and was fascinated by them.

Dahmer Novelty Collectors Coin

Artist: Professor Tooth
Nickle Plated Brass Coin, 1.25 in. x 3mm
IG: Professortoothsodditorium
Website/Sales: professortooth.bigcartel.com
Mailing: P.O. Box 61033 Richmond, VA 23261

Artist Statement

I wanted to create something using a medium that hadn't already been used or tapped out. Crossing over into a realm that hasn't been exhausted by previous artists. In turn, creating and producing a product that is completely new to the market of Serial Killer Culture and Novelty Coin Collecting. Giving the collector a new sense of what coin collecting can entail. Whether it being by displaying the coins themselves or carrying a selected one with other personal effects. It gives the owner full control of what they want to do with their purchase. And gives the product itself more uses than just a sim- ʼple one. In the end I'm trying to essentially introduce a culture to a hobby that may not have been appealing until now.

Now as for having Jeffrey Dahmer in the series, that was a no brainer. The Milwaukee Cannibal was not only fascinating due to his childhood and his accused crimes during his reign of terror. His attraction to create a "sex slave/zombie" and what he was willing to do to make it happen is something that has always stuck out to me. The process itself was quite barbaric and experimental which made it that much more memorable and noteworthy. So that ingenious aspect is what I took into consideration to aid in the creation of his specific coin.

Dahmer's Attraction

Artists: Charles D. Moisant/Hailan Gong
Mixed Media 8.5"x11" matted to 16"x20"
silverphoenix.net - rogallery.com/Hailan/Hailan-bio.htm

Artist Statement

The Serial Killer Calendar, I developed as a curiosity for the general public. My motivation was to have a new product for a new convention "Dark History", the Convention's theme was devoted to True Crimes against humanity. I wanted to develop a product that would disturb the public and at the same time draw them in. I chose 6 Serial Killers. Ed Gein, Richard Speck, John Wayne Gacy, Albert Fish, H.H. Holmes and finally Jeffery Dahmer. Since I am a cartoonist, I enlisted the help of internationally acclaimed fine artist Hailan Gong. We decided to approach this project with a mixture of realistic surrealism. Working with common photos for reference and working with mixed media. (Water Color Pastel, and photoshop) first quick glance one could see the six images as realistic until one took a closer look. For example, Jeffrey Dahmer, we made him more glamorous in looks, blush, and lipstick. I felt this helped the audience to realize how Dahmer may have looked to a homosexual male and why Jeffery had an easy time attracting his prey. All of the 6 serial killers had unique symbolism denoting their internal thinking as to how and why they attracted their prey. All of the images evoke a sense of uneasiness and dread.

I also made the calendar "Educational" with the hope of minimizing the gross assumption of sensationalism or glorification of Serial Killers. I had taken quotas from Wikipedia. I felt this gave the calendar legitimacy.

At nearly every venue where I offered the calendars for purchase, they sold out. Mostly to women in law enforcement, or from an educational setting.

Teamwork

Artist: Brian Cain aka bentWitch
Acrylic, 20 x 20 canvas, 2017
etsy.com/shop/bentWitchcreations

Artist Statement

This is a painting about duality and giving a face to the devil that makes us do it.
I'm a 50-year-old two time cancer survivor with three years experience in painting. I
assume that painting is the superpower I gained from radiation treatment.

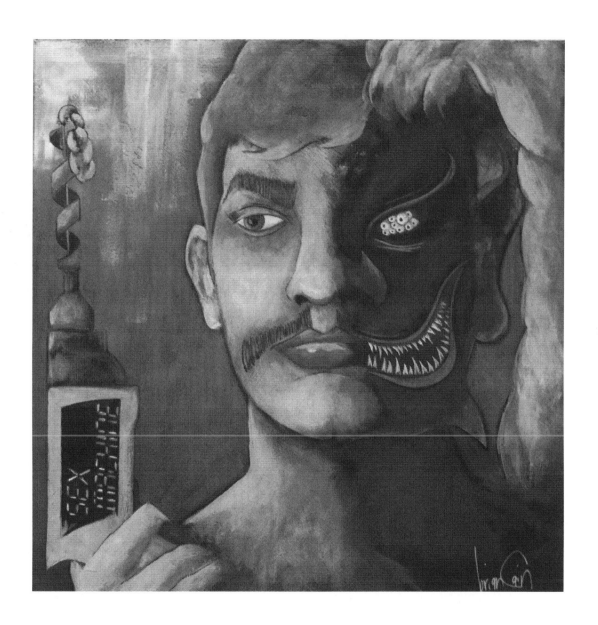

Psychotherapy session, 1987

Artist: Tania Larionova
50"x45" oil on canvas

Artist Statement

I learned of the period of Damer's life devoted to visiting psychotherapists, which clearly affects the personality formation. So I focused on sessions with his doctor, whose work was incorrect, unprofessional, and contrary to medical ethics. Dahmer would prefer to be in jail than visit the sessions. Therapist humiliated external, social, and financial aspects of patient. During this therapy, 4 days after one the session, Dahmer commits the first murder in last 8 years and he kills Steven Toumi.

Alternate Book Cover Courtesy of Erica Kauffman - atomiccotton.com.

Eyes of a Serial Killer
Jeffrey Dahmer at Shakers and the Celebrity of Hangman Tours

Who could have imagined that my life as a Chef and restaurateur at Shakers in Milwaukee would collide with America's most notorious serial killer and cannibal.

Shakers World Café and Cigar Bar in Milwaukee has been in business since 1986 and is housed in a beautiful 1894 historic building, replete with a mahogany bar installed in 1924 in the main room by the Capone brothers from Chicago and repurposed to serve as a Speakeasy and Brothel.

Shakers is known today for world class spirits, award-winning foods, and superior customer service; as well as being the lone licensed Cigar Bar in Milwaukee and selected as one of the five most Haunted bars in America

Shakers location played a big role in my meeting Dahmer. Shakers is located in the former warehouse district of Milwaukee, where many buildings are constructed of Cream City bricks in what was the city's vibrant gay entertainment district.

Shakers was not a gay bar; however it was located directly in the middle of the gay entertainment district, filled with extravagantly creative types.

Weekday mid-day business was mostly corporate clients with a heavy accent on advertising and design houses whiling away the day over late martini-laden lunches.

In 1991, we began to notice a very odd chap coming in sporadically during the midday segment, beginning somewhere around the early part of the year.

Where everyone else was in chic suits or shades of black, this one guy, although not unstylish, was certainly not cut of the same cloth.

This chap often had a simple zip-front jacket over an ordinary shirt and jeans.
He'd come in and look around and migrate to one particular barstool at the front bar.

This one stool matched the other two dozen in the house, being an antique bentwood old oak chair atop an oak base with the exception that when it was made, the makers had put an extra oak spacer under the seat. This made this stool about 1.5" taller than its mates. This stool is still in residence at Shakers, albeit moved to our Dillinger speakeasy side bar.

Shakers, then and now, is known for the many attractive female bar staff at its front bar; a visual which has proven to be popular with our clientele.

When said patron would come in, the bar staff noticed he didn't fit in with the average clients and had a persona and look about him which made him stand out due to his oddness. He didn't say much, however he was adamant that one of the female bar staff not make his drinks for him. Instead, he demanded that they get me or a male member of my culinary team to come out of the open kitchen to make his Gin & Tonic drink for him.

He had eyes that I can only describe as being like a shark's eyes and which I shall never forget. Dead, hollow, yet piercing you with a look of that unsettled and inspired absolute terror. After getting his drink, he'd turn around in the chair and stare at the other patrons, perhaps sizing them up for his next adventure. He'd stop by every once in a while, yet always stood out.

On a hot day in July 1991, Shakers was transformed into an ad hoc command post for the local media and police as Jeffrey Dahmer was arrested and many body parts were discovered in his apartment.

Why Shakers, you ask?
Shakers has, since inception in 1986, had a more than solid rapport with the myriad law enforcement and police agencies from Federal Department of Justice and FBI, down through the Milwaukee County District Attorney's office and Milwaukee Police Department. Shakers also has always enjoyed a stellar relationship with the local media, which came into play in July 1991.

As I remember it, Dahmer was arrested on a hot summer night in Milwaukee. There was a period of intense police and emergency sirens piercing the evening and the beat cops commented to me on their normal patrol that some freak had been arrested and human heads found in his refrigerator.

When Dahmer was arrested, Wisconsin reporters knew where their best shot at gleaning the behind the scenes story was and that was at Shakers, where the otherwise silent authorities came to decompress and perhaps spill a story along with their bourbon.

Queuing up the next day, Tuesday, we had a bevy of reporters in Shakers for lunch, and

I was hanging out behind the bar. At some point, one of the reporters, perhaps Alan May, pulled out mug shots of Jeffrey Dahmer and passed them around. As the pictures went past me, I went from being the fly on the wall to stopping the handoff from one reporter to the next and spoke up.

Something, like "Hey, I recognize this guy, this is that one scary guy who comes in here with those weird eyes who won't let the women wait on him and who drinks gin and tonics"

That entire day was filled with detectives and District Attorney's coming to Shakers for a blast of reality with their peers and to grab a few whiskies in a safe environment to numb the images in their minds.

Later that night, Tom Jacobson, who owned the environmental clean-up company and was the guy in the yellow hazmat suit seen on TV and on covers of news magazines carting barrels out of Dahmer's apartment, was in Shakers to drown the memories with Scotch.

Tom consumed Scotch that night and the rest of the week, likely spending the entire fee the City paid him for the cleanup work.

Throughout Dahmer's incarceration, booking and interviewing process, we had reporters, coppers and ordinary people talking incessantly about the 'Cannibal'.

Years later, a girl friend and I were in Key West, researching cemeteries and Ghost Tours. I noticed that whenever someone would ask where we were from and we'd say Milwaukee, they'd get bug-eyed and say "oh, Jeffrey Dahmer". We had the same experience when we were in New Orleans, Austin or Savannah.

Years earlier, I had been in France and when people there would ask where we were from and I'd say Milwaukee, they'd ask where that was and Id say, about 90 miles North of Chicago, which prompted them to comment something like, "Chicago ...Dillinger, bang bang".

I decided that with the high awareness with Jeffrey Dahmer as Americas' Serial Killer, Shakers should include his story in our collection of historic Tours, as Hangman Tours, hangmantours.com. After all, I had personal experience serving Dahmer in my restaurant over several occasions, had seen his creepy side in person at Shakers and experienced his dead staring, gimlet-like eyes, all the while in our own home town of Milwaukee.

Shortly after we announced plans to create this as a viable historic tour, I heard that a Chicago group was considering a sensationalist tour of Dahmer. I decided that our tour would not only be historic, but rather would be rigorously researched with my myriad real-life contacts to give it enough factual and solid anecdotes to be used as a serious piece of work for various psychology, modern history and criminal justice programs.

To date, we have been used by Special Agents from the FBI who were studying serial killers, as well as several collegiate programs dealing with the lax prosecutors and Judges, to those studying the psychology of Dahmer's actions.

In 2017, Shakers/ Hangman Tours was picked by the "world's largest entertainment content provider", for filming a new series, as one of the eight most unique adventure tours in the world. We also have designed a line of merchandise with Jeffrey Dahmer tour images that we sell globally, and Shakers has been used for numerous television broadcasts, documentaries and adventure tours.

By Bob Weiss

Made in United States
Orlando, FL
29 October 2022

23974988R00159